The Price of War

To
Austin Robinson
who got me into all this (and much else).

Alec Cairncross

THE PRICE OF WAR

British Policy on German Reparations
1941 – 1949

Basil Blackwell

© Alec Cairncross 1986

First published 1986

Basil Blackwell Ltd
108 Cowley Road, Oxford OX4 1JF, UK

Basil Blackwell Inc.
432 Park Avenue South, Suite 1503,
New York, NY 10016, USA

British Library Cataloguing in Publication Data
Cairncross, *Sir,* Alec
  The price of war: British policy on
  German reparations 1941–1949.
  1. World War, 1939–1945 —— Germany ——
  Reparations
  I. Title
  940.53'14   D819.G3

ISBN 0–631–14919–8

Library of Congress Cataloging in Publication Data

Cairncross, Alec, Sir, 1911–
  The price of war.
  Bibliography: p.
  Includes index.
  1. World War, 1939–1945—Reparations. 2. Great
  Britain—Foreign relations—Germany. 3. Germany—Foreign
  relations—Great Britain. I. Title.
  D819.G7C34 1986   094.086   86–1136
  ISBN 0–631–14919–8

Typeset by Lovell Baines Print Ltd, Newbury, Berkshire.
Printed in Great Britain by Billing and Sons Ltd, Worcester

The West Germans were lucky. It was the East Germans who paid the full price of Hitler's war.

Theo Sommer, Editor-in-chief, *Die Zeit* (1985)

Contents

Preface

Forty years have passed since the four powers in military occupation of Germany reached agreement in Berlin on a Reparations Plan. The agreement was short-lived and never whole-hearted; even the title of the document was the subject of a long dispute and a footnote was enough to put its publication in doubt. It was almost the last occasion on which the four powers united in planning a future for the German economy; and the fruits of their failure to agree are still with us in the division, first of Germany, then of Europe.

I took part in these events as the Treasury representative in Berlin, succeeding Austin Robinson and Donald MacDougall in late October 1945 as head of the Economic Advisory Panel that was preparing a British plan for Germany, and returning to London just before the publication of the Reparations Plan at the end of March 1946. My duties before and after this episode lay in very different directions since I had just completed four years in the Ministry of Aircraft Production and was about to join the staff of the London *Economist* when I was asked to go to Berlin. I was not able to satisfy a natural curiosity as to what had been going on before October 1945 or what happened after March 1946 until I embarked on this book. I had, however, so far indulged myself as to write five chapters of a personal memoir of the negotiations in Berlin while recovering from mumps in 1952.

My interest revived when an inquiry from Charles Kindleberger brought home to me that there was no available account of the Berlin negotiations from the British side. In 1947 my American colleagues, Ratchford and Ross, had published in *Berlin Reparations Assignment* a detailed narrative of events as they recalled them. But comparatively little was said about British views. I also reflected that the lapse of 40 years meant that the records were now open and that it should be possible to obtain a much fuller picture of the evolution of British policy towards Germany. To my surprise, however, the Berlin records of the Economic Advisory Panel had disappeared or been destroyed. Even the full report which I prepared on my return from Germany in March 1946 was no longer to be found. My correspondence with the Control Office for Germany could not be traced. Fortunately I retained a copy of many of the key documents, including my report and various letters, and could supplement them from the mass of Control Commission records which have recently been released.

My first thought was to complete and publish the memoir, leaving the first five chapters as they stood in 1952 but adding two further chapters to fill out the picture and give a more adequate account of the reparations negotiations in 1945–6 and their consequences. Memoirs of such distant events are, however, of limited interest. The reader would be left wondering what went before and what happened afterwards, and asking how the quadripartite negotiations in Berlin were linked with ministerial discussions and policy in London. I decided therefore to do a full-scale study of British reparations policy during and after the Second World War that could be read on its own. The memoir might add colour and piquancy, but I did not think that I could merge it with a more scholarly study, given the wide difference in subject matter and the limited interaction between ministerial policy and events in Berlin.

I have confined the study to *German* reparations, conscious that half the countries of Europe (and many others) were claiming or paying reparations after 1945. Albania, Egypt, Ethiopia, Greece and India were among the claimants and Austria, Bulgaria, Finland, Hungary and Italy among the payers. The amounts involved were often substantial but none raised problems comparable in international importance with the claims on Germany. I have also refrained from pursuing the activities in Brussels of the Inter-Allied Reparations Agency (IARA), which was intended to allocate reparations between the claimant countries. The narrative stops in 1949 with the creation of the Federal Republic, and makes no reference to the later voluntary payment of reparations by the Federal Republic to Israel.

It was difficult to decide how to deal with the political setting of the reparations story. The quarrels over reparations cannot be understood in isolation from other quarrels between the powers concerned. But international relations during and after the Second World War is an enormous subject of which my knowledge is quite inadequate. I have stuck fairly closely to the theme of reparations, recognizing its powerful political overtones but limiting myself to

such asides on the larger issues as seem necessary to explain why
events took the course they did. Readers interested in the wider
issues should turn to Mastny's *Russia's Road to the Cold War*, the
three volumes on the 1940s by Herbert Feis, and Lord Bullock's
Ernest Bevin, Foreign Secretary, 1945–1951. Also recommended are:
W.H. McNeill's *America, Britain and Russia*; and *The Semblance of
Peace* by Sir John Wheeler-Bennett and A.J. Nicholls.

Although German reparations are now a distant memory, the
story is not without its relevance to current preoccupations.
Reparations are a form of unilateral transfer akin to the transfers
that fall to be made by countries with large international debts such
as now abound. They were also the main bone of contention
between Russia and her war-time allies in the West, so that the story
of reparations is also the story of how Germany and Europe came to
be split in two.

Until I had almost completed the manuscript I was unaware of the
excellent, but unpublished, study of German reparations by Philip
Baggaley ('Reparations, Security and the Industrial Disarmament of
Germany: Origins of the Potsdam Decisions'), in Yale University
Library, which traces the story to mid-1946 from the point of view of
each of the three main powers involved. I was able to take advantage
of Lord Bullock's account of the part played by Ernest Bevin and of
some (but only a little) of the recent work of German scholars like
Josef Foschepoth and Rolf Steininger. In the main I have gone to the
original documents in the Public Record Office, concentrating on
British policy rather than trying to do full justice to the views of the
other countries involved. I am correspondingly grateful to the PRO
for their assistance.

My particular thanks are due to Francis Wyman and Tony
Nicholls, both of whom read a draft of the manuscript and made
many helpful suggestions. Others who lent a hand include Charles
Kindleberger, Richard Demuth and David Ginsburg, Klaus Hennings,
Dr Johannes Kuppe, Wendy Carlin, Martin McCauley and Sally
Marks (National Archives, Washington DC). I am indebted to Anne
Robinson for transforming my illegible scribbles into such a work of
the typist's art that I hesitated to amend it. As always, however, the
most important contribution has come from my wife in the
forbearance with which she has borne my obsession with the
manuscript and seclusion from her company.

The preparation of this study has been assisted by the grant of an
Emeritus Fellowship by the Leverhulme Trust to which I should like
to express my gratitude.

A.K.C.

1

Introduction

The problem of reparation was in no sense a technical economic problem whose 'answer' depends on the estimation of a whole complex of elasticities and various other parameters; if the will had existed, the technical problems of an inadequate market mechanism could certainly have been overcome . . . . Reparation was always far more a political than an economic problem.

Trachtenberg, Reparations in World Politics

Over the years there have been many attempts on the part of the victors in war to extract reparations from the vanquished. Sometimes they have succeeded, sometimes they have been disappointed with what they got.

An outstanding example of the successful exaction of an indemnity was the payment of 5 billion francs (£200 million) by France to Germany after the Franco-Prussian War in the 27 months between June 1871 and September 1873. Even for a rich country like France, 5 billion francs was in those days a large amount, equal to over 20 months' exports. But the payment was made without appearing to interrupt the economic development of France. Indeed, it was the effect on Germany that was thought at the time to be more open to question: it helped to sustain, and perhaps aggravate, the post-war boom that culminated in 1873 and was followed by what seemed a prolonged depression.

Most of the money needed by the French Government was raised by three large loans: one for 1.5 billion francs from the Bank of France; and two issues of bonds, for 2.25 and 3.5 billion francs respectively, that were either taken up on the day of issue or heavily overscribed by private investors attracted by an effective rate of interest of about 6 per cent. Some bonds, probably about one-third, were taken up by foreigners, particularly Germans, while others were sold to Frenchmen swapping out of foreign investments. Thus initially the money paid over came largely from capital borrowed abroad or realized from the sale of foreign assets. The strain on the French balance of payments was very much reduced – so much so that although the franc was inconvertible between 1870 and 1878 it suffered little or no depreciation.[1]

The whole operation was an early demonstration of the rôle of capital movements in bringing about balance of payments adjustments: it is much easier to operate on the capital balance than on the current account. Not that the current account remained unaffected. There are no reliable figures for invisibles, although it is known that there was a large and fairly stable surplus, consisting mainly of interest on French holdings of foreign bonds. The balance on visibles, that is, the balance of trade, swung from a consistent deficit averaging 340 million francs a year in 1868–71 to an equally consistent surplus in the next four years, 1872–5, averaging 240 million francs, and then swung back again in the following four years, 1876–9, to a growing deficit that averaged 750 million francs per annum.[2] It is natural to see in these fluctuations the influence of the the the indemnity, and to conclude, perhaps rashly, that by 1875 a real transfer had been effected out of current income equal to perhaps half or more of the total indemnity, the other half being carried as an impairment of France's net external assets.

The boot was on the other foot after 1918, when it was Germany that was asked to pay reparations to France and other countries; the situation then was a very different one. Whereas in 1871 a relatively short war had left the French economy largely intact – French exports hardly fell in value in 1870, rose in 1871 and rose again, by over 30 per cent, in 1872 – in 1919 Germany was just emerging from a long and exhausting war, on the verge of revolution, blockaded and unable to trade freely. Other countries in central Europe were in an equally impoverished condition and this both inflamed the call for reparations and complicated the problem of exacting them.

Very large sums were demanded. Lord Cunliffe, a former Governor of the Bank of England, and Hughes, the Australian Prime Minister and a member of the War Cabinet, wanted to make Germany pay the full cost of the war, estimated at £24,000 million.[3]

[1] H. H. O'Farrell, *The Franco-German War Indemnity and its Economic Results*, 1913, pp. 1–19; F.W.Taussig, *International Trade*, 1927, chapter 22.
[2] I have used the figures given by Rueff (1929, p. 394 n.) although these differ slightly from those quoted by O'Farrell (1913, p. 14)
[3] Harrod (1951), p. 230.

Others, like Keynes, thought that Germany might be able to pay no more than £1,000 million, but were prepared to recommend an indemnity of between £2,000 million and £3,000 million.[4] Agreement was eventually reached in Paris on claims, including the cost of war pensions and separation allowances, that were later estimated to amount to £6,600 million.

It has been usual to pillory the French for the outrageousness of these claims. But it was the UK, not France, whose reparations policy at the Paris Peace Conference was most exacting and intransigent. Lloyd George professed moderation and reconciliation with Germany. But he also wanted justice and justice for him meant punishment. In the general election that followed the armistice of November 1918 he yielded to the popular clamour to make Germany pay, and throughout the peace negotiations continued to support demands that he knew to be impossible. His stance, which was by no means dictated by political pressure, committed the British Government to a harsh and punitive policy.[5]

Such a policy was not at first favoured by the French. At the armistice they looked to co-operation between the Allies rather than to reparations from Germany for a solution to their economic problems. Their Minister of Commerce, Clémentel, had plans in 1918 for a new international order which would continue into the peace some of the kinds of international collaboration that had grown up in the war. The main feature would have been a permanent inter-Allied system for the pooling and control of raw materials, with preferential tariffs within the Allied bloc. Allied co-operation was to provide a framework for the ultimate reintegration of Germany into the international economic system and at the same time restrain German ambitions. As for reparations, Clémentel thought vast payments neither feasible nor desirable: they might, however, be demanded as a means of extracting 'concessions' (e.g. supplies of coal) from Germany and inducing recalcitrant allies to support the idea of a world fund for the rebuilding of the devastated areas.[6] These ideas foundered, however, on the refusal of the Allies to play the role assigned to them.[7] The French then hoped for agreement on a moderate fixed sum in reparations with a German bond issue in the USA to raise the money and the payment of a

[4] Hessian (1984), pp. 131–2.
[5] Trachtenberg (1980), pp. 46–9.
[6] One of Clémentel's advisers, the historian Henri Hauser, argued that, apart from other undesirable effects, huge reparations payments would transform France into a country incapable of working, 'like Spain in the sixteenth century' (ibid., pp. 18–19).
[7] Ibid., pp. 31–41.

substantial part of the proceeds into the French treasury. This, too, failed. The British would not agree to the naming of a fixed sum and it is questionable whether the Germans could have sold bonds in America.

As a condition of the armistice the Germans had agreed to make compensation 'for all damage done to the civilian population of the Allies and their property by the aggression of Germany by land, by sea and from the air'. But to war damage the British proposed to add war costs, hoping in this way to increase their share of the total. The French, while supporting British claims, wanted reparation, strictly defined, to have priority. They would have liked to pool war costs and reapportion the inter-Allied debt, each nation paying acording to its ability. The Americans, to whom a large part of the burden would have been transferred, would have none of this. They were also opposed to the inclusion of war costs and the attempt to include them was abandoned. From that point on, French proposals fell below the British demands and the French were prepared, while the British were not, to name a fixed sum.[8]

The attitude of the British Government during the negotiations did not long command popular support. Public opinion quickly swung round, first among the troops quartered in Germany who saw the extremities to which the Germans were reduced, and then increasingly among the public at large. A mood of disillusionment and hostility to the Treaty of Versailles spread as it became clear that there would be no reconciliation, no assurance of lasting peace; the treaty would have to be upheld by force. The French, who had most reason to fear for their security, stood firm by the Treaty, and in so doing attracted to themselves the condemnation of those who wished to revise it. The idea took firm root that it had been French vindictiveness and vengefulness that accounted for the harshness of the terms of peace.

The subsequent history of German reparations has been well summarized by Professor Backer:

> first, a short period with Germany meeting its obligations, to be followed by a request for a moratorium; second, an Allied refusal to grant relief and the Franco-Belgian occupation of the Ruhr; third, a German policy of passive resistance accompanied by the rapid collapse of the German currency; fourth, the introduction of a new currency and a greatly reduced reparations programme primarily financed by American loans; fifth, a period of artificial prosperity, with inflowing loans exceeding the balance of payments; and sixth, the crisis of 1930, the final collapse of the German economy, and the end of all reparations payments.[9]

From first to last the amount actually collected in reparations was a little over £1,000 million.[10] The original obligation was to make an immediate payment of that amount plus an annual payment that would have worked out at £300 million thereafter. By the time the Young Plan had been adopted in 1930 the average annuity, spread over 60 years, had come down to an average of £100 million – the amount that Keynes had thought reasonable before the negotiations in Paris began. Meanwhile in the seven years 1925–31 Germany's foreign indebtedness had grown by £910 million more than her foreign assets. Over those years Germany borrowed abroad nearly twice as much as she paid in reparations.[11]

The experience of those years left a deep impression on those who lived through them. On the one hand 'the attempt to extract reparations dominated European politics during the critical period following the conclusion of peace [and] in large measure determined the structure of power in Europe'.[12] On the other, reparations were blamed for Germany's slide into hyperinflation and chaos and for the continuing uncertainty and turmoil in the 1920s in international financial markets. It came to be believed that the effort to extract reparations would do injury to all concerned: as like as not, little would be paid and that little might well be exceeded by what the victors had first to contribute. Either the burden would prove insupportable and cause the economy of the payer to collapse; or the normal flow of trade would be distorted to the detriment of the receiver by the efforts to make additional transfers across the exchanges in reparations.

These views in their turn coloured British thinking when reparations were again under consideration during the Second World War. Not that ministers gave much thought to reparations while the war was in progress. They were in no hurry to discuss the subject, and never did so in Cabinet until after the war was almost over. But on the few occasions on which their wartime views are recorded, ministers tended to appeal to the record of earlier experience as they interpreted it. Officials were more alive to the need to work out a policy in advance and were not deterred by the absence of ministerial guidance from reviewing the issues that would have to be settled. The thinking of those most concerned was dominated by Keynes who had been in the thick of the negotiations in 1919, had

[8] ibid., p. 63.
[9] J. H. Backer (1971), p. 62.
[10] Wheeler-Bennett (1933), p. 255, gives a figure of £1,029 million.
[11] Ibid., p. 89.
[12] Trachtenberg (1980), p. vii.

written extensively both on the history and theory of reparations transfers, and was active throughout the war in stirring up interest in Whitehall in the post-war settlement. What he wrote on reparations between 1941 and 1945 fills 74 pages of Vol. XXVI of his *Collected Writings*. But this falls well short of a complete record of his written contribution to the subject over those four years and is an inadequate measure of his participation in the framing of advice on policy. He was for ever drafting, querying, catechizing, and making suggestions that were almost always constructive.

The Lessons of the Past

Four main lessons were drawn from past experience by ministers and officials. The first was the importance of what came to be known as the transfer problem in assessing a country's capacity to pay reparations. A second moral was the supposed advantages of requiring such payments to be made in kind rather than in cash. A third was the need to take precautions against paying reparations to the defeated country instead of receiving them. Finally there was a lively awareness of the fickleness of public opinion in the aftermath of war.

So far as the first of those is concerned, much of the argument immediately after the First World War was at a low level of sophistication. British negotiators, for example, at one stage took as a satisfactory measure of what Germany could pay her national wealth – as if one could buy and sell entire cities. It was not always appreciated that there were two quite separate problems facing the paying country: how to release resources for the production of reparations; and how to make additional sales abroad to raise the necessary foreign exchange. The first of these problems was essentially a budgetary one: by additional taxation or by curtailing expenditure, the Government would have to accumulate in local currency the purchasing power required. The counterpart to this attempt to create a budget surplus would be a falling-off in demand and a consequent release of resources that might or might not be re-employed in the production of goods for export. The second problem was one of trade and payments: in order to transfer the funds accumulated into foreign currency, the Government would first have to acquire the necessary foreign exchange. This would only be possible (unless it held very large reserves) if it could effect a corresponding improvement in its balance of payments by boosting exports, limiting imports, or borrowing abroad.

Most people could see as far as the first of these problems but had more difficulty with the second. Yet even the first problem was highly complex. What was the limit to a country's taxable capacity? How far was it possible to depress consumers' incomes without drying up the flow of savings into investment and undermining the incentive to produce? It was not a question to which there was a hard and fast answer since it depended on human reactions that were bound to vary with circumstances. A Germany defeated but not occupied by Allied armies in 1919 could develop a resistance to high taxation that was not possible in Soviet-controlled East Germany after the Second World War.

The problem of transferring German purchasing power across the exchanges was quite another matter. There were some like Prime Minister Hughes who simply shut their eyes to it. There were others who regarded it as virtually insoluble, treating the *existing* balance of payments as a measure of what could be transferred. There were others again who found any disturbance to existing trading patterns unwelcome and were correspondingly alarmed at the prospect of *receiving* reparations. Economists recognised that there were mechanisms enabling some financial transfer to take place if appropriate changes occurred in prices and incomes. But there was much controversy as to the additional burden that this might impose on the paying country by obliging it to deflate and lower the level of economic activity or, even if this could be avoided, to accept less favourable terms of trade. There was no agreement how large this additional burden might be, or at what point the mechanism of transfer might break down.

Indeed it must be confessed that the economic theory of capital transfer was still rather primitive in 1920 – not surprisingly, since although capital investment by one country in another had been on a growing scale throughout the nineteenth century, the textbooks discussed international trade as if it did not occur at all. It was Keynes's insistence that it was one thing to raise money for the payment of reparations in local currency and quite another to effect a transfer of the money across the exchanges that prompted a reconsideration of the theory of capital movements. In a famous controversy with the Swedish economist Bertil Ohlin in 1929, Keynes argued that Germany was faced with an acute transfer problem that could only be solved by a reduction in money-wages to make her more competitive in international markets. To get back into external equilibrium without borrowing, she would have to increase the value of her exports of finished goods by perhaps 40 per cent. The increase in volume would have to be still larger since the effort to sell more abroad would involve a reduction in export prices. If, for example, prices had to be lowered by 10 per cent in order to effect an increase in the volume of trade by 20 per cent (i.e. with an elasticity of 2), the increase in the value of exports would be only 8 per cent. In some situations, where the elasticity of demand was less than unity, a cut in export prices would produce, not an increase but a reduction in the value of exports. Keynes did not, as is sometimes suggested,[13] assume that this was in fact the situation confronting Germany: to do so would have been to represent the transfer problem as completely insoluble. But he laid stress on possible reactions in foreign markets (e.g. higher tariffs, parallel wage-cuts in competing countries) that would intensify the difficulty of making a large adjustment in Germany's balance of payments.

Ohlin pointed out that Keynes took no account of the transfer of purchasing power from one country to the other that reparations payments involved. The transfer was bound to reduce demand in the paying country and add to it in the receiving country and these 'income effects' would react on the trade balances of both countries, reducing imports in the one case and increasing them in the other. Thus before it became necessary for either country to put pressure on imports and exports through price movements and variations in the level of activity, a large step towards restoration of equilibrium would already have been taken as an almost automatic consequence of the reparations transfer. How large would depend on the propensity to use additional income for the purchase of imports; if that propensity were, say, 25 per cent in each country, and if only two countries existed, half the transfer would be quasi-automatic.[14]

Ohlin's conclusions were more optimistic than Keynes's. But they were far from demonstrating that there was no transfer problem or indeed that the problem might not become acute. As a practical matter it could not be assumed that governments would vary their budget surpluses (or deficits) in exact accord with the amount of reparations transferred each year. Indeed, they might make little or no immediate adjustment. Similarly the banking systems of the

[13] Trachtenberg (1980), pp. 341–2, quoting Fritz Machlup.

[14] It is over 50 years since I grappled with the theory of capital transfer in my Cambridge PhD dissertation on *Home and Foreign Investment*. The key variables were marginal import propensities, the elasticity of substitution between home-produced goods and imports, and the elasticity of transfer of resources into, or out of, industries making traded goods. Most of the theory, as I later discovered, had already been worked out by Roland Wilson, the Australian economist, in his *Capital Imports and the Terms of Trade*. In modern theory similar results are now expressed in terms of 'expenditure switching', that is, a combination of changes in incomes and prices induces consumers to switch their purchases to the extent required.

paying and receiving countries might not allow the money supply to respond promptly or sufficiently to gains or losses in foreign exchange resulting from reparations transfers.[15] The experience of Germany also showed that if capital was transferred in one direction this might be offset or more than offset by capital flows in the opposite direction. Moreover the two might be casually connected. One of the effects of exacting reparations, and so removing capital, might be to force up interest rates and stimulate the sucking in of new capital from abroad. The net transfer of capital would be abated *pro tanto* and the train of events depicted by Keynes would simply not occur. But if the reparations obligations were very heavy there would be much greater reluctance to lend to or invest in the paying country and the transfer problem would be aggravated.

All this suggests that there is indeed a transfer problem which may be mitigated in various ways, but may also raise almost insurmountable difficulties when the transfer is large and the trade of the countries concerned is small and difficult to expand. These difficulties may well arise if the transfer is left to be effected through the operation of market forces. But since the transfer is from one government to another, one has also to allow for administrative action. The import propensity of a receiving *government* is precisely what it makes it. It can find within its programmes of expenditure, or by adding to them, ways of enlisting the services of the paying country if it so chooses. It need not be a centrally planned economy to make deliberate provision for increased imports. Similarly what the paying country

[15] Trachtenberg (1980), p. 341.
[16] Much of the discussion of the transfer problem is vitiated by the assumption of 'normal' trading conditions. But trading conditions fluctuate and when world markets are contracting the difficulty of making a transfer can become acute. As Roy Harrod reminds us (Harrod, 1951, p. 230) Britain claimed in all good faith to be unable to pay £35 million a year to the USA in 1931 when the world depression was at its worst. Equally, the difficulty of making a large reparations transfer cannot be judged from the ease with which a country makes large investments abroad. Trachtenberg, in an otherwise excellent analysis, draws a parallel between British success in exporting capital in the first decade of this century, when investment abroad rose in ten years from 1.6 per cent to 8.7 per cent of GNP, with the demand for annual payments by Germany of £300 million or 7 per cent of average German GNP in the period 1925–9 (Trachtenberg, 1980, pp. 67–8). But the two situations are quite different. The same conditions as made for high British investment abroad made for a large balance of payments surplus. To a large extent, the areas affected by the changes in the pattern of British trade and investment were an extension of the British economy. An obligation to make 7 per cent of her GNP immediately available to a group of countries only loosely connected with her economy would have been a quite different matter and would almost certainly have led to extensive foreign borrowing by the British Government – an eventuality which the textbooks disregard but which the negotiators at Versailles had very much in mind.

finds it possible to do is not just a technical matter but depends on the will to make the necessary adjustments.

Under the conditions of the 1920s it was right to emphasize the transfer problem when Germany's markets lay mainly in other industrial countries.[16] But from 1924 onwards, with capital flowing *into* Germany at twice the rate it was flowing out, the point was academic. It was even more academic at the end of the Second World War when Russia, the main claimant of reparations, had an almost unlimited capacity to absorb them. In relation to reparations from Germany to Russia, the transfer problem was simply irrelevant.

Emphasis on the transfer problem gave rise to a second misconception. It came to be taken for granted in the Second World War that it would be a mistake to require payment of reparations in cash across the exchanges. As we shall see, this view did not go unchallenged. But it was generally accepted, in all the Allied countries, including the USSR, that if reparations were demanded they should take the form of payment in kind, either through removals of plant, etc., or out of current production, or alternatively should consist of labour services by prisoners of war or other workers detained in the receiving country. Loot and slavery, the traditional forms of reparations, had returned to favour.

A third misconception was that reparations were paid in the end to Germany, not by Germany. It is true that the Germans were able to borrow twice what they paid and that little of what they borrowed was ever repaid. But it was not the Allied governments that lent the money: it was investors, mainly American, who made a commercial loan or investment that, like many other loans and investments between the wars, turned out badly. They made it easier for the German Government to go on paying reparations; and in a balance-sheet sense the Allies were the losers. But the situation was quite different from that in 1945 when the Western Allies feared that the more was sucked out of Germany in reparations, the more they would be obliged to pump in to keep the economy from collapse or to prevent disease and social unrest.

Most of all, ministers and officials were perplexed by the question: how is Germany to be prevented from waging yet another war? They had seen how the obligations imposed on Germany in 1919 had kindled a spirit of revenge and how at the same time, the will of the Allies to enforce the Treaty of Versailles had been sapped by lack of conviction that it was fair and reasonable. Neither those who sought reconciliation with Germany nor those who put security first and proposed to keep her disarmed and dismembered had had their way.

The divisions of opinion continued in the Second World War.

Both sides were conscious that what popular opinion would demand when hostilities ceased might differ widely from what it would sustain in later years. While one side put its money on changing the German will to war, the other wished to take no chances and wanted to destroy Germany's war potential. Neither side saw much to be gained from reparations unless they were incidental to measures of economic security.

Ministerial Attitudes in 1945

When the war with Germany ended in May 1945, British ministers had made few public commitments as to the treatment to be accorded her. On the one hand they had insisted on unconditional surrender; on the other they had forsworn extreme economic policies. In July 1941, for example, Eden had said that 'it is not part of our policy to cause Germany or any other country to collapse economically. . . . A starving and a bankrupt Germany in the midst of Europe would poison all of us who are her neighbours'.[17]

Similarly Churchill declared: 'it is not the purpose of the Allies to leave the people of Germany without the necessary means of subsistence'.

With his deep sense of history he looked back to the mistakes of the peace settlement at Versailles and was determined to avoid them. He had long denounced the failure to take adequate precautions against German rearmament. He now contrasted the effort, as he interpreted it, to ruin German trade after 1919 with the lesson that it is 'not in the interests of the world and of our two countries that any large nation should be unprosperous or shut out from the means of making a decent living for itself'.[18]

It was not an attitude to which he held consistently and there was a time in 1944 when, for reasons still in dispute, he was prepared to put his name to a watered down version of the Morgenthau Plan. But his was normally a magnanimous temperament and he soon returned to a more hopeful view of Germany's place in Europe. Within a few months he was urging that the dangers and difficulties of reparations should be brought home to the Russians.

Ministers had not, however, any clear-cut policy for the treatment of Germany when the war was ended. It was not easy to foresee how it would end and what kind of government, if any, would conclude an armistice or sign a treaty of peace. Other countries were involved,

[17] Speech on 29 July 1941.
[18] Broadcast on 24 August 1942.

other armies were advancing, other armistices were being signed. When hostilities ceased in Europe they still continued in the Far East. What part Britain would play and what influence she would be able to exert on the final settlement, no one could be sure. The situation was constantly changing and there had to be corresponding flexibility in the terms proposed.

Reparations in particular were not the subject of much debate among ministers while the war was in progress. So far as they gave thought to the future of Germany it was issues such as disarmament, democratization and dismemberment that occupied them. But these in turn affected policy on reparations and made it seem natural to defer decisions on reparations until it was possible to form a clear view of what would be left of Germany.

It is highly likely that if the peace settlement had been a purely Anglo-German affair, ministers would have plumped for a peace treaty in which reparations would either not have figured at all or would have been on a very modest scale. They felt far more strongly the need to take measures to prevent Germany from ever again threatening the peace of the world. As Dalton scribbled on a note by James Meade, demonstrating that the payment of reparations might well injure Britain commercially, 'economic security for us matters most'.[19]

But there was plenty of room for disagreement over how, if at all, economic security was to be achieved on a continuing footing. If the method favoured was to dismantle the heavy industry on which Germany had built her war machine, then there would automatically be surplus plant that could be taken in reparations. This not only made dismantling more attractive, but also made it harder to stand out against reparations. So long as it was thought to contribute both to economic security and to reparations, dismantling was seen as serving two otherwise conflicting objectives and may for that reason have been given less searching scrutiny on its own merits.

There were, however more powerful reasons for acquiescing in substantial reparations. Other countries which had suffered more – some of them much more – than Britain were sure to demand them. On moral and political grounds – whatever the economics of the matter – these countries had an irresistible case. They would expect solid compensation for 'unspeakable maltreatment' and what people expected was a fact that could not be left out of political calculations.[20] The reparations they would expect would not be confined to second-hand plant but would extend over the whole

[19] Meade to Dalton, 1 December 1942, 'Reparations and the Terms of Trade', in PRO T230/121.
[20] Dalton, 'Reparations', 28 August 1942 (RES(423)6, in PRO T230/121).

range of German outputs and stocks and would certainly include labour services. As Churchill told Roosevelt in November 1944: 'Uncle Joe certainly contemplates demanding two or three million Nazi youths, Gestapo men, etc., doing prolonged reparation work and it is hard to say he is wrong'.[21]

The strength of these reasons depended on how easy it was to satisfy the expectations others had built up. If the UK was doubtful on her own account of the wisdom of taking large reparations from Germany she could hardly change her mind merely because others were more pressing. Admittedly, some were in a position to sidestep the transfer problem and take directly for their own immediate use. If Russia, whose normal trade was less than that of Switzerland, took goods in replacement of what she had lost, there could be little consequent distortion of trade flows and British fears on that score (although not on other grounds) would be baseless. The bigger difficulty might remain that what was taken put too heavy a burden on what was left of the German economy and struck at her power to contribute to European economic recovery.

A second consideration was the fear that reparations, if set too high, would be paid by the occupying powers, not by Germany. It was Keynes's *bête noire*: 'That is how all these things tend to end up', he wrote. 'I should like to imbue all Departments from the outset with the doctrine that, in no circumstances or on any terms do we supply anything or pay for anything, so far as Germany is concerned'.[22]

This fear was shared by the Americans and was the basis of the so-called 'first charge principle' introduced into the Potsdam agreement, which had appeared earlier in Sir John Anderson's paper to the War Cabinet in March 1945 in a passage drafted by Keynes:

> We must. . . put it in the forefront of our conditions that relief and other supplies, which are agreed to be necessary to put Germany in a position to pay any reparations at all, shall be a first charge on any deliveries taken from her, and must be paid for in the first instance (in the appropriate proportions) by those receiving the deliveries, so long as supplies exceed the value of Germany's overseas earnings apart from reparations.[23]

[21] Churchill to Roosevelt, 24 November 1944 (quoted in PRO CAB 127/272).
[22] Keynes to Playfair, 14 February 1944, in PRO T247/87.
[23] 'Reparations', Memorandum by the Chancellor of the Exchequer, 7 March 1945, WP(45)146 in PRO CAB 66/63. A slightly different version (with 'her' misprinted as 'here') appears in Keynes, *Collected Writings*, Vol. xxvi, pp. 387–8. Neither version achieves Keynes's customary lucidity. The meaning seems to be that goods taken in reparations will have to be paid for if Germany's overseas earnings are insufficient to meet the cost of relief and other permitted imports.

Keynes's fears on this score were only too realistic. By 1946 Dalton was loudly proclaiming that we were in fact meeting the cost of most of Germany's imports and, in effect, paying her reparations. A substantial slice of the dollar loans negotiated at the end of 1945 from the USA and Canada went in paying for food to feed the starving Germans. How it was affected by reparations deliveries, I shall discuss later (see pp. 150–1).

In the background was a third consideration that came to the surface as early as 1941. With both Russia and the USA in the war it was natural to reflect on the relationship between these two countries once the war was over. It seemed obvious even then (to me at least) that the future lay with them and not with Germany or the UK; and that if Germany were thoroughly defeated in an increasingly destructive war, she was unlikely to resume her position of dominance in Europe. As Marcus Fleming put it in a prescient note of 1 September 1942:

> Is it certain that Germany will retain its rôle as the chief potential disturber of the peace and aspirant to European hegemony? In the past five centuries many nations have appeared in this rôle – Austria, Spain, France, Germany . . . . In fifteen or twenty years [won't] the German power . . . be overshadowed by another power no less dangerous to British interests and not much less inimical to the spirit of our civilisation.[24]

But if that were so, what became of the argument from economic security? If it were Russia that had to be reckoned with in future, not Germany, and the war-time alliance was doomed to dissolve, did it make sense to set about dismantling plants across half of German industry, the half that allowed her to make war but also supplied Europe with much of its industrial equipment and earned the means of payment for Germany's imports? Was it not likely that both Russia and the UK would come to woo the defeated Germans, each fearing the success of the other, would speak soft words to them in public and try to conceal the big stick of reparations until forced in the end to put it away.

If that was to be the situation it would be necessary to make peace with Russia as much as with Germany. The issue of reparations would then be one in the whole complex of relations with Russia, linked with all the other matters in dispute, just as it was linked with all the other elements in the post-war treatment of Germany. Instead of being an isolated intellectual issue on which different

[24] J.M. Fleming, 'Economic Disarmament and Reparations', undated but before 1 September 1942, in PRO T230/121.

opinions might prevail in this country or that, or among different people in any one country, it would become one ingredient only in the post-war settlement, the subject of bargaining in a political confrontation that embraced all other differences. Russia might genuinely need reparations and want them for their own sake as part of a plan of recovery; but she might also insist on having them from the Western zones in order to expose the occupying powers to the odium of large-scale dismantling, set back the recovery of industry, and create such uncertainty, confusion and delay in the Western zones that the population would turn to Russia and the Communist party for a way out of their difficulties. Equally, the Western powers, reacting to Russian expansionism, might do exactly what the Russians feared, abandon reparations and rebuild the heavy industries from which they were to be taken, initiating the resurgence of Germany's military potential that was previously anathematized by both sides.

The interest of a study of German reparations after the Second World War is thus very different from that of a similar study of reparations after the First World War. Some elements, mainly economic, are common to the two: the damage to European reconstruction from any delay in the recovery of Germany; the difficulty of extending a programme of reparations over more than the first few years; the failure of the USA and the UK to avoid paying Germany more than they received in reparations; the difference in the attitude between countries that have and have not suffered invasion and massive destruction. There was the same lack of any clear policy before the war was over; the same hope of encouraging German separatism; the same oscillation between an 'idealistic' vision of continuing allied collaboration in pursuit of the restoration of European prosperity, and a 'realistic' attempt to prolong German weakness and subordination. The French had the same aspirations to strike a different balance between their coal and steel industries and the coal and steel industries of the Ruhr. In the eternal triangle formed by Britain, France and Germany, the future of the Rhineland, the Ruhr and the Saar was a continuing preoccupation.

Other elements, mainly political, present a sharp contrast. The power relationships were fundamentally different. The chief claimant to reparations, Russia, was in the ascendant, not stunned like France after the First World War. The USA retained a military presence in Europe and an increasing involvement in European economic affairs. Germany was under military occupation, divided into separate zones and without a government. There were other contrasts in the stress on transfers in kind rather than in cash; in the extensive use of 'slave' labour; and in the rapid and enduring economic recovery in Europe and elsewhere. These had little or no counterpart in the years after 1918 and provide a very different background to the reparations debate. The economic dilemmas were also different. Economic security took precedence over reparations and, taken to its extreme in dismantling of steel and engineering plants, ran counter to the aim of a steady flow of reparations from current production. The most striking contrast in the whole affair is that between the flood of reparations from the Eastern zone to Russia and the trickle from the Western zones as they absorbed massive injections of capital from outside.

But above all, the interest of the second period lies in the struggle for Germany between former allies divided by ideology and interest, in which reparations came to be the most obvious bone of contention.

2

Early Wartime Views: The Malkin Report

> The chief thing that matters is that Ministers should not suppose that the chief thing that matters is to avoid the mistakes made last time.
>
> *Keynes to Sir Horace Wilson, 20 October 1941.*[1]

The treatment of Germany after the war was the subject of elaborate discussion at the official (but only the official) level in Britain long before peace was in sight. Keynes in particular took a keen interest from the end of 1940 onwards in the policy to be adopted. At that stage Britain was fighting alone and Germany was holding out to her neighbours the prospect of a 'New International Order' when the war was over. Invited to prepare a statement to counter this Nazi propaganda, Keynes circulated a short draft which was revised in the light of Departmental comments and shown in January 1941 both to the Prime Minister and to Roosevelt's emissary, Harry Hopkins.

The starting point of Keynes's proposals was the need to avoid the mistake at Versailles in 1919 of 'neglecting the economic reconstruction of Europe [because of] preoccupation with political frontiers and safeguards'.[2] To this reconstruction Germany could make an indispensable contribution and she should be offered opportunities of reconstruction not less than those of her liberated neighbours. 'It would be senseless to suppose that her neighbours can develop an ordered, a prosperous, or a secure life with a crushed and ruined Germany in their midst.'[3] Punitive and preventive measures should therefore be concentrated in the political and military settlement.[4]

---

[1] Quoting Hubert Henderson (Keynes to Ronald, 14 October 1941, in PRO T247/86).
[2] Keynes, *Collected Writings*, Vol. xxv, p. 11.
[3] Ibid., p. 15.
[4] Ibid., p. 10.

The draft made no reference to reparations; but by implication it assumed that, if levied, reparations would be limited by the needs of German economic recovery.

Interdepartmental discussion of reparations did not begin until towards the end of 1941. Then, at Keynes's prompting, a group of officials from the Foreign Office and the Treasury met to consider how Germany should be treated. Keynes circulated to this group a series of questions relating mainly to the claims likely to be put forward by Allied countries at the end of the war and giving more prominence to conflicts of priority in claims to restitution than to the related issue of reparations. The conclusions the group arrived at are not recorded, but a Treasury memorandum on 'Compensation to be Required from the Enemy' presumably reflected its discussions.[5]

The memorandum, dated 5 December 1941, argued that there should be no payments of reparations in cash; 'we should not demand reparations as the term was understood after the last war.' Compensation should be limited to deliveries in kind over, say, five years – a period long enough to allow German exports to recover. Thereafter any excess of exports in reparations 'might displace the products of Allied industry and give German exports a lasting advantage in European markets.' Other countries might insist on reparations, and Russian demands in particular were difficult to predict. But it was not in Britain's interests to make large demands. British policy should be guided by the principle that claims on Germany (other than restitution in kind) should be restricted to compensation for 'depredations by the occupying power'. Claims for restitution in kind, which were dealt with separately, were likely to take precedence over reparations.

As Keynes explained subsequently, one of the purposes of the memorandum was to prevent premature declarations being made by a responsible minister. As the memorandum put it: 'Ministers should be guarded in public statements and not give undertakings which may be impossible to fulfil or lead to charges of bad faith.' Ministers, however, continued to show little interest in the subject until August 1942, when Hugh Dalton, then President of the Board of Trade, produced a memorandum headed 'Reparations'.[6] This explained that when he had seen the Treasury memorandum some months previously, he had liked neither its conclusions nor its

---

[5] The paper was circulated in 1942 to the (Malkin) Committee on Reparation and Economic Security as RES3. This and other RES papers can be found in PRO T230/121–4. For the final report, see PRO FO 942/52.

[6] This was circulated to the Malkin Committee as RES6. The views expressed in it help to explain why nothing came of the Treasury memorandum.

approach. It did not provide a good basis for discussion. Rather than let officials go on working on the wrong lines, he suggested that they should put themselves in the position of experts advising a victorious Hitler, work out a plan for dealing with a defeated Britain on the basis of German interests only, turn it round and apply it to the UK with whatever amendments were necessary in the interests of Allied countries, and then ask themselves why it should not be adopted. What Dalton mainly objected to was the Treasury view that 'very large inter-governmental payments cannot be made without doing the greatest harm to all concerned?' This seemed to him absurd. Would Hitler agree? Or Stalin? Would we be worse off if we received outright gifts from other governments? Or better off without any foreign investments? If so, it could only be because of faulty organization. It had suited us between the wars to maintain that it was a great mistake to exact reparations from Germany. But the truth was that that experience was an unnecessary muddle.

Reparations, he concluded, had a threefold aspect; moral, economic and political. Moral considerations set no limit, given Germany's behaviour. Economic considerations needed re-examination. As for politics, the Slav nations would be bound to expect 'solid compensation for the unspeakable maltreatment' they had suffered, and even the UK would expect to recover occupation costs, of which no mention was made in the Treasury document. Such expectations were a political fact that could not be set aside.

Dalton ended by proposing that the reparations question should be studied by a committee drawn from the Treasury, Foreign Office, Board of Trade, Paymaster General's Office and the Economic Section of the Cabinet Secretariat. The committee should report to the Chancellor of the Exchequer, the Foreign Secretary, the Paymaster General and the President of the Board of Trade. While the composition of the committee appointed was not quite as Dalton proposed – the Paymaster General's staff was not represented while the Admiralty was – his suggestion bore fruit. An influential interdepartmental committee under Sir William Malkin, the Foreign Office's legal adviser, started work in November 1942, had drafted a lengthy report by June 1943 and circulated a revised draft at the end of August 1943.

The Malkin Committee

The membership of the committee included Keynes, Lionel Robbins and James Meade. The 'official' Treasury was represented by E. W.

Playfair, the Board of Trade by Percivale Liesching, the Foreign Office by Gladwyn Jebb and Nigel Ronald, and the Admiralty by Rear-Admiral R. M. Bellairs. Other officials attended from time to time and papers were submitted by many different departments. The committee was clearly dominated by Keynes who contributed two papers and wrote a large part of the Report. Other members of the committee, however, were also active and there is evidence of a good deal of controversy among officials who did not serve on the committee. Marcus Fleming, of the Economic Section, for example, wrote a lengthy note to Lionel Robbins to which reference has already been made (above, p. 14) and which is discussed below.

A major contribution came from Lionel Robbins, Director of the Economic Section. This seems to have been written before the appointment of the Malkin Committee but was not circulated until late November.[7] Robbins started from the proposition that since all claims on Germany could not be met, it would be necessary to make use of some arbitrary principle in deciding between claims of different degrees of urgency. The UK could expect only a small share and might suffer injury if the need to make large reparations payments to other countries forced down German export prices and intensified competition with British exports just when the UK was struggling to remedy an unprecedented deficit. Even if reparations payments continued for only a limited period, the UK would lose the opportunity in the critical post-war years of forming trade connections that would be of great value later on. A clean sheet might therefore suit British interests best, but since other countries would insist on reparations, what was needed was a policy to satisfy the claims of others with minimum disturbance to British trade and perhaps some incidental advantage.

This line of argument had been given logical rigour in a minute from James Meade to Dalton. This demonstrated that if Germany were required to make large payments of reparations, with only a small proportion of the total coming to Britain, the net effect was highly likely to be to Britain's disadvantage. Meade's conclusion was that

> *if* there is a transfer problem (which there probably is) and *if* the United Kingdom's terms of trade are closely affected by the German terms of trade (which they are) and *if* the United Kingdom would receive only a small part of any total payable in reparations, the United Kingdom would probably lose more from the change in the

[7] The paper in its original form is undated and can be found in PRO T230/121. It was circulated as RES8 under the title 'Notes on Reparations and Economic Security' on 23 November 1942.

terms of trade brought about by the payment of reparations to third parties than she would gain from her own receipt of reparations.[8]

Robbins thought it better to go for the imposition of permanent economic disarmament rather than prolonged reparation payments. The Allies were already committed under the Atlantic Charter to the economic disarmament of Germany and the eradication of means to wage future wars. Military and economic considerations had to be balanced against one another in deciding how far to take economic disarmament and there was no hard and fast line that one could draw. The measures Robbins had in mind stopped well short of 'disindustrialization' which, even then, long before the Morgenthau Plan, had found 'very powerful advocates'. He took disarmament to mean the destruction of the armament industries and perhaps also machine tool production; a reduction in stocks to normal levels; and a reversal of autarchic policies giving support to ersatz industries and creating obstacles to trade with other countries. Some international body might be set up to control the chief German manufacturing companies that could be converted easily to the production of arms by acquiring a majority holding of their shares.

In the light of these considerations, Robbins found the 'arbitrary principle' that he sought in limiting claims to 'the repair or replacement of material damage'. This would keep the total down to what was manageable, pointed towards methods of payment that would be less likely to damage UK interests, and had a certain rough justice about it if, as he believed, the recollection of other losses faded once the material damage of war had been made good. Whatever principle was adopted there was a presumption in favour of speed – penalties should be visited on the current generation only – and also in favour of payments in kind: a presumption satisfied by deliveries of materials and labour services for physical reconstruction.

Much of Robbins's memorandum was an amplification of what was already contained in the Treasury's paper. Where the latter took as its criterion 'depredations by the enemy as an occupying power', Robbins favoured the rather broader principle of 'repair or replacement of material damage'. There was general agreement on the need for speed, a limited period, and so far as possible, payment in kind. The new element in Robbins's memorandum was his discussion of disarmament: particularly the suggestion for an international body with a controlling interest in German industry and the proposal to force freer trade on Germany in the interests of world peace. International shareholding did not win the outright

---

[8] Meade to Dalton, 1 December 1942, in PRO T230/121.

support of the Malkin Committee but the idea of requiring freer trade did find an echo in its report.

In his undated note to Robbins, Marcus Fleming took a much more radical line.[9] He saw little sense in economic disarmament. If Germany was made militarily impotent, would that ensure the peace of Europe when German power was likely to be overshadowed in future by Russian, and policy ought to be directed to preventing a coalescence of the two? Apart from that, what was there to be said in favour of economic disarmament? Nobody thought it could continue indefinitely; indeed, 'given the short memories and generous temper of the English and American electorates' it was unthinkable that they would persist in armed occupation for more than a decade or so. And once the occupation ended, any German Government would be able to rearm cautiously and by imperceptible stages.

Germany's initial disarmament would provide a breathing space for the establishment of a general system of European political security. If, as he feared, we did not succeed in this or did not even try, our main hope must be that Germany had 'learned her lesson' and, having given militarism a long and thorough trial, accepted a more modest role in the world. If that happened, as he thought quite likely, Germany would 'seek to attach herself to whichever of the two great power groups,the Anglo-Saxon or Russian, will afford her the more tolerable and dignified form of existence.' Our aim must therefore be to ensure that when Germany recovered her natural position in Europe, there was no legacy of bitterness to prevent co-operation with the West and nothing that savoured of exploitation in the interests of Anglo-Saxon industrialists.

Turning to reparations, Fleming found two rational justifications. They helped to demonstrate that aggression does not pay; and they helped to relieve distress and restore productive capacity in countries that suffered material damage at Germany's hands. But to exact reparations as a form of punishment would arouse bitterness and a desire for revenge. There should be simple restitution of identifiable objects and securities looted by Germany; and beyond that Germany should be made to participate in an international relief and rehabilitation scheme, at first perhaps as a net recipient of relief in the immediate post-war years, then as a net contributor, with payments likely to cease within a decade. Fleming visualized a great co-operative effort on an international scale to restore the economic life of the war-shattered areas, wherever they were, with Germany helping to bear the ultimate financial burden of the scheme. A separate reparations scheme would render these arrange-

[9] 'Economic Disarmament and Reparations', undated, in PRO T230/121.

ments less efficient; reparations and relief should be co-ordinated so as to permit of a centralized assessment of the needs of the various regions and of the means for meeting these needs. In this way Germany would no longer be paying a form of tribute as an isolated defeated country but would be an active participant in European recovery.

Fleming then addressed himself to the mechanics of getting reparations out of Germany, beginning with a rather airy dismissal of the transfer problem ('I believe that, under suitable conditions, much vaster sums can be transferred internationally than most people . . . . are willing to admit'). He then recommended a long succession of measures of control for this purpose that are in striking contrast to the earlier part of his memorandum. Control of the German banking system, and in particular of the Reichsbank, seemed to him an 'obvious and vital' step; this would include control over all foreign payments. Control over taxation and government expenditure was a more doubtful requirement; but in the interests of avoiding inflation, powers over broad categories of revenue and expenditure would probably be necessary. A study should be made of the German fiscal and social insurance scheme with a view to varying weekly contributions as a brake on inflation – a device favoured by the Economic Section as a regulator of the British economy. The exchange rate would have to be allowed to fall so as to make the balance of payments sufficiently favourable for the transfer of reparations. If this gave rise to wage demands in sympathy with import prices, wage-control would have to be imposed. As for trade, there was a strong political case for compelling Germany to adopt a liberal policy so that she could not create a self-sufficient, blockade-proof war economy by building up 'ersatz' industries. Rationing of consumer goods, licensing of investment goods, quotas on imports and other war-time controls might have to be continued.

Given such a catalogue, one might well ask whether it would not be simpler to make reparation payments in kind. Fleming thought not. The sole advantage of such an arrangement, which would share some of the disadvantages of barter, was that it assessed Germany's obligation in terms of a given quantity of her own products. But this result could be achieved more simply by fixing the amount to be paid in marks and adjusting it at intervals by reference to an index of German wages and prices.

Fleming's views do not seem to have persuaded the Malkin Committee that reparations should be merged with relief or that they should be paid in 'cash'. Yet in fact when the war was over,

Germany – or at least the Western zones – did become a net recipient of relief and reparations in kind were limited – again, in the Western zones – almost exclusively to capital goods made available by dismantling. If large scale payments *had* been made, many of the controls envisaged by Fleming might well have been necessary.

The Malkin Report

Many other views were put before the Malkin Committee, to whose conclusions we now turn. They are conveniently summarized in a paper from which Keynes spoke, and which he subsequently handed over, at a discussion with members of the US Department of State on 28 September 1943.[10] Even the Summary is a lengthy document, the most thorough and comprehensive treatment of the subject by any British committee. But, as is only too apparent in retrospect, it was erected on insecure foundations. The economic treatment of Germany was inevitably linked with the eventual military and political settlement, and what that settlement would be, no one in 1943 could say. The length and circumstances of any military occupation, the loss of territory, the extent to which Germany would be dismembered, the measures of economic disarmament that would be adopted – all these remained to be decided and all of them affected the scale on which reparations could be paid and the form that reparations might take.

An even more fundamental issue had first to be settled. If what took precedence over everything else was the need for security and the prospect of a lasting peace, was the more hopeful course to offer generous terms and seek reconciliation between victor and vanquished or to take every possible precaution against a revival of Germany's military strength? There was an obvious danger of repeating the failure after the First World War to pursue either course with sufficient singlemindedness, neither insisting on necessary safeguards that were enforceable and would be enforced, nor offering opportunities of economic recovery that would overcome German alienation and resentment. The choice, moreover, did not rest with the UK alone. America and Russia were likely to have a bigger say in the post-war settlement and their views at that stage in the war were still obscure.

The Malkin Committee began by setting out the hypotheses which they had used in order to give definition to the position for which they were seeking to prescribe. They were making recommendations

[10]. The paper is reproduced in Keynes, *Collected Writings*, Vol. xxvi, pp. 348–73.

intended to apply to Germany only, without considering other enemy states; they were assuming that Germany would remain a substantial unitary state, whatever changes were made at the frontiers, and that there would be no dismemberment; and they were concentrating on the most suitable methods of exacting reparations if they formed part of the peace settlement, not passing judgement on the advisability of such a policy. They assumed also that the Atlantic Charter 'clearly ruled out such measures as the total deindustrialisation of Germany', and that

> while it would be manifestly unfair to ensure that the German
> standard of living is maintained at a higher level than that of the
> countries she has overrun, measures which would have the effect of
> unduly depressing that standard or impairing the opportunities for
> peaceful employment would be inconsistent with the Atlantic Charter.[11]

Other assumptions took account of likely changes in public feeling over the post-war period. As much as possible of what had to be done should be done quickly on a once-for-all basis within a limited period after the termination of hostilities; and what was intended to remain in operation over a longer period should be such as to appear sufficiently just to command full co-operation from the United Nations, not only when introduced, but also for the critical 10 or 20 years after the war.

As for economic security, it would be a mistake to multiply safeguards that a later generation would regard as arbitrary and unjust, infecting the will to use force to suppress a potential aggressor. There was no possibility of devising any measures, economic or otherwise, which would of themselves permanently keep Germany impotent if her conquerors lost the will to enforce them. On the other hand, if that condition were fulfilled, use could undoubtedly be made of economic measures to make the task of recreating Germany's war economy 'difficult, protracted and unpromising'. The more important of such measures would have to be on a long-term footing, with a high degree of control, since the danger of renewed aggression could develop only after a considerable period of time. Long-continuing controls over normal activities in Germany had obvious drawbacks, however, and would either have to be exercisable from outside Germany or appeal to public opinion as thoroughly justifiable and interfering very little with normal economic life, so that in the event on infringements sanctions could be applied without popular opposition.

From these principles the committee drew a number of concrete

[11] Keynes, *Collected Writings*, Vol. xxvi, p. 349.

conclusions. Germany should not be allowed to make armaments of any kind (including under this heading civil aircraft), and any existing plant for their manufacture should be destroyed or removed. She should, however, be allowed to retain a machine tool industry since it formed an integral part of her engineering industry, and a progressive engineering industry was a necessary part of her economic life. She should also be allowed to make use of oil and various non-ferrous metals such as manganese and nickel that entered into the production of armaments and had a high value in war-time. But she would be forbidden to hold more than six month's stocks of any of these materials, obliged to supply full statistics of production, consumption, imports and stocks, and subject to the threat of an import ban if these conditions were not fulfilled. The production of synthetic oil was to be forbidden and existing plants destroyed, but, after careful consideration, the Committee came down against extending this recommendation to synthetic rubber and plants for the fixation of nitrogen. Many of these recommendations, as we shall see, reappeared in later discussions on economic disarmament.

Without going so far as to recommend that Germany be required to adopt free trade, the Committee wanted to see Germany abstain from 'undue autarchy' and conform to any arrangements made by the United Nations to promote mutually advantageous economic conditions between nations. They were opposed to stringent measures of financial control, especially efforts to control the central bank (the Reichsbank), and refrained from any general recommendation in favour of international shareholding in German industry. Finally, they considered the effect on economic security of possible transfers of German territory, assembling information in relation to the Saar, Upper Silesia, East Prussia and Austria.[12] Since the economic aspect of such transfers was only one, and by no means the most important, of the considerations involved, they made no definite recommendation, but struck no note of discouragement, pointing out that some of the transfers could add up to a considerable influence on Germany's capacity to wage war.

Reparations occupied a much larger place in the committee's report. They set out to cover all economic and financial claims that could be made against Germany at the end of the war, classifying these claims under four headings: reparation; restitution; Germany's contribution to the cost of peace-keeping; and pre-war private claims.

[12] On 8 December 1942 Meade asked Arnold Toynbee to put in hand a study of the effect on Germany's war potential of the loss of these four areas. The work was undertaken by Professor A. J. Brown and circulated as RES22 (PRO T230/121).

Restitution was a highly complex issue that need not concern us. All property taken by Germany was to be restored in so far as it could be identified, whether taken without payment, requisitioned and paid for, or acquired by 'voluntary' sale at the market price. The more important claims would include gold and precious stones; works of art; industrial and other securities; rolling stock, ships and other transport equipment; factory equipment; and other items such as pedigree livestock and miscellaneous loot.

The third set of claims corresponded to the relief that Germany would enjoy through the absence of a defence budget. Germany would be prohibited from spending money on armaments and military service but these would continue to be a burden on the victorious powers, 'charged with the task of preserving the peace of Europe and of the world'. That so large an economy should accrue to Germany while a corresponding burden had to be shouldered by the UK would seem intolerable after a time to public opinion. The Committee proposed, therefore, that so long as the disarmament provisions remained in force, Germany should be required to make a substantial contribution to the financial cost of keeping the peace. Indeed, when reparation proper ceased after the first few years, any continuing contribution from Germany should be used exclusively as a contribution to the cost of peace-keeping. This, the most novel of the Committee's recommendations, was clearly attributable to Keynes. It ultimately found expression in Germany's financial contribution to NATO.

The treatment of pre-war claims, including the Dawes and Young loans, need not concern us, except to note that the more they were satisfied, the less would be Germany's capacity to make other payments on account of reparations (or peace-keeping). The committee was in some perplexity how best to handle the matter and expounded three possible solutions without picking on any one of them.

With regard to reparations proper, the Committee took it to be evident that the various claims, even if confined to limited categories of damage, would greatly exceed Germany's capacity to pay. From this it followed that no Allied country could hope to receive more than a small proportion of its claim, and that the amount that Germany would be required to pay – the maximum that it was advisable to demand – would be unaffected by any classification or justification of individual claims such as was thought to be necessary at Versailles. The only purpose of considering which claims should rank would be to assist in establishing how the aggregate payable in reparations should be divided between the countries entering claims.

For such a division it was simply not worth while to enter into detail and debate the merits of different classes of claim. In the Committee's view: 'round figures for the proportionate share of the different members of the United Nations should be settled by the governments concerned as part of a broad-bottomed bargain'.[13]

But on what broad principles should such round figures be arrived at? The committee's answer to this question was reached via a series of exclusions. First it argued that a fair division would be difficult if it were based on the costs of the war incurred by each Ally. Occupation costs, and the like, levied by German authorities on occupied areas, claims in respect of German bank notes circulating in these areas, and similar exactions and sacrifices were also excluded as somewhat similar in principle to the costs of the war in countries doing the fighting. Claims in respect of personal injury and loss of life should also be excluded. They would be extremely difficult to assess and compare with other claims, and were unlikely to yield an answer significantly different from that reached by the method favoured by the committee.

This was to confine the basis of claims for reparation to the loss of non-military property, movable and immovable, directly caused by the enemy in the course of military operations. They agreed that in strict logic it was hard to distinguish loss of property caused directly by the enemy and property expended for the purpose of defeating the enemy. But if no line were drawn, one category of claims would lead on to another until not only the whole costs of the war but losses arising out of disorganization of the internal economy, the costs of re-settling people who had been evicted, and all kinds of other claims would have to be included. There was no reason to suppose that 'to bring all these claims into hotch-potch would improve the essential justice' of the simpler formula. Much the same reasoning had prevailed in 1940 when the British Government decided to confine compensation for war damage in the UK to damage resulting from 'the fire of the enemy'.

Thus claimant Governments were to be awarded a share of the compensation obtained from Germany in roughly the same ratio as that of their losses of non-military property to total losses. Heads of governments would have to exercise a broad judgement on the facts produced by each claimant government, and should be free to take into account such other considerations as they deemed relevant. If no agreement could be reached, 'some impartial authority' should settle the matter. Each government should be free to put the compensation it received to whatever use it thought fit, irrespective

[13] Keynes, *Collected Writings*, Vol. xxvi, p. 352.

of the basis on which its claim had been assessed in the international share-out.

But how much could Germany pay and in what forms? The Committee thought it 'useless and unwise' to name a specific figure rather than 'aim at an elastic formula that [would] be automatically adjusted to the facts of the future as they disclosed themselves'. They were only too well aware of the enormous damage that Germany had suffered and would continue to suffer and, on the other hand, of her 'immensely efficient industrial organisation' and the swift recovery of which she was capable if economic conditions in the post-war world were favourable. In spite of their natural caution they did, however, at a later point in their report, venture an estimate that Germany's total contribution in all forms within the first five years might be 'of the order of, say, $4 billion at 1938 prices, or possibly $6 billion at the level of prices prevailing after the war'.[14]

What forms of reparations did the Committee have in mind? They listed seven:

1 once-for-all deliveries of financial or capital assets;
2 once-for-all deliveries of materials, raw or manufactured, out of stock;
3 annual deliveries in kind from current output;
4 the performance of tasks in Allied territory by organized German labour;
5 the services of labourers not organized for special tasks to be made available outside Germany;
6 the provision of the requirements within Germany of the armies of occupation;
7 annual payments in cash to be provided out of the excess of Germany's exports over her imports.

Of these, the last had already been rejected by the Committee except in the form of a contribution to peace-keeping met out of an annual cash payment across the exchanges. Occupation costs (item 6), so far as they involved expenditure in local currency, should be met by the German authorities without charge, leaving only costs arising outside Germany to be met by the Allied government concerned (at least until the peace-keeping contribution became available after the first five years). This left the first five items. Deliveries in kind (items 1–3), especially where they contributed to reconstruction in the devastated areas through the repair of buildings and transport facilities, could be of great value in

[14] Ibid., p. 365.

the early post-war years and matched the committee's view of reparations as compensation for enemy damage to property. But deliveries in kind, if unduly prolonged, would be an artificial element in the economic life in Europe, delaying the restoration of normal trade flows, and disadvantageous both to Germany and her neighbours and competitors. The committee recommended, therefore, that they should be terminated within a short period after the war, say five years. There were even stronger reasons for restricting the period over which German labour should be employed abroad, and a limit of three years should be set.

The Committee went on to spell out in more detail what deliveries in kind and labour services they envisaged. They recommended that all German property rights and interests in the territory of any of the United Nations should pass to the government concerned. This would include not only property located there but any claims by German nationals against the nationals of any of the United Nations. Where German claims and assets in German ownership exceeded her liabilities to any neutral country the excess should go towards the cost of post-war relief in Germany.

Deliveries in kind should be only of such articles as could be employed in work of reconstruction, all other articles obtained from Germany being purchased in the ordinary way. Deliveries in kind might come either from stock or from current production. The first of these would include machine tools and factory equipment; ships, rolling stock, and inland transport equipment of all kinds; stocks of raw materials in excess of normal requirements; and livestock. From current production might come building materials, including steel, timber, bricks and cement; and semi-manufactured and finished products required for the erection or equipment of buildings and the restoration of the means of transport. New ships and transport equipment and agricultural machinery and fertilizers could also be included.

Finally, labour services might consist either of work done by organized groups of Germans in the restoration of buildings and means of transport, or of work not involving such organization for special tasks. The maximum number of Germans engaged in such forced labour should be three million in the first year, two million in the second, and one million in the third year after the war. Housing, subsistence and any pocket-money paid to them should be at the charge of the governments employing them, while the German Government would be responsible for the provision of clothing and the supply to their dependants in Germany of any necessary subsistence.

The Committee recognized that at the end of the war, Germany would require more imports than she could pay for out of exports so that she would be in need of relief. They did not attempt to reconcile this with their recommendations on reparations deliveries in kind, but addressed themselves to ways in which such relief could be paid for. Any gold remaining after restitution should be drawn upon and there might be payments due from neutral countries out of the surrender of German property rights (see p. 30). The rest would be a charge on export proceeds in later years collected in instalments by relief authorities.

The machinery for this purpose would be the same as for the Germany contribution to the cost of peace-keeping. This involved canalization of all receipts due to Germany for her gross exports through an international institution and the retention in a special account of a proportion of those receipts. The proportion suggested was 10 per cent, rising to 20 per cent on any excess of exports receipts above the equivalent of $1 billion in any year and 25 per cent on any excess above $2 billion. The cost of this deduction from the value of exports would fall on the German budget, not on the exporters who would be paid in full by the German Government.

Since it would not be possible, even at the end of the war, to make any final estimate of Germany's capacity to pay, the Committee proposed that is should be left to an inter-Allied organization, which might be called the Reconstruction Commission, to decide what deliveries Germany should make and in what form. The commission would have to satisfy itself on a number of points: for example, that the required deliveries would not reduce unduly the German standard of living, or impair, disproportionately to their value, Germany's productive capacity, or be needed as exports to pay for necessary imports. How the Commission should be constituted would have to depend on the political situation at the time.

The recommendations of the Malkin Committee showed foresight and realism in insisting on the need for a broad-bottomed agreement on shares in reparations, in refusing to settle at once on a total that Germany could be expected to pay, and in proposing a limited period for such payments as fell to be made. The idea of a continuing 'peace-keeping' contribution after the first five years was imaginative and constructive. There was also much to be said for the view that reparations should be linked with reconstruction of the devastated areas, both in the way the total was divided and in the form that deliveries took. The recommendations to avoid cash payments across the exchanges and allow labour services for a limited period were both in keeping with later views. Much of what was said on deliveries in kind, whether from stock or from current production, was thoroughly sensible. Given how little was known in 1943 about the changes in the condition of Germany, or the political and military conditions to which the Allies would have agreed by the time the war was over or at the Potsdam Conference that followed, the Malkin Report was a masterly exposition, reaching far more definite conclusions than the uncertainties of the situation appeared to permit.

And yet, looking back, one is struck by a certain ingenuousness. Would other countries be content with the limited measures of economic disarmament proposed if, as seemed likely, economic security was foremost in their minds? Would the Russians in particular be content to see reparations restricted to articles required for the restoration of buildings and means of transport? Would a Reconstruction Commission that included the Russians ever agree about what depressed 'unduly' the German standard of living? What if the post-war relief needed to put Germany back on her feet ran to $1 billion or more?

Two years later the Committee would no doubt have produced a different report. But for the purpose of bringing ministers face to face with the major issues, the Report was well conceived and timely. Unfortunately it received little attention from ministers although submitted well ahead of the Conference of Foreign Ministers in Moscow in October 1943 at which the post-war treatment of Germany was first discussed by the three major powers.

The Report was given a wide distribution in Whitehall at the end of August 1943.[15] If it came before ministers a month later, it was only because Keynes had sought authority to discuss it with officials in the State Department in the course of a visit to Washington. By the time ministers met on 29 September, their delay in replying had been interpreted as consent; on the previous day Keynes had both spoken at some length (leaving the Americans 'considerably interested and even excited') and handed over to them a full summary of the argument of the Report.[16] Unaware of this, ministers refused permission for the disclosure of the substance of the Report. The Foreign Office, however, subsequently concluded that no harm had been done and that no further action need be taken.

The meeting of ministers on 29 September, with Eden in the chair, was very much *ad hoc*.[17] Anderson, then Lord President, thought

---

[15] The printed copy in PRO FO 942/52, dated 31 August 1943, is numbered 121. Copies were later made available to the Dominion Governments (APW(44)15M in PRO CAB 87/66).

[16] Keynes, *Collected Writings*, Vol. xxvi, pp. 348–73.

that the Report's assumptions that there would be no dismemberment and no deindustrialization were 'rather large assumptions to make without reference to the Cabinet'. Others picked on one or other of these assumptions for attack, and Eden explained that a paper on dismemberment was under preparation.[18] The most forceful criticism came from Cherwell and Selborne (Minister of Economic Warfare), both of whom insisted that Britain should take over Germany's export markets, for example in steel and machine tools. But apart from random expressions of dissatisfaction, there was no adequate consideration of the Report, and ministers parted under the impression that they would have a further opportunity of discussing it once policy on dismemberment had been settled. They also appeared to believe that they would then be able to instruct the Malkin Committee how to continue its work.

In this they were very much mistaken. When the Cabinet met to discuss Eden's paper on 5 October, no decision on dismemberment was taken and ministers engaged in no further discussion of it for nearly a year. The Malkin Report was never again explicitly considered by ministers (although it sometimes figured in the documentation submitted for discussion). As for the Malkin Committee, its labours had already ceased.

Yet the committee did exercise considerable influence on thinking both in Britain and in the USA. As we shall see, its recommendations on reparations were virtually reproduced in the next major official report in August 1944.[19] They also had an admitted influence on the paper tabled by the American delegation at the Moscow conference of Foreign Ministers in October 1943.[20]

[17] PRO FO 371/35309, Malkin Report. Those attending the meeting included, in addition to those mentioned, Attlee, Dalton and Sir William Malkin.
[18] Below, p. 33.
[19] 'Report by the Economic and Industrial Planning Staff on issues affecting the economic obligations to be imposed on Germany', EIPS(44)23, 15 August 1944, in PRO FO 1005/959.
[20] Below, pp. 50–53.

3

Later Wartime Views

There is no point to oppose these desires of Stalin [to extend Russian territory], because he has the power to get them anyhow. So better give them gracefully. . . . Communist regimes [will] expand, but what can we do about it? . . . The European countries will have to undergo tremendous changes in order to adapt to Russia, but . . . in ten or twenty years the European influence would bring the Russians to become less barbarian. . . . The European people will simply have to endure the Russian domination.[1]

Roosevelt to Cardinal Spellman, 3 September 1943

My guiding thought . . . is that nothing must happen which might in the future separate the four powers who came together in the war. To preserve this entente, I will make any sacrifice.

Clemenceau, in Chambre des Députés, 29 December 1918

Even before the *ad hoc* meeting at the Foreign Office on the Malkin Report in September 1943, ministers had begun to turn their attention to the way in which Germany should be treated after the war. There were three occasions in 1943 on which Eden raised the matter in the War Cabinet: once in March before he left for Washington; again in June when he asked for authority to talk without commitment to the American and Soviet ambassadors; and finally in September before leaving for the Moscow Conference.[1] A Cabinet committee was set up in August 1943 under Attlee to advise on armistice terms and instruments of surrender, the military

[1] The papers submitted to the War Cabinet by Eden in 1943 began with 'The Future of Germany', WP(43)96 on 8 March, followed by 'Armistice and Related Problems', WP(43)217 on 25 May 1943 and 'Germany', WP(43)421 on 27 September 1943, in PRO CAB 66/ 34, 37 and 41 respectively.

administration of occupied enemy territory, and other matters involving discussion with the Allies.[2] But in none of the discussions in Cabinet or on the new committee was there more than a passing reference to reparations.

A variety of other issues engaged the interest of ministers. First of all it was necessary to agree on the arrangements governing the military occupation of Germany. The Chiefs of Staff wanted total occupation so as to bring home to Germans throughout the country that the Nazi system had failed in the military field as it had elsewhere: there was to be no second attempt to put the blame for military defeat on a 'stab in the back' from politicians. Zones of occupation for each of the Allied armies should be fixed before the cessation of hostilities, with boundaries that should not depend on the positions reached by the various armies at the armistice.[3] This of itself raised controversial issues. Cripps, for example, objected to a division of Germany into three zones of occupation;[4] Eisenhower, for different reasons, wanted a single zone; Roosevelt made endless difficulties, and did not finally accept the zones suggested by the British until the Quebec Conference in September 1944.

A long list of other questions arose. How lasting were the zones to be? Were they to be mere lines of demarcation between armies that would soon withdraw, or permanent divisions into separate states? Was Germany to be dismembered? What territory should she be required to give up? Would the surrender, when it came, be made by a central German Government that was to be kept in being, or would there be turmoil and guerilla warfare and no German authorities willing to assume responsibility? How was Germany to be administered when civilian government was resumed? Would it be possible to decentralize without dismemberment and yet administer Germany as a single economic unit?

These were the kind of questions about post-war Germany that

[2] Woodward (1962) p. 445; PRO CAB 87/65. The Armistice Terms and Civil Affairs (ACA) committee continued the work of an *ad hoc* committee set up to consider armistice terms for Italy. It was superseded in turn by the Armistice and Post-War Committee (APW), in April 1944, still with Attlee in the chair. A sub-committee of the Chiefs of Staff Committee, the Post-Hostilities Planning Sub-Committee (PHP), was also appointed in August to prepare Draft Instruments of Surrender and remained in being after February 1944 with a Foreign Office chairman, Gladwyn Jebb.

[3] 'The Military Occupation of Germany'. Report by the Chiefs of Staff Committee, ACA(43)20, 12 December 1943, in PRO CAB 87/65.

[4] 'Armistice and Related Problems', Memorandum by the Minister of Aircraft Production, WP(43)243, 15 June 1943, in PRO CAB 66/37; WM(43)86, 16 June 1943, in PRO CAB 65/34.

troubled ministers in 1943–4 and that took precedence in their minds over reparations. Yet since they were linked with Germany's capacity to pay reparations, and the attitude of ministers to the one set of questions throws light on their attitude to the other, it is useful to outline the course of the debate before reparations emerged as a major issue at Yalta.

There was a natural reluctance on the part of ministers to come to firm decisions of principle, or even to engage in discussion of post-war arrangements on Germany, when events were moving so fast and the situation at the end of the war was so difficult to foresee. For those reasons, Eden told the Cabinet in June 1943 that it was neither desirable nor practicable to lay down principles to govern the treatment of Germany after the war. Nevertheless he saw dangers in leaving it to the last minute to try to reach agreement on matters of such complexity; and since the Americans and the Russians were giving thought to the subject, he asked to be allowed to talk to their Ambassadors. The only specific questions that he wanted to pursue, at that stage, however, related to zones of occupation and the choice between partial and total occupation of Germany.

On later occasions Eden showed a similar unwillingness to press for decisions on Germany while the future remained so uncertain,[5] hoping like Keynes that 'history and the course of events will provide something better for us than we are capable of inventing for ourselves.'[6] Churchill was even more reluctant to try to reach agreement on the post-war treatment of Germany while the war was in progress. He felt strongly that his first duty was to get on with winning the war. He had no lack of anxieties over what might follow but these were increasingly concentrated on Russia rather than Germany, and so long as these anxieties were not shared by the Americans, he might well conclude that there was limited scope for taking a firm stand on British policy towards Germany or any need to be in a hurry to arrive at one. A further difficulty lay in the close links between the many different aspects of the matter which made it hard to settle one set of issues in isolation from the rest. All the various blows to Germany's industrial capacity, and all the various claims on it, interacted on one another and could not be the subject of separate adjudications. This, he argued as late as June 1945, when the war with Germany was already over, made it impossible for the Cabinet to give detailed consideration to the complex recommendations officials submitted to them.[7]

[5] Below, pp. 48–52.
[6] Keynes, *Collected Writings*, Vol. xxvi, p. 383.
[7] CM(45)8, 15 June 1945 in PRO CAB 65/53.

Nevertheless it was a mistake to wait so long before trying to form a view of British interests in so important a matter. Churchill did not avoid being drawn into discussion on what was to be done with Germany by failing to ensure that he was adequately briefed in advance. At Teheran in November 1943, at Yalta in February 1945, and even more at the Quebec conference with Roosevelt in September 1944 when the Morgenthau plan was unveiled, he showed little sign of familiarity with the work done by British officials. What is more doubtful is whether any amount of briefing would have brought more success in arguing against American and, still more, Russian views.

Most of the discussion between ministers in 1943–4 related to economic security and the need to prevent a revival of Germany's power to make war. Officials tended to pursue a rather different line and concentrate on matters of *will*: either on Germany's will to aggressive war or on the will of the United Nations to restrain her. The four main themes of ministerial discussion were: disarmament and demilitarization; decentralization; dismemberment; and dismantlement.

Disarmament and Demilitarization

There was never any disagreement, after two world wars, that Germany must be completely disarmed and remain disarmed. All munitions of war were to be destroyed and all facilities for making them removed or dismantled. The manufacture of armaments of all kinds was to be prohibited.

As far back as 1941, Churchill had insisted that the mistake of acquiescing in German rearmament after the First World War must not be repeated, and that this time the measures taken to ensure this must be effective. But how could one be sure that they were effective? Still more, how could one be sure that they would be enforced? The more stringent they were, the more likely it was that efforts would be made to evade them, at first secretly and on a small scale, then more openly and on a progressively bigger scale, while at the same time the public opinion by which the measures were sustained in the Allied countries would weaken and offer no support for necessary sanctions. In those circumstances might it not be necessary to think of other measures to limit Germany's military power either by way of re-insurance or as an alternative to extreme measures of disarmament?

Decentralization

One such measure – the mildest – was decentralization of political power so as to strengthen local authorities. This was very much in Eden's mind, as an alternative more to dismemberment than to any measures of disarmament. In the conditions of chaos to be expected after the war, he pointed out, the various regions would be thrown back on their own resources and this situation would lend itself to the creation of a more decentralized system of government.[8] On the other hand, when Attlee argued strongly in July 1944 for smashing up the central government machine, rather than giving priority to the early restoration of orderly life, Eden insisted that a central authority of some kind, German or Allied, was indispensable and that economic turmoil would not be in Britain's interests.[9]

On the European Advisory Commission, the American and Russian repesentatives were still arguing in September 1944 that it was necessary to plan on the assumption that a central government existed in Germany and for the Allies to begin by using it. The Prime Minister at the Quebec Conference in the same month took a similar view. A report in October argued that, even if there were no formal surrender by a German government, some form of central government would have to be re-established, if only as an interim measure. All the controls which the Nazi regime had instituted – as in any war economy – were planned from the centre and would have to be continued if the economy was to function at all. The only choice was between an Allied governing authority and a German authority under Allied control. On considering this report the ACA Committee opted for the second of these alternatives and did not pursue the issue of decentralization.[10]

Dismemberment

The most frequent subject of discussion was dismemberment. Eden kept saying that he had an open mind on the subject but was never entirely convinced that it would be right to force dismemberment on Germany rather than rely on separatist tendencies, encouraged by

[8] 'Germany', Memorandum by the Secretary of State for Foreign Affairs, WP(43)421, 27 September 1943, in PRO CAB 66/41.
[9] 'Policy towards Germany,' Memorandum by the Deputy Prime Minister and Lord President, APW(44)43, 11 July 1944, in PRO CAB 87/67; 'Policy towards Germany', Memorandum by the Secretary of State for Foreign Affairs, APW(44)47, July 1944, in PRO CAB 87/67; and APW 10th Meeting, 20 July 1944, in PRO CAB 87/66.
[10] Woodward (1962) pp. 466–9.

the Allies, to bring it about. Some other ministers – for example, Selborne, the Minister for Economic Warfare – were in favour of dismemberment from 1943 onwards.[11] No one seemed to be strongly against it.

At the *ad hoc* meeting of ministers in September, Eden had promised a paper on dismemberment. But the paper that he put to the War Cabinet did not discuss the matter at any length.[12] Policy, he argued, should aim ultimately at the readmittance of a reformed Germany into the life of Europe. Of the action that might be taken after the war, dismemberment was the most drastic but it would need a very long period of political control if the reunion of the dismembered parts was to be prevented. Action such as decentralization and control of Germany's economic potential would be less demanding from that point of view. There should be total occupation of Germany, total disarmament and administration by an inter-allied body for possibly two years.

When Eden went to the Moscow Conference of Foreign Ministers in October 1943 he was still without a policy on dismemberment (or, for that matter, on reparations). He had suggested to the Cabinet that they should go on record as having an open mind on the forcible dismemberment of Germany, but as welcoming indigenous separatist movements. This recommendation was supported by the Prime Minister who proposed that no attempt should be made to reach a binding conclusion.[13]

At the Moscow Conference, the American and Soviet delegations were in a similar position. Cordell Hull, the leader of the American delegation, explained that dismemberment was generally favoured by the American leaders but considered to be impracticable by their experts.[14] Molotov, who led the Soviet delegation, and Eden, who led the British, agreed that the position was much the same in their countries. Whether the reasons advanced by the experts were also similar we do not know.

Before Hull's departure for Moscow, Roosevelt had expressed strong views to him and other senior advisers on the measures necessary in the post-war treatment of Germany. He appears to have been in favour of dismemberment for some time, in spite of the very

[11] Lord Selborne argued the case in a memorandum to the War Cabinet, 'The Future of Germany', WP(43)144, 8 April 1943, in PRO CAB 66/35.
[12] 'Germany', Memorandum by the Secretary of State for Foreign Affairs, WP(43)421, 27 September 1943, in PRO CAB 66/41.
[13] WM(43)135, 5 October 1943, in PRO CAB 65/36.
[14] Balfour (1956) p. 18, quoting Moseley, 'Dismemberment of Germany', *Foreign Affairs* (1950).

different views held by State Department officials. When told in March 1943 by Eden that Stalin was likely to insist on it, he had expressed no dissent: even if, contrary to his hopes, separatist movements did not develop, a division of Germany into separate states would have to be brought about.[15] Germany must be disarmed and broken down into three or more states, linked by a customs union and other common services, while Prussia was completely detached.[16]

Roosevelt elaborated his views a few weeks later, just before he left for Cairo and Teheran, when he told his Chiefs of Staff that there would be three separate states, possibly five: a South German state of Baden, Württemberg and Bavaria, a North-Western state extending as far east as Berlin and an eastern state including West Prussia and Pomerania. The boundaries he had in mind were very different from those for the proposed occupation zones, and this difference created immediate problems for the staff who were planning the invasion of Europe.[17] At Teheran in November 1943 Roosevelt repeated his proposal, which had now become one for a fivefold division of Germany with the Ruhr and the Kiel Canal under international control.

It was Stalin, however, who made the running at Teheran on the treatment of Germany. He wanted Poland's western frontier to be extended to the Oder and dismissed Churchill's proposal that some of the South German states should be detached and joined to a new Danubian Confederation, arguing that it would simply allow the Germans to rebuild a powerful state on the Hapsburg model. He was equally opposed to Churchill's suggestion for some form of international supervision over German industry. Even the manufacture of metal furniture might be converted to assist in the production of aircraft while the making of clocks and watches could provide facilities for making fuses for shells. Germany must be destroyed, not reconstructed or re-educated. His aim seemed to be a weak and dismembered country, preferably under Russian tutelage, at the opposite pole from those who maintained that a healthy Europe required a healthy Germany.[18]

Stalin's ideas met with little opposition from Roosevelt who took an equally Carthaginian view and lent towards the deindustrialization

[15] Balfour (1956), p. 15.

[16] Wheeler-Bennett and Nicholls (1972), p. 108.

[17] The occupation zones ultimately fixed were those originally proposed by a British Cabinet committee under Attlee in the late summer of 1943, accepted by the Russians in February 1944 and not finally agreed to by Roosevelt, after much argument, until September 1944 at the Quebec conference (Wheeler-Bennett and Nicholls (1972), chapter 13).

[18] Wheeler-Bennett and Nicholls (1972), pp. 148, 166, 179; Mastny, pp. 128–9.

proposals soon to be put forward by Morgenthau. Churchill himself was not against dismemberment and favoured putting the Ruhr area and Westphalia under some form of international control. He came away convinced that 'the British, United States and Russian Governments are . . . agreed that Germany is to be decisively broken up into a number of separate states'.[19] This assertion was challenged by Herbert Morrison, the Home Secretary,[20] and as we have seen, it was the Prime Minister himself who persuaded the Cabinet to take no binding decision. Churchill was basing himself on the Teheran discussions but all that had been agreed at Teheran was that plans for dismemberment should be referred to the newly established European Advisory Commission.[21]

By the beginning of 1944, however – and indeed throughout the year – opinion in Whitehall was running strongly in favour of dismemberment. Even Keynes was attracted by the idea and envisaged uniting Bavaria and Wurtemberg with Austria.[22] By July it was possible for Sir Alexander Cadogan, Permanent Under-Secretary of State at the Foreign Office, to tell Ministers that 'it was our accepted policy to promote separatist tendencies but not to impose them.'[23] Yet there does not appear to have been any discussion of the matter earlier in the year to overturn the decision of the Cabinet to keep an open mind.

Discussion between ministers in the second half of 1944 and in early 1945 went on in the Armistice and Post-War (APW) Committee of the Cabinet which was set up in April 1944 to advise on armistice terms, the administration of liberated or conquered territories and general political and military questions in the post-

---

[19] 'Unconditional Surrender', Note by the Prime Minister, 15 January 1944, WP(44)33 in PRO CAB 66/45.

[20] Pimlott to Bridges, 20 January 1944, in PRO CAB 127/272. Attlee, who was at this stage against dismemberment 'enforced by the victor', but in favour of 'the severance

[21] Stalin said at Yalta that the discussion at Teheran had been only an exchange of views (*Foreign Relations of the United States* (henceforth FRUS), *The Conference at Malta and Yalta*, 1945, p. 612). At the third Moscow Conference in October 1944,

[21] Stalin said at Yalta that the discussion at Teheran had been only an exchange of views (*Foreign Relations ofthe United States* (henceforth FRUS), *The Conference at Malta and Yalta*, 1945, p. 612). At the third Moscow Conference in October 1944, when Stalin took a more favourable view of Churchill's proposal, Roosevelt was not present and no decision was taken.

[22] Keynes to Playfair, 28 January 1944, in PRO T247/87. He later changed his mind and claimed that he was never in favour of making dismemberment permanently compulsory, but wanted to gain 20 years' time (Keynes, *Collected Writings*, Vol.xxvi, p. 382).

[23] APW(44) 10th meeting on 20 July 1944 in PRO CAB 87/66.

war period.[24] Most of the papers on the post-war treatment of Germany submitted to the committee by officials came from the Economic and Industrial Planning Staff appointed in February 1944.

The question of dismemberment came to the fore at the tenth meeting of the new Ministerial Committee. A report on 'Transfer of German Populations'[25] had been submitted by a committee under a Foreign Office chairman, J. M. Troutbeck. This had been asked to consider Germany's capacity to absorb immigrants form the territories that it was proposed to cede to Poland and Czechoslovakia including East Prussia, Danzig, a large part of Silesia, and the territory taken from Czechoslovakia in 1938.[26] It estimated that these proposals, which had been enlarged to include a bigger slice of Germany to compensate Poland for territory she would lose to Russia, would result in the expulsion of over 10 million Germans. The committee expressed doubts about so large a transfer of population: 'The heavy extra burden on Germany which the transfers would impose might create an economic problem which would prove insoluble and lead to a complete German collapse.'

It was this paper which touched off the first major discussion by ministers of the post-war settlement. Attlee circulated a paper to his colleagues attacking officials for their excessive concern to get organized life going again in Germany as quickly as possible.[27] The papers they submitted, in his view, too readily took for granted that everything should be done to facilitate Germany's economic, commercial and industrial revival. There wer three arguments for this: the need to help German industry to recover for the sake of reparations; the contribution that Germany could make to European welfare; and the desire to run the country with a minimum of trouble. But the last of these was misguided. He would willingly accept a good deal of inefficiency and disorder in the interests of rooting out 'the whole German military machine, the whole Nazi system'. He was strongly in favour of smashing the central

[24] For the terms of reference see APW(44) 1, 19 April 1944, in PRO CAB 87/67. The members were Attlee (Chairman), Eden, Bevin, Lyttelton, Cranborne and Sinclair. Grigg was entitled to attend to attend as Minister of War whenever questions of military administration of enemy territory arose.

[25] 'Transfer of German Populations', Memorandum by the Minister of State, covering 'Report of the Interdepartmental Committee on the Transfer of German Populations', APW(44)34, 26 June 1944, in PRO CAB 87/67. The Report is dated 12 May 1944.

[26] Eden had made these proposals to the Cabinet on 27 September 1943. Benes had been told in July 1942 that the Government approved the principle of transferring German minorities to Germany.

[27] 'Policy towards Germany', Memorandum by the Deputy Prime Minister and Lord President, APW(44)43, 11 July 1944, in PRO CAB 87/67.

government machine and returning to what he referred to, rather oddly, as the Germany of Bismarck – an idea that appealed to other ministers present, including Cranborne (Secretary of State for the Dominions).

These views were somewhat different from those of Eden who submitted a memorandum arguing that chaos in Germany was not in the interests of the UK.[28] As Grigg (Secretary of State for War) kept insisting, there might be no central government to surrender, but it was indispensable that there should be a central *Allied* authority which could work through local German authorities. (Sir William Strang pointed out that the draft terms of surrender prepared by the European Advisory Commision *did* assume that there would be a central German government, but no one enquired what this implied.) It was left to Lyttelton to suggest that, were Germany dismembered, the newly created states had better be given a good start and competent government, or there would be a strong tendency for them to reunite.

Dismemberment had the support both of Attlee and Cranborne. Bevin said he would have liked to see the southern states of Germany attracted into a union with Austria, towards the Mediterranean basin and away from Germany. In his view there was little natural affinity between the people living in the different German states. Strang explained that the three zones of occupation had been demarcated so as to permit of dismemberment without re-creating any of the old states. Eden, however, stuck to Cadogan's formula and was not prepared to go further than advocate all possible measures to promote the disruption of Germany into separate states.

By the middle or 1944 Churchill at least was more or less reconciled to many of the territorial components of what became the Potsdam Agreement. All foreign territory acquired under Hitler would be surrendered; Russia would acquire East Prussia and occupy Poland up to the Curzon line; in compensation, Poland would absorb a large slice of German territory between her Western frontier and the river Oder; the rest of Germany would be divided into three (later, four) zones under military occupation; and these might either come to form separate states or give place to some other form of dismemberment. By the middle of the year, moreover, it was recognized that the changes in frontiers would lead to massive transfers of population, estimated at 10 million.[29] All this was in the

[28] 'Policy towards Germany', Memorandum by the Secretary of State for Foreign Affairs, APW(44)47, 19 July 1944; and 'Policy towards Germany', Note by the Secretariat, APW(44)52, 26 July 1944, in PRO CAB 87/67.
[29] 'Transfer of German Populations', APW(44)34, 26 June 1944 in PRO CAB 87/68.

wind without Cabinet agreement, virtually without Cabinet discussion, and without regard to the views that France had yet to express.

After the inconclusive meetings of the APW committee in July, discussion continued over the next few months. At the end of August a telegram from General Eisenhower, raising the possibility of a complete breakdown of all central authority in Germany, brought the subject up again, and on this occasion the committee recorded their support for dismemberment but agreed to take no decision pending a report from the Foreign Office. A paper was prepared and a meeting arranged, but the meeting was cancelled and the paper withdrawn.

Foreign Office versus Chiefs of Staff

The reason for this lay in a dispute between the Chiefs of Staff and the Foreign Office. The views of the Chiefs of Staff had been invited in June 1944 – not a very opportune time – and were not submitted until 9 September. They were in favour of dismemberment for reasons which the Foreign Office, now against dismemberment, regarded as dangerous and fantastic. The reasons that excited this reaction added up to the need to insure against a hostile Russo-German combination. The UK could count on no help against Russia from a united Germany, since the Russians would never allow Germany to rearm unless under Russian domination. If however, Germany were dismembered, the North-West and perhaps also the South might gravitate to a Western European group.[30]

The Foreign Office, on the other hand, was against dismemberment, on the grounds that it would be evaded and come to be regarded in Britain and America as unjust. The idea of reversing

[30] The controversy is reviewed in Julian Lewis, 'British Military Planning for Postwar Strategic Defence 1942–47', 1981 (Oxford D. Phil. thesis. See also Woodward (1962) pp. 189–90; Elizabeth Barker (1983); D. Cameron Watt, 'Britain, the United States and the Opening of the Cold War' in Ovendale (ed.), *The Foreign Policy of the British Labour Government* (1984); Burridge (1981); and PRO CAB 81/45, CAB122/1566 and FO 371/43336. For the Foreign Office's view of relations with the USSR in 1941–5, see Graham Ross (ed.), *The Foreign Office and the Kremlin* (1984).

The Chiefs of Staff seem to have been more alive than the politicians to shifts in the Soviet attitude to dismemberment. At a meeting with Eden in October 1944, Portal (Chief of Air Staff) suggested that a change had occurred in the course of 1944 towards keeping Germany as a single unit. At that stage Churchill was maintaining that both Stalin and Roosevelt were more in favour of dismemberment than he was (PRO FO 371/43336; and Lewis, pp. 143–4).

policy towards Germany and using it as part of an anti-Soviet bloc struck them as unrealistic and futile, since Russia was a great military power and to rearm Germany against her was to revive the danger of future German aggression. The only hope lay in preserving the unity of the United Nations and doing nothing to endanger the Anglo-Soviet alliance. This still left open other ways of diminishing the authority of the central government: the French proposal for Rhenania (a scheme for permanent international control over an area from the Ruhr to the Black Forest), for which there was some half-hearted support in parts of Whitehall; the dissolution of Prussia, much favoured by the Prime Minister; and either a return to a confederate or federal system or some form of decentralization.

Further discussions failed to resolve the difference. The Chiefs of Staff argued that they were bound to take account of the possibility that the United Nations might break down owing to differences with Russia, leaving Britain face to face with a hostile Russia and a Germany under her domination. The British were just as much entitled to take wise precautions as the Russians. Eden, on the other hand, thought that 'by focussing our attention on the distant danger we might fail to guard against the immediate danger which was the resurgence of Germany. . . . If study and talk about Russia as an enemy became widespread, it would almost certainly come to the ears of the Russians' and encourage their 'innate suspicions . . . that our talk of collaboration was not sincere.'[31]

The conflict of views on the dismemberment of Germany between Eden and the Chiefs of Staff was a reminder that policy towards Germany was inseparable from policy towards Russia. In the autumn of 1944 it tended to be taken for granted that the war-time alliance and collaboration with Russia must and would continue into the peace, and that there would be a corresponding prolongation of war-time antagonism towards Germany. Pro-Soviet feeling in Britain ran high. It found abundant expression in *Times* leaders and Foreign Office memoranda.One such *Times* leader in November (presumably written by E. H. Carr) declared that 'Russia, like Great Britain, has no aggressive or expansive designs in Europe. What she wants on her Western frontier is security'; and, further on, 'in Poland, Russian policy is clearly aimed at a compromise Government in which different elements of Polish opinion are represented.'[32]

[31] Minutes of meeting between the Foreign Secretary and the Chiefs of Staff, 4 October 1944 in PRO FO 371/43336. For a development of the Chiefs of Staff's argument, see PHP (44) 15 (0) Revised Final, 15 November 1944, in PRO CAB 81/45.
[32] 'Russia, Britain and Europe', *The Times*, 6 November 1944.

One official in the Foreign Office went so far as to instance the views of the Chiefs of Staff in justification of the Russian contention that 'nests of Fascists' were still at work in the West; 'the recent PHP papers on the dismemberment of Germany, the Western European bloc and the Middle East', he argued, 'show that the authors (or, more probably, those whom they serve) have not the slightest faith in the Anglo-Soviet Alliance.'[33]

Eden was hopeful but guarded. The Soviet Government might decide 'to break all the rules . . . to come out in open antagonism of everything which Russian propaganda has associated with "capitalism" and "imperialism" and to use their immense power and influence in support of extreme Left-wing movements in the countries of Europe, including even Germany.' But he thought it far more likely that they would try a policy of collaboration so long as they were convinced of their Allies' intention to keep Germany weak. For at least five years, while they concentrated on internal rehabilitation, it could be assumed that they would refrain from territorial aggression and from attempts to enhance Russian influence in foreign countries 'by methods and to an extent that would seriously indispose opinion in this country or the United States'.[34] The conclusion to be drawn was that it should be the constant aim of British policy to strengthen the hands of the collaborationist school of thought in the USSR, of which Eden regarded Stalin as the protagonist.

Others at the time took a less hopeful view. One correspondent of the Foreign Office argued that, in the light of recent events, 'domination by Soviet Russia of a given territory means the exclusion from affairs of everybody else, including Russia's present Allies, from that territory.'[35] President Beneš of Czechoslovakia, when told by Eden that 'the Russians genuinely wished to work with us', also reacted rather sceptically. He thought that Stalin would wait for a year after the defeat of Germany before coming to any final decisions. He would then be able to see more clearly the real position of Germany and the real sentiments of the Western Allies towards Russia, and weigh up the balance of forces. But Stalin and his associates might not be able to decide policy freely without regard to the wishes of the Party and the new military caste; and, what worried him more, he was by no means sure how far Moscow would be able to control the various Communist parties in other countries.[36]

[33] Minute by Geoffrey Wilson, 23 September 1944, in FO 371/43336.
[34] 'Soviet Policy in Europe', Memorandum by the Secretary of State for Foreign Affairs, 9 August 1944, WP(44)436 in PRO CAB 66/53.
[35] Preston to Foreign Office, 5 December 1944, in PRO FO 371/43336.
[36] Interview with Beneš, 27 November 1944, in PRO FO 371/43336.

The most sober and far-sighted assessment of Soviet post-war policy was submitted by the Joint Intelligence Sub-Committee to the Chiefs of Staff in December 1944.[37] 'Russia', the Sub-Committee thought, 'will contain within her own frontiers such military and economic resources as would enable her to face without serious [risk of?] defeat even a combination of the major European powers.' Apart from her 'great advantages in depth of defence and dispersal of economically important targets', Russia was immune from any serious threat to her security, except on her Western frontier between the Baltic and the Carpathians, and could concentrate her immense strength on the defence of that frontier. But after the devastation she had suffered she would not be prepared to take any chances; and while experimenting with a policy of collaboration with the British Empire and the USA, she would insure against a breakdown by building up a protective screen of buffer states closely linked with her and treated as falling naturally within her special sphere of interest. These would include Finland, Poland, Czechoslovakia, Hungary, Romania, Bulgaria 'and to a lesser extent Yugoslavia'. It would be the keystone of her post-war policy to ensure that Germany was kept weak and she would regard as the acid test of the sincerity of the Western powers' collaboration their determination to make and keep Germany weak. Any trend towards reconciliation would be regarded as a potential menace and might be met by efforts to win Germany over to the Russian side. If her suspicion of British and American policy deepened and she could put no trust in their collaboration in the interests of world security on the lines she thought necessary, she would move on from 'tactlessness in the handling of international affairs' to pushing her military frontiers forward into the border states in Europe, stirring up trouble in Greece, the Middle East and India, and using her influence over Communist parties abroad to stimulate opposition to anti-Russian policies. There was not likely, however, to be an aggressive policy of territorial expansion especially as Russia would above all wish for a prolonged period of peace in which to restore her devastated economy and embark on a programme of internal development.

The paper reached the Foreign Office but not the Cabinet. The Joint Chiefs of Staff no doubt feared that it would give rise to renewed ministerial attacks on such views and risk a veto on further

---

[37] 'Russia's strategic interests and intentions from the point of view of her security', Report by the Joint Intelligence Sub-Committee, 18 December 1944. JIC (44) 467 (O) (Final), in PRO FO 371/47860. The paper appears to have been largely the work of Sir A. Noble although he was not a member of the Committee.

studies. Thus they decided not to circulate it, although invited to do so. There were others in Whitehall, however, who thought along similar lines without reaching quite the same conclusion. Bruce-Lockhart, for example, issued a warning in April 1945 that in her obsession with security Russia might overreach herself and reawaken pro-German feelings in the UK and the USA, 'leading inevitably to the establishment of the Sanitary Cordon which Russia presumably wishes to avoid and which she uses adroitly as an excuse for a policy of expansion.'[38]

In November 1944 Eden was still hopeful of collaboration with Russia and of reaching agreement with her on policy towards Germany. In a memorandum at the end of the month he argued against an enforced dismemberment, and reviewed alternative ways such as federalism and decentralization of providing additional security against German aggression.[39] He accepted the need to break up Prussia although he was sceptical of any close connection between Prussia and the rise of Hitler, and equally sceptical of the benefits expected by Labour ministers from the elimination of the Junkers. The memorandum did not advance matters much. It was accompanied by the promise of yet another paper on dismemberment, but none was circulated before the Yalta Conference, the Prime Minister preferring to reserve any decision until discussion had taken place there.

There was thus no agreed British policy when the Yalta Conference took place in February 1945 and there had been no consideration of dismemberment by the War Cabinet. There was not even any agreement on the form that dismemberment should take if agreed upon. The term could be used to mean no more than stripping Germany of territories like Austria and the Sudetenland acquired under Hitler, or alternatively it could mean partition or a complete break-up into separate states. By the beginning of 1945 it had become mixed up with French proposals for the creation of a separate province of Rhenania, and with the plans being made for the military occupation of Germany in three separate zones.

At Yalta Stalin pressed for dismemberment, with support from the Americans; Churchill agreed in principle but was unwilling to fix on precise boundaries there and then. He personally would cut off Prussia, but was Germany to be further divided? In the end it was agreed that a report should be submitted to the three governments

[38] PRO FO 371/47860.

[39] 'Confederation, Federation and Decentralization of the German State and the Dismemberment of Prussia', Memorandum by the Secretary of State for Foreign Affairs, 27 November 1944, APW(44)118, in PRO CAB 87/68.

by a suitable group before any final decisions were taken and that the Foreign Ministers should find the best way of introducing the Allies' intention to dismember Germany into the terms of surrender.[40]

It was at this session also that Churchill persuaded Stalin to agree to a French zone carved out of the British and American zones. Since the President did not believe that Congress would allow American troops to stay in Europe for much more than two years, Britain would need help from elsewhere in the long-term control of Germany and this was something the French could offer if they had a large army and a share of the administration of Germany. Churchill was unwilling, however, to discuss French claims to German territory up to the Rhine.

After Yalta all talk of dismemberment died away. The War Cabinet had just adjourned a preliminary discussion of their attitude on 22 March when the Soviet Government informed the Foreign Office that they did not regard the decision at Yalta as implying an obligation to dismember Germany but more as a means of exerting pressure on her to render her harmless. The tripartite committee set up to consider plans for dismemberment decided on 11 April, at its second meeting, that such plans should be communicated by any of the three representatives to his colleagues as soon as they were ready. No such plans were ever submitted and no further meeting of the committee was ever held. The Allied declaration after Germany's unconditional surrender made no mention of dismemberment; and Stalin announced in a proclamation on 9 May that the Soviet Union did not intend to dismember Germany.[41]

Dismantling and Deindustrialization

From time to time in 1943–4 ministers stressed the need for economic security, by which they meant placing restrictions on Germany's industrial development so as to reduce or eliminate her power to make war. A report on economic disarmament was put in hand in April 1944 by the Economic and Industrial Planning Staff, and was submitted to the APW Committee in August. Fourteen working parties were set up, with a membership drawn from the government departments concerned, and asked to make recommendations in respect of a corresponding number of German industries. They were asked to consider 'arguments if any' against continuing production, either at all or above a proposed ceiling. They were also to report on how far production should be maintained or increased,

[40] FRUS, *Malta and Yalta*, pp. 611–16.
[41] Woodward (1962), pp. 326–7.

the implications this would have for labour, transport and raw material requirements, and the likely repercussions 'on important British commercial interests'.

On the basis of this and other work, a lengthy report was prepared by the EIPS on 'Issues affecting the economic obligations to be imposed on Germany'.[42] This first discussed the issue of economic security, then reparations, and finally the reports of the working parties on the restrictions to be imposed on German industries. These reports were summarized in an Appendix; a further Appendix tried to establish the effect of all the proposed measures on the German balance of payments. A separate report on the economic aspects of dismemberment proposals was prepared and two documents on the subject were circulated a few weeks later.[43] These were followed in December 1944 by a report on 'De-industrialization'.[44]

When the EIPS reported in August 1944, it accepted that Germany should, 'if possible', be required to pay 'substantial' reparations. The Committee also assumed that for an indefinite period after the war Germany would be disarmed and would not be allowed to manufacture armaments. Measures to eliminate, restrict or control the economic and industrial basis of Germany's war potential should be taken so far as they could 'effectively contribute to the avoidance of future war . . . . even at considerable economic cost to Germany or the United Nations'. Such measures should not treat the German standard of living as a paramount consideration, and the commercial interests of the Commonwealth, particularly the UK, should not be overlooked. Germany was to derive no economic advantage from disarmament for an indefinite period or from taking no direct part in the later stages of war with Japan, but might be required to supply goods and services for the prosecution of the war.

The Committee recognized that there was a conflict between these objectives, since measures of economic security would limit Germany's capacity to pay reparations and might even make it necessary to offer help in buying necessary imports. How was a balance to be struck between such measures and the set-back they would involve to European rehabilitation and world prosperity? There were those who, at one extreme, thought the maintenance of peace dependent in the long run on the will of the United Nations to keep Germany disarmed; they expected no strengthening of that will from measures

[42] EIPS (P)(44)23, 15 August 1944, in PRO FO 1005/959.
[43] EIPS (P)(44)24, 7 September 1944 and EIPS(44)30, 4 September 1944, in PRO FO 1005/959. The first of these was purely factual and non-committal, but the second argued the case against dismemberment.
[44] EIPS (P)(44)42, 5 December 1944, in PRO FO 1005/959.

of economic security. At the other extreme were those who thought industrial potential so important in modern war that Germany must be crippled industrially as an insurance against any weakening of the will of the United Nations. Nobody seems to have put the prior question how *Germany's* will to peace might be affected by whatever measures were taken.

Without taking sides on this issue, the report laid down a number of principles of economic disarmament. For example, it would be preferable to take measures, such as the destruction or removal of plant, that did not involve continuing controls; controls that were intended to outlast the period of military occupation should be few in number and capable of enforcement from outside Germany; 'uneconomic industries' or industries over-expanded in war-time should be treated more drastically than others; and so on. 'Peaceful industries' were to be encouraged and Germany was to be made more dependent on other countries (and other countries – or some of them – less dependent on Germany). There was concern too about the effect on labour movements in other countries of widespread unemployment in Germany resulting from restrictions on her industry. In short, the principles of the report were so many and so general that they did not establish a definite line of policy. They did introduce a misleading distinction between 'peaceful' and other industries – of which much was to be heard later – that presumed a ranking of industries in some absolute order of war potential without regard to ease of substitution at the margin.

With regard to specific measures, the Committee contented itself with a list of candidates for discussion with the Americans and Russians. Five branches of production had been suggested for elimination – civil aircraft, shipbuilding, synthetic oil, nitrogen fixation and synthetic rubber – and four for restriction – engineering (particularly machine tools and ball-bearings), iron and steel, light metals (aluminium and magnesium) and chemicals. Another candidate was compulsion to follow a liberal commercial policy, with only a moderate degree of protection. During the period of military occupation such controls would be unnecessary and their value, therefore, in terms of economic security, was dependent on their continuing effects. These took the form of a decline in the skilled manpower available to those industries, the growth of a vested interest in a pacific German economy and the rise of foreign sources of supply for Germany's former customers. Such natural forces were a surer safeguard against the rebuilding of Germany's war potential than any continuing obligations laid on Germany in a Peace Treaty; but if they were to operate successfully the period of occupation or control should not fall short of ten years. If the period were shorter, the measures taken would have to be much more drastic in order to yeild an equivalent degree of economic security, thus possibly reducing Germany to a state where she was dependent on the charity of the rest of the world.

At this point the report again contrasted the two extreme views: one regarding it as culpable weakness not to include in the Peace Treaty the measures of economic security adopted during the period of occupation, while the other argued that the Peace Treaty should limit itself to prohibitions on maintaining armed forces, the possession and manufacture of munitions and, possibly, the manufacture of civil aircraft, on the grounds that a breach of non-military obligations would not be held in, say, 20 years time to warrant recourse to effective sanctions.

Ministers were asked to decide between these opposing points of view. Three questions were put to them;

1　Was it better to rely for security on the will of the United Nations to keep Germany disarmed by effective sanctions, or to look for some reinsurance against any weakening of that will through the destruction or limitation of Germany's industrial capacity? If so, how far should this go?

2　Should any such measures continue beyond the period of occupation and be written into the Peace Treaty in spite of the risk that a new generation might be unwilling to enforce them?

3　Was it possible to count on a period of occupation not appreciably shorter than ten years?

These questions were considered by the APW Committee at the end of August.[45] Eden had put round a rather discouraging cover note, pointing out that 'Ministers have as yet taken no decisions in regard to a policy for the future economy of Germany [which was, at best, only half true]. Nor do I think that they would wish to consider a detailed programme now.'[46] He explained, however, that he was under pressure from the American Embassy to embark on exploratory discussions at the official level on reparations, restitution and kindred subjects, including the re-starting of trade. He would like to associate the USSR with those discussions, to put them under the aegis of the European Advisory Commission, and to extend their

[45] APW 13th meeting, 31 August 1944, in PRO CAB 87/66.
[46] 'Comments on EIPS Report on Issues affecting the Economic Obligations to be imposed on Germany', Memorandum by the Secretary of State for Foreign Affairs, APW(44)72, 29 August 1944, in PRO CAB 87/68.

scope to cover the whole field of policy towards Germany. Officials should be authorized to take the EIPS report as a framework.[47] Eden also supported the proposal of the EIPS Committee that the Malkin Report should serve as a basis for discussion by ministers on reparations and other matters. (It had already gone to Dominions governments.)

On the direct questions put to them, ministers returned categorical answers. They were not prepared to rely simply on the will of the United Nations to keep Germany disarmed; they wanted to impose continuing obligations on Germany coupled with the physical dismantling and removal of plant, rather than the imposition of restrictions on economic activity; and they agreed that Germany should be occupied for a minimum of ten years in the first instance. On economic disarmament Lyttelton argued for a selective but Draconian policy; his views were endorsed by the committee. A small number of industrial activities that were both vital in war and difficult to conceal should be eliminated while the others should be allowed a large measure of latitude.[48] Similar views had been expressed at the meeting of the Committee a month previously, when Sir John Anderson, Chancellor of the Exchequer, argued that there must be a consistent occupation policy sustained by public opinion for a long period of years, and that support could be retained for the complete elimination of key industries and severe restrictions on some others.

The Morgenthau Plan

Shortly afterwards came the Quebec Conference and the Morgenthau proposals for the deindustrialization of Germany. These went far beyond 'the removal or destruction of . . . key industries which are basic to military strength'.[49] In the key section it was proposed that 'the Ruhr area', (including the Rhineland and all German territory up to and beyond the Kiel canal) should be 'so weakened and controlled that it cannot in the foreseeable future become an industrial area.' Within six months, if possible, after the cessation of hostilities, 'all industrial plants and equipment not destroyed by

---

[47] 'Report by the EIPS on Issues affecting the Economic Obligations to be imposed on Germany'. This had been circulated to the APW Committee on 26 August as APW(44)66.

[48] APW(44) 15th meeting, 31 August 1944, in PRO CAB 87/66.

[49] Morgenthau's programme in the form in which he circulated it after the Quebec Conference is in Keynes, *Collected Writings*, Vol. xxvi, pp. 376–9. The quotation above is from para.1.

military action shall be completely dismantled and transported to Allied Sections as restitution, all equipment shall be removed from the mines and the mines closed.' In the execution of this policy, the area was to be made an international zone under the United Nations.

Whatever impression one might form of the rest of the plan – much of which would have been by no means unacceptable to British ministers – this proposal to put an end to all industrial employment and close down the coal mines was preposterous. It might seem to be the logical consequence of trying to reduce Germany to a state in which she was incapable of waging war. But it would do this only by depriving most of the population of a livelihood.[50] The shutting of the coalmines could have equally disastrous repercussions on Germany's neighbours. As Keynes commented to Anderson as soon as he saw it, this part of the plan was 'hopelessly impractical, creating intolerable conditions of a kind which world opinion could not conceivably allow, without any hint as to how they can be ameliorated.'

It was not a plan that appealed to the Foreign Office nor, for that matter, to the Prime Minister when he first saw it at the Quebec conference with Roosevelt in September 1944. He had come to Quebec primarily to obtain financial aid from the USA after the war with Germany was over, and to argue for a larger role thereafter in the war with Japan. But his mind was 'singularly untrammelled by considerations of what should befall Germany after her defeat', despite the fact that defeat seemed imminent.[51] Roosevelt for his part neither listened to the other members of his committee on post-war policies for Germany (Stimson, Cordell Hull and Harry Hopkins) nor studied Morgenthau's memorandum with proper care.[52] After much argument between the two heads of state, and much drafting by Lord Cherwell, Morgenthau and Churchill himself, a memorandum of agreement was signed calling for the metallurgical, chemical and electrical industries of the Ruhr and the Saar to be 'put out of action and closed down', and 'looking forward to converting Germany into a country primarily agricultural and pastoral in character'.[53]

It has been suggested that Churchill's agreement was wrung from

[50] E.F. Penrose, *Economic Planning for the Peace* (1953), Chapter XIV.
[51] Wheeler-Bennett and Nicholls, p. 178.
[52] He told Stimson, when the US Secretary of War read to him passages from the document he had signed, that he had 'no idea how he could have initialled this' (ibid., p. 183).
[53] Ibid., p. 180.

him as the price of the aid he was seeking ($6.5 billion). This seems highly unlikely. Morgenthau himself was a strong supporter of aid to Britain – indeed one of the objects of his plan was to relieve Britain's post-war financial problems by eliminating her strongest competitor.[54] Roosevelt, too, was 'anxious to keep Britain from going into complete bankruptcy at the end of the war. I just cannot go along with the idea of seeing the British Empire collapse financially and Germany at the same time building up a potential rearmament machine.'[55] It was reasoning of this kind, urged on Churchill by Cherwell, that reconciled him to the Morgenthau Plan. With the prospect that Britain would emerge from the war as the greatest international debtor in history, he was open to persuasion that the plan cleared the way for a great expansion in British exports. Nonetheless he made vigorous attempts to water it down.

From the American point of view, the plan would save the USA money by helping Great Britain to help herself.[56] Just as American reparations policy was dominated from 1947, if not earlier, by the aim of promoting European recovery, so in 1944 the promotion of British recovery played a major role.

It is doubtful whether Roosevelt, any more than Churchill, really changed his mind about the plan. But, under pressure from his ministers and advisers, he withdrew his approval of it within a few weeks, and even went so far on 25 October as to put a comprehensive stop on all post-war planning. A month previously some of Morgenthau's thinking had been reflected in a directive, JCS 1067, prepared by the Joint Chiefs of Staff which was intended to govern American Military Occupation policy and remained in force until mid-1947.

Eden, who arrived in Quebec on the very day Churchill accepted the plan, could hardly be expected to approve so disastrous a proposal, which ran counter both to the principles of the Atlantic Charter and to the work of the European Advisory Commission since the beginning of the year. Before leaving for Quebec he had warned the Cabinet that the Morgenthau Plan might be under discussion, and had undertaken to prepare a note for the Prime Minister in consultation with the Chancellor and one or two other ministers.[57] No such note was ever circulated to the Cabinet, presumably because of Churchill's reaction to Eden's forceful

---

[54] Penrose (1953), pp. 256–7.
[55] *Malta and Yalta*, p. 155, quoted by Baggaley (1980), p. 241.
[56] Baggaley (1980), p. 241.
[57] WM(44)122 on 11 September 1944, in CAB 65/43.

criticism on the spot: 'I don't want you running back to the War Cabinet trying to unsell this proposal before I get there.'[58]

So far as the UK was concerned, the Morgenthau Plan soon faded out.[59] At the end of the year Eden circulated to the APW Committee a report on deindustrialization prepared by the Economic and Industrial Planning Staff.[60] This made it abundantly clear that pastoralization was no answer to the German question. Even if the purchasing power of the community in the area affected was sustained by subsidies from the rest of Germany, 30 per cent of the population would be out of work before taking any account of the 3.5–5 million refugees that would have to be absorbed. As for the advantages to British trade that Morgenthau and Roosevelt foresaw, the net gain in visible trade to the UK was put no higher than £30 million a year, and against that had to be set the need to write off substantial British investments in Germany and the loss of virtually all reparations.

Abandonment of the Morgenthau Plan did not put an end to its influence. It was not publicly repudiated and no new plan took its place. The Russians were left asking themselves how seriously they should take it, aware that their Allies now contemplated extensive dismantling and deindustrialization as a considered policy. Churchill, when he saw Stalin in October, encouraged the idea that he favoured such measures. Asked by Molotov what he thought of the Morgenthau Plan, he avoided a direct reply. But it was clear that he held to the views urged on him by Cherwell in Quebec. 'Russia's intention to take away German machinery', he told the Russians, 'was in harmony with Great Britain's interest in filling the gaps left by Germany. This was only justice.'[61] This representation of reparations as a morally justifiable claim, and now in keeping with British interests, may have misled the Russians into thinking that their allies would accept a programme of economic dismantling going far beyond the needs of economic security.[62]

Nor did the setting aside of the Plan put an end to consideration of economic disarmament. In April 1945 a further report on the subject

[58] Harry White, Memorandum of meeting on 20 September 1944, quoted by Wheeler-Bennett and Nicholls, p. 183.
[59] On 30 December 1944 Keynes claimed to have been the last man at that date to have discussed the plan with Roosevelt (Keynes to Playfair, 30 December 1944, in PRO T247/87).
[60] 'Deindustrialization of the Rhineland-Westphalia-Saar Area', Memorandum by Secretary of State for Foreign Affairs, APW(44)127, 27 December 1944 covering report by the EIPS.
[61] Baggaley (1980) p. 258.
[62] Ibid., p. 259.

was submitted by the EIPS to the APW Committee, based on that committee's conclusions at its meeting on 31 August 1944.[63] The report was considered, first by the APW Committee on the 10 May and then, rather perfunctorily, by the Cabinet on 15 June, when the war with Germany was already over and the war-time coalition had given way to a new (Conservative) government.

The EIPS pointed out that no measures of industrial restriction or control could be devised which would effectively prevent Germany from developing weapons of the V1 or V2 type, or for purposes of biological warfare. Had they been aware of it, they might have made a similar comment about atomic weapons. They judged that the economic effect of the restrictions they proposed, taken by themselves, was not likely to be very great but that, if account were taken of other adverse factors, the combined effect would be very different. Not only might reparations from current production be made impossible, but the restrictions might even make it necessary to provide outside help to Germany for the first five to ten years after the war.

With these emphatic warnings, which were very different from the tone of ministerial discussions, they submitted a long list of proposed restrictions, divided between those on which a decision should be taken at once (Catagory A) and those where a decision could be deferred (Category B). The list was as shown in table 3.1.

The Committee did not provide any rationale of these restrictions, but extracted them from the reports of the working parties set up a year previously, some of which had still to report their findings. It simply took the more obvious candidates from the industries that contributed to, or could be utilized for, the production of armaments, and tacked on some branches of the chemical industry that were thought to make Germany, in some sense, too self-sufficient. Other German industries would have to be encouraged to expand if severe unemployment was to be avoided and new sources of exports developed. This would involve competition with the corresponding industries in Britain but there should be some net gain to British industry from restrictive measures and, if not, the risk of loss was the price that would have to be paid for economic security.

The Committee also sought to assess the impact of its proposals on the German standard of living and the German balance of payments. It put the loss of exports at RM(Reichsmarks) 1,140 million for

---

[63] Above, p. 52. The EIPS 'Further report on issues affecting the economic obligations to be imposed on Germany' was circulated as APW(45)57 on 19 April 1945 by Richard Law, Minister of State at the Foreign Office, in PRO CAB 87/69.

Table 3·1   Industries to be restricted

Industry	Restriction	Duration of restriction
Category A (Restrictions proposed for immediate decision)		
Civil aircraft	Eliminate plant, prohibit production	Indefinitely
Synthetic oil	"	"
Ammonia and methanol (high pressure hydrogenation)[a]	"	"
Ball and roller bearings	"	At least 10 years
Merchant shipbuilding	Remove up-to-date equipment. Prohibit sea-going vessels except small fishing craft	" "
Merchant shipping	Prevent reconstitution of fleet by acquisitions from abroad	–
Machine tools	Eliminate surplus capacity. Reduce holdings to peace-time requirement	At least 10 years
Steel	Reduce capacity by about half (i.e. to 11.5 million tons).	"
Category B (Restrictions to be decided later)		
Chemicals (including synthetic rubber	–	–
Locomotives	–	–
Motor vehicles	–	–
Agricultural tractors	–	–
Aluminium and Magnesium	–	–

[a] Might need to reconsider after report from German Science and Industry Committee.

Category A industries and RM 225 million for Category B, with steel and synthetic oil accounting for over half the first of these. The total forfeited would be about one quarter of the value of imports into Germany in 1937. But this was not the whole story since the full impact on engineering exports had yet to be estimated. As for the net loss to the German standard of living, this worked out at no more than RM 850 million in the early stages, a mere 1–2 per cent of pre-war consumption, and much less than Germany would suffer from other causes.

The discussion of the report in the APW Committee at one of its last meetings started at a more general level. Lyttelton said that the various interrelated aspects of policy towards German industry must be addressed in the right order of priority. In his view, once the political boundaries had been settled, economic security came before reparations and that in turn before German exports. Anderson saw the sequence rather differently, with the German standard of living to be decided before reparations and trade; while Sinclair (Secretary of State for Air) wanted all aspects of the matter to be considered simultaneously if Germany was not to be reduced below the subsistence level. Grigg showed a similar concern for the German standard of living, asking that the Zone Commander be instructed to secure the maximum production of food. The three Labour ministers on the Committee took the view that economic security − or, as Bevin put it, 'disarmament of Germany's industrial war potential' − was overriding. Cripps (then Minister of Aircraft Production) suggested that the machinery manufacturing branches of the engineering industry should be restricted and controlled, and Alexander gave expression to the navy's view that *all* German shipbuilding should be suppressed indefinitely. Cripps, however, was opposed by Bevin who argued that decisions on the engineering industry could safely be left to the Allied Control Council, while Anderson and Lyttelton insisted that Germany must export to live, and put it to Alexander that it was enough for the present to forbid Germany a merchant marine.

On the specific restrictions proposed, the Committee agreed that so long as the hydrogenation plants were needed in order to maintain the supply of fertilizers they should remain in production, but they were not willing to postpone the destruction of synthetic oil plants as proposed by the Foreign Office. Synthetic rubber, aluminium and magnesium, which Lyttelton wanted moved up to Category A, and banned, were to remain in Category B. Machine tools were to be limited to peace-time requirements as estimated by the EIPS who were also to look at the possibility of regulating the use of raw materials through international customs control. Finally, steel production, as proposed, should be limited to half the pre-war capacity of 23 million tons.

On 11 June, after the interim Conservative Government was formed, Churchill insisted that policy on economic disarmament should be reviewed by the Cabinet before any indication of its likely terms was given to the European Advisory Commission. But when a paper was submitted by the Foreign Office he found the recommendations too complex for discussion and was content that the EIPS report (APW(45)57) should be used by the British representative (Sir Walter Monckton) on the Allied Reparations Commission in Moscow and by Field Marshal Montgomery in the British zone as general background for guidance in the destruction of Germany's war potential.[64] Consideration of the report itself was deferred and no further discussion of economic disarmament occurred before the Potsdam Conference. The UK delegation to the Reparations Commission left for Moscow on 18 June 1945 with the EIPS report and the minutes of the meetings of the APW Committee on 31 August 1944 and 10 May 1945 for guidance.[65] As we shall see, even when the Labour Government came back to the subject on 13 September, nothing had changed.

[64] CM(45)8, 15 June 1945, in PRO CAB 65/53.
[65] 'Industrial Disarmament of Germany', Memorandum by the Minister of State at the Foreign Office (W. Mabane), CP(45)36, 14 June 1945, in PRO CAB 66/66.

4

Reparations from Yalta
to Potsdam

There has never been a full discussion of the manner in which the American plan conflicts with the idea of German economic unity and it is doubtful whether its implications have been fully realized, in particular the fact that Russia will receive no current deliveries from the Western zones and that there will thus be no normal interchange of goods between the east and west of Germany.

Coulson to Cadogan, 31 July 1945

Soon after the completion of the Malkin Report, and reflecting the influence of Keynes's exposition of the Report in Washington, the Americans put forward proposals on reparations at the Moscow Conference in October 1943.

The proposals originated with the experts in the State Department, who tabled a short paper prepared after consultation with the British Embassy in Washington.[1] Although the paper did not say so, it based itself on the total military occupation of Germany and its division into zones of occupation. Cordell Hull, the US Secretary of State, who led the American delegation, wanted Germany to remain a single economic unit with a decentralized, democratic regime, shorn of her capacity to make armaments, but not dismembered — East Prussia alone excepted. She was to contribute towards the restoration of physical damage inflicted in other countries but was to be allowed 'a tolerable standard of living' — a provision that caused Molotov to growl 'Why Germany?'[2]

The aim of reparations, according to the paper circulated, should

[1] The paper is in PRO FO371/35309 and in FRUS, 1943, Vol. I, p. 740. It is dated 25 October 1943, covers one page only, and was hastily drafted after the delegation had left for Moscow (Baggaley (1980) p. 93).
[2] PRO FO 371/35309.

be to speed economic recovery and help in the establishment of the kind of world economy desired by the United Nations. Ironically, in the light of after events, reparations were to be the means of strengthening the post-war economic and political order. Germany should be required to contribute, in goods and services – not money – for a period co-extensive with the first stage of European reconstruction; to an extent acceptable to claimant countries; without injury to third countries; and without so affecting Germany's living standards and productive plant as to create serious economic and political problems. Determination of the amount to be raised in reparations, its distribution between claimants and supervision of the discharge of the obligations imposed should be the responsibility of an Allied Reparations Commission.[3]

The paper represented the views of State Department officials when that Department had little pull with Roosevelt, and it was in striking contrast to the Carthaginian plan put forward less than a year later by Morgenthau. It was referred to the European Advisory Commission set up by the Conference under strong pressure from Eden. There it disappeared from view. It was to be another year before reparations reappeared on the international agenda – at Yalta. Virtually no discussion of reparations took place during that year in Whitehall.

When the Yalta Conference opened in February 1945, neither the Americans nor the British had a policy on reparations. The Morgenthau plan had torpedoed earlier work done in the State Department, put an end to interdepartmental discussion in Washington

---

[3] There is no foundation for the view expressed by Professor Clemens (*Yalta*, p. 38) that Russian reparation plans were based on Hull's paper, which expresses a very different philosophy from theirs. It is more likely that Russian plans reflected the advice of Varga, a close friend of Maisky, who expresses deep gratitude to him for his 'valuable contribution to working out the post-war programme of the USSR' (Maisky 1967, p. 383). Varga's article on 'The Reparation of Damage by Hitlerite Germany and her Accomplices' was reprinted in *Trud* on 24 October 1943, while the Moscow Conference was in progress. It claimed that from 1933–9 Germany had spent RM 15 billion (about $4–5 billion) a year on armaments and as this would cease after the war, Germany could pay at least as much in reparations. Later research suggests that Varga's figure should be cut almost in half (Klein 1959, p. 117, cited in Baggeley (1980) p. 52). It is true, however, that in 1938–9 German military expenditure was RM 17 billion (Overy 1984, p. 95). While one Foreign Office official, on reading Varga, thought that 'it should be by no means impossible for the Americans, Russians and ourselves to reach agreement on the principles that should govern reparations', Keynes thought it 'in some respects . . . a dangerous article' which was at least semi-official and ought to be carefully analysed (Keynes to Ronald, 2 December 1943, in PRO FO371/35309, which also contains a copy of Varga's article). Keynes was disappointed that the idea of a German contribution to peace maintenance had not been put to the Russians.

and led Roosevelt to impose a ban on *all* post-war planning.[4] In the UK, concentration on matters of machinery and on issues of economic security and dismemberment had pushed reparations policy off the stage; even when ministers met to discuss the Malkin Report in September 1943 it was only to settle whether the Americans should see the document, not to consider its recommendations. It is doubtful whether in that discussion (or even in Cabinet over the ensuing year) the word 'reparations' was so much as mentioned.

This left the initiative to the Russians and it was an initiative they retained.[5] No attempt was made by the Americans and British to engage in joint planning; and no attempt could have been made when Ministers took no steps to offer guidance. Both the Americans and the British were afraid of exchanging views directly for fear of being accused of 'ganging up' against the Russians; and both were liable to feel that they would have to act as intermediaries between their Western partner and the Russians. Yet the only hope of achieving a consistent and feasible policy would have been to reach preliminary agreement between the two Western powers and make this agreement, rather than the extravagent claims of Russia, the basis for further negotiation.

The Russians had made clear their interest in reparations since 1941, when Stalin raised the question with Beaverbrook in September and again with Eden in December. They accepted, as Maisky told Eden in March 1943, that reparations should be in kind, not in money, and accepted also, as became clear at Yalta, the principle already expressed in the Malkin Report and in the State Department's paper, that reparations should be related to the physical damage inflicted. They had no clue to the thinking of their Allies on the subject except what they could gather from the single page tabled in October 1943 and the apparent commitment of Roosevelt and Churchill to the Morgenthau Plan – a commitment that had vanished well before Yalta.[6]

[4] For a full account of the evolution of American thinking about reparations see Baggaley (1980), chapters II, IV–VI. One school of thought early in 1944 wanted to confine reparations to a relatively short period (although ten to twelve years was mentioned) with payment primarily in the form of raw materials, industrial equipment and labour; another school of thought favoured payment in cash spread over a longer period and reaching a total estimated at one stage at $37 billion compared with $14 billion on the other hypothesis. These ideas, and still more these figures, underwent many radical changes over the following year. Roosevelt himself took the view in December 1944, after the controversy over the Morgenthau plan, that there should be no reparations.
[5] For Russian war-time planning on reparations see Baggaley, chapter I.
[6] Clemens (1970) p. 37.

The Yalta Conference

It was at Yalta that the first international discussion of reparations took place, and it was the Russians who made the running. They were within sight of their first victory in a major war since 1812 – a war in which they had had to confront never less than two-thirds of the German armed forces[7] – and were in no mood for the kind of soft peace which they suspected Britain of favouring. They viewed with intense suspicion the argument that a prosperous Germany was necessary to the prosperity of Europe as a whole and Great Britain in particular.[8] A letter from the Embassy in Moscow had already warned the Foreign Office that 'all available indications go to show that the Russians are firmly determined that Germany shall provide the goods and labour required to repair destruction caused in the Soviet Union and that they will take steps to see that their demands for this purpose are fulfilled to the hilt', even if this meant retarding the recovery of other European countries.[9]

The Russians had suffered enormous loss of life and far more extensive damage than any other country.[10] They were planning an ambitious 15 year programme of reconstruction to make good the damage and create a much enlarged industrial machine. They spoke of raising steel-making capacity to 60 million tons, and of leaving in the Urals the plant moved there during the war, while new factories were built and equipped with German machine tools in place of those destroyed.[11] Against this background, the Russians needed all the help they could get in reparations or in long-term credits from the USA.

Maisky, the Russian Deputy Foreign Minister, outlined their proposals at the first plenary session of the conference on 5 February

[7] Ibid., p. 75.

[8] Annex I, Germany, to 'Soviet Policy in Europe', Memorandum by the Secretary of State for Foreign Affairs, 9 August 1944, WP(44)436, in PRO CAB 66/53.

[9] Balfour to Warner, 17 July 1944, in FO 371/43336.

[10] They put the damage at $128 billion (a figure repeated by Voznezensky in 1949) but this was clearly an exaggeration. On their own showing it exceeded the whole of the pre-war wealth of Germany; and if, as is likely, the damage did not exceed, at most, one-third of the wealth of the USSR, the estimate implies a total Soviet national wealth in excess of that of the USA. Nutter (1962, pp. 214–15) estimates Soviet war damage at no more than $13–16 billion, which is actually lower than the net war-time impairment of the British capital stock (including debt obligations to other countries). A British estimate in June 1945 put the damage at £4,640 billion or $18.6 billion (CR/P36. 5 June 1945. in PRO T236/257). Bergson, in Appendix 18 to the Pauley Report to the President, gives an estimate of $20 billion.

[11] Harriman to Stettinius, 11 April 1945, *Malta and Yalta*, p. 994; Keynes, conversation with Maisky, in PRO T 247/86.

1945. Reparations were to be paid in kind, half in the form of capital removals over a period of two years and half in current deliveries over ten years. Economic disarmament was to be accomplished through the destruction or removal of 80 per cent of German heavy industry (by which the Russians meant iron and steel, heavy engineering, electrical power and chemicals) and the complete removal of all branches of industry that could be used only for military purposes, including all aircraft factories and synthetic oil refineries. Capital removals would also include ships, rolling stock, German investments abroad and shares of industrial, transport and other enterprises in Germany. There was to be a tripartite control of the German economy in the interests of international security and this was to extend beyond the ten years over which reparations would be paid. Representatives of each of the occupying powers would sit on the boards of all German enterprises that could be utilized for war purposes. Finally a Reparations Commission should be appointed to meet in Moscow and study the details.

All this was largely, although not entirely, common ground. The really critical question was the total claimed; there might also be disagreement over the share-out. Maisky had proposed that reparations should be allocated in accordance with war damage suffered and the contribution made towards winning the war, and this was accepted with a minor modification. But on the total there was an acrimonious dispute throughout the conference. The Russians had settled on a figure of $20 billion of which they would take half, i.e. $10 billion, while the other half would be split between the UK and the USA, who together might take $8 billion, and other countries who would then be left with $2 billion.

The British, on the other hand, were strongly against naming any figure at that stage when it was impossible to assess what Germany could pay. Churchill thought the Russian figure far too high. He pointed to the experience of reparations after the First World War, when the Allies had received no more than £1,000 million or so, in spite of the pumping in of extensive loans and credits from abroad (put by Roosevelt at $10 billion). Britain was now so burdened with debt that if there were large benefits to be gained from the payment of reparations, he would want his country to participate. But he had grave doubts whether, once again, the effort to extract reparations would not result in leaving Germany unable to pay for necessary imports, and thus oblige the Allies to foot the bill. He was quite sure that Germany would never pay anything like $1 billion a year. What would happen, he asked, if Germany was reduced to a position of starvation? 'Did we intend to stand by and do nothing and say it served her right? Or did we intend to provide enough food to keep the Germans alive and if so who would pay for it?'[12]

Roosevelt agreed that the USA had advanced money to Germany after the First World War and lost most of it. The USA would not repeat that mistake. She wanted no reparations but at the same time did not propose to offer help to Germany. Enough industry should be left in Germany to keep her people from starving, without raising German living standards above those in Russia.

Stalin assured Churchill that there would be food for the Germans – an assurance that soon proved to be without foundation in the British zone where the ration fell at times as low as 800 calories per day, and was never higher in 1945–7 than 1,550 calories per day, in spite of heavy expenditure on food grains by the UK from her dwindling reserves of dollars.

It was left to Maisky to make a plausible case for his proposals. After the First World War, he argued, demands for reparations had been much larger: they were $38 billion over 58 years. The plans of those years, however exorbitant, had not broken down because of Germany's inability to match requirements with production, but because of the transfer problem. Payment in kind instead of in cash would eliminate that problem. Experience after the First World War was therefore irrelevant – all the more so if, this time, there was no inflow of capital from the Allies.[13] Maisky went on to point out that Germany had formerly spent six million dollars a year on arms alone and would now have no military expenditures of any kind. The $10 billion that Russia asked for was no more than 10 per cent of the US budget. It was also a relatively small amount in comparison with the war damage that Russia had suffered.

There were other ways of looking at the Russian total of $20 billion. It coincided with Keynes's first estimate in October 1918 of the maximum that Germany could pay over 30 years without being crushed – an estimate he later cut in half; with the German offer in May 1919 as a final capital payment;[14] with the amount fixed under the Young Plan in 1929 to be paid in instalments averaging £100 million a year over the next 60 years. It happened also – as Keynes [15] in particular was painfully aware – to coincide with the total external debt accumulated by the UK at the end of the war. The reparations that Russia proposed from Germany tallied with the external debt

[12] 'Record of the Yalta Conference', WP(45)157, 12 March 1945, in CAB 66/63.
[13] The force of this aside is obscure but rests on Maisky's contention that the investment of capital in Germany *encouraged* default on reparation obligations.
[14] Wheeler-Bennett (1933), p. 256.
[15] Keynes, *Collected Writings*, Vol. XXIV, p. 278.

burdens contracted during the war by the UK.

At a meeting of the three Foreign Ministers, Maisky explained how the Russian total was arrived at. The pre-war national wealth of Germany had been $125 billion, of which perhaps 40 per cent should be deducted for war-time losses (including, presumably, losses of territory, although Maisky did not say so). This left $75 billion and of this, the 'mobile' proportion would be about 30 per cent or $22–23 billion. If $10 billion out of this was removed in reparations Germany would still have enough to exist 'on a modest and decent central European level'.

Maisky's estimate of $125 billion was on the basis of Germany's 1937 frontiers, at 1938 prices plus 15 per cent, and using a rate of exchange of RM 3.5 to the dollar. His total is close to a more recent estimate by Hoffman of RM 373 billion at current prices in 1938, which works out at about $120 billion on Maisky's basis.[16] There is a bigger difference in what Maisky calls 'mobile capital' if by this he meant industrial equipment. Hoffman's total for industrial plant in 1938, excluding working capital and buildings, is only $18 billion for the whole of Germany (including territory ceded to Poland) and for Western Germany in 1949 he gives an estimate of about $12.5 billion at 1938 prices.[17] When the Russians themselves came to itemize the total of $10 billion for reparations, the most they were able to tot up in industrial plant (including port equipment, power stations, etc.) was $6–7 billion, the rest consisting of foreign investments, shares and miscellaneous items.[18]

As for the $10 billion in current deliveries over ten years, it had to

[16] Hoffman (1956) p. 256.

[17] British estimates in 1945 (below, pp. 79–80) put the value of plant within post-war Germany frontiers at $11.65 billion for the metal, engineering and chemical group of industries, but this is likely to have been on the high side. At RM 3.5 to the dollar instead of RM 2.5, the figure would come down to $8.3 billion. An American estimate, showing that the Soviet zone had 40 per cent of the *movable* capital equipment in manufacturing industries within Germany's *1937* frontiers at 1 January 1945, put the value of such equipment at $12.3 billion, of which $6.6 billion was in iron and steel, chemicals, etc., and $5.7 billion in light industries. Only 27 per cent of the total for heavy industry was attributed to the Soviet zone as compared with 55 per cent for light industry (FRUS 1945, Vol. II, p. 885).

[18] The make-up of the $10 billion was given subsequently in a memorandum submitted by the Soviet Delegation at Potsdam: (a) war and chemical industries (production of aircraft, tanks naval vessels, arms and ammunition, power and explosives, synthetic rubber and fuel, artificial fibres, cellulose, coal derivatives – $2–2.2 billion; (b) iron and steel, non-ferrous metals, engineering (including electrical industry), coal, power stations – $2.3–2.7 billion; (c) building industry, textiles, food industry, printing, transport (including water transport), communications (radio, telephone, telegraph), equipment of ports, warehouses, etc. – $1.8–2 billion; (d) foreign investments and claims of Germany – $1.1–1.4 billion; (e) shares of

be related to Germany's pre-war national income of $30 billion, less perhaps 30–35 per cent to adjust to post-war conditions.[19] To take $1 billion a year from this would impose a burden of no more than 5 or 6 per cent which Germany could easily carry.[20]

Maisky did his best to make his figures sound modest but without much success. It was not easy to see how so much capital plant could be taken without prejudicing the flow of reparations from current production. Even on Maisky's showing, nearly half the surviving 'mobile' capital of the country would be removed; and if it had suffered the 40 per cent war-time loss which he assumed, Germany would end up with only one-third of the 'mobile' capital she had before the war. Since most of the 'mobile' capital that would be taken in reparations was in the heavy industries producing metals, chemicals and engineering products, or in power and transport facilities – equally vital to a healthy economy – the impact of the proposed removals on the level of production was unlikely to be limited to 5–6 per cent. When in due course the matter was put to the test in the Level of Industry negotiations in Berlin in 1945–6, it was only with the utmost reluctance, and after long and unyielding argument, that the Soviet representatives accepted the need to leave in Germany enough equipment to produce 55 per cent of the 1938 volume of production within the new frontiers.

It is true nevertheless that in the immediate post-war years there was a vast superfluity of equipment in the Western zones at a time when many countries, and Russia most of all, were desperately short of it. Much of the plant was old and likely to be replaced eventually in Germany by more modern plant; nevertheless it was capable of meeting the urgent requirements of other countries for at least a few years until new plant became available and was at last within their means. There was nothing novel in principle about transferring such plant from one country to another, since a large and well-organized

German enterprises (railways, ports, canals, etc.), foreign currency, precious metals – $1.9–2.3 billion; (f) miscellaneous – $0.9–1.2 billion. Total – $10.0–11.8 billion.

German property, for this purpose, was defined as property within Germany's 1937 frontiers as well as German property abroad. Values were at 1938 prices plus 15 per cent on equipment and 10 per cent on raw materials and finished goods. The rate of exchange was taken to be $1=RM3.5 (Butler and Pelly(1984), pp. 494–5).

[19] For 'net social product' at market prices in 1938, Hoffman (p. 826) gives RM 98 billion or a little over $30 billion allowing for a small rise in prices.

[20] 'Record of the Yalta Conference', WP(45)157, 12 March 1945, in CAB 66/63. See also *Malta and Yalta*, pp. 620–3, 702–4, 707. Deliveries in kind were to consist of: coal, briquettes; chemicals (drugs, dyes, potassium, etc.); machinery, tools; cement, building materials; timber, paper; sugar; cattle, agricultural produce; ceramics; mechanical instruments, optical apparatus; river ships (Butler and Pelly, 1984, pp. 494–5).

market in second-hand plant and machinery had long existed in Europe.[21] But a market is one thing; the compulsory dismantling, packing, transport and re-erection abroad of millions of tons of heavy machinery within a matter of months is something entirely different – as was soon to become apparent.

The proposal to take $10 billion in current deliveries over ten years was rather more plausible. It was twice as much as Germany paid in the ten years after the First World War, but that experience was a poor guide to what was possible under military occupation. Germany was potentially much richer (GNP in 1938 was some 80 per cent higher than in the mid-1920s), had spent a comparable total on arms in the 1930s, and, if allowed to recover, could supply just the things that Europe needed for her own reconstruction. Maisky was quite right in arguing that there need be no transfer problem, not because payment would be in kind, but because if the transfer was mainly to the USSR the repercussions on world markets would be minimal.

It was not possible at Yalta to foresee the scale on which deliveries from Germany might be made. There was no agreement on Germany's post-war frontiers and no reliable estimate of the damage, destruction and disorganization to be expected by the time the war came to an end. Ten billion dollars was not far short of the entire national income in 1936 of the territory that is now West Germany. In the post-war years, too, there would be the added burden of some ten million refugees. As Churchill pointed out, with the loss of territory to Poland and the influx of refugees, Germany would have greater difficulty in feeding herself. Even to pay for the pre-war level of imports, and at the same time supply goods to the value of $1 billion a year in reparations, she would have to double the pre-war volume of her exports. It was natural, therefore, to feel some hesitation in accepting Maisky's total of $10 billion.

But perhaps the main objection to the Russian proposals was not the magnitude of the annual deliveries they proposed. If Russia could absorb $500 million of German goods a year into her domestic economy without throwing Germany into deficit on the rest of her trade and leaving the Western powers to foot the bill, well and good. Maisky took it for granted that because his proposal avoided the transfer problem it created no difficulties in Germany's trade accounts. But both the UK and the USA held that there was no scope for the payment of reparations until Germany had a balance of payments surplus. If the Russians started taking deliveries of reparations from their own zone without payment and the Western

[21] IARA Report for the year 1947, Foreword by the Secretary General.

Zones were obliged to import at their own expense food normally obtained from Russian-occupied territory, they were bound to regard this as an infringement of the first charge principle. They, not the Germans, would be paying reparations to the Russians.

This issue, of which so much was to be heard, had been looming up ever since the middle of 1944. Sir William Strang had then asked whether it was possible to count on Germany's being treated as an economic whole, regardless of zonal boundaries, so that the Western zones would be able to continue to rely on the agricultural Eastern zone to meet their large deficiencies of foodstuffs. If this were not possible, Britain would find herself obliged to purchase millions of tons of grain, almost certainly for dollars, to prevent starvation in her zone. This was a burden she could ill afford even if repayment might eventually take place.[22]

Both Churchill and Eden did not conceal British concern over the probable shortage of food. Churchill said that he was haunted by the spectre of a starving Germany that might have to be helped with food for which Britain could not pay. Eden at a later session emphasized the danger that it might eventually become necessary for Britain to finance and feed Germany because of the payment of reparations.

Throughout the conference the Russians pressed to have the sum of $20 billion mentioned in the terms of reference of the Allied Reparations Commission which was to pursue the problem in Moscow. Stalin said that the figure was not sacrosanct but that it should be taken as a basis for discussion. Conceivably he had it in mind to accept a rather lower total once the bargaining started – the Russians made large reductions in their original claims against Finland and some of the satellites[23] – but it was noticeable that they were not content with the American delegation's suggestion that the figure of $20 billion should merely be 'taken into consideration'. Churchill, strongly supported by the Cabinet in London, was adamant that no figure should be mentioned and that any agreement on reparations made at Yalta should be limited to matters of principle. The Conference Protocol on reparations, which was not published until 1947, showed the American and Russian delegations

---

[22] 'Food situation in Germany and Austria during the occupation period', Memorandum by the UK representative on the European Advisory Commission (Sir William Strang), with a draft letter to the US and Soviet representatives on the Commission, APW(44)50, 24 July 1944, in PRO CAB 87/67.

[23] PRO T 236/255. At the first meeting of the official Committee on Reparations on 6 April 1945, Mark Turner said that in the satellite armistices the USSR's calculations had been more accurate than the UK's.

agreeing that 'the Reparation Commission should take in its initial studies as a basis of discussion the suggestion of the Soviet Government that the total sum . . . [in the form of capital removals and current deliveries but *not* labour services] should be 20 billion dollars and that 50 per cent of it should go to the USSR.' The British delegation, however, was minuted as opposed to the mention of any figures before the Commission started work.[24]

In discussion with Molotov and Stettinius, Eden raised a whole series of points; the incompatibility between large reparation payments and the depletion of German manufacturing capacity; the need for a lower total in the event of dismemberment; occupation costs; the priority to be given to the pre-war claims of the United Nations and to payment for imports into Germany in the use made of goods taken from Germany; the restitution of looted property; labour services. He asked for the inclusion of France in the Reparations Commission and suggested the limitation of the period over which reparations would be paid to five years instead of ten.

So far as the Russians were concerned, Maisky said that Eden seemed to want as little as possible to be taken from Germany – a charge which Eden strongly denied. Maisky then tried to meet him on some of his points, admitting that the reparation plan would need adjustment once the shape of dismemberment had been decided. The period need not be extended to ten years: in the end it might be five or six. By agreeing to take the Soviet total as a basis for discussion, the British Government would not be committed to it.

Molotov was less accommodating. At one point he asked in exasperation if there was anything Eden *did* agree about. In the last session at which Churchill, Roosevelt and Stalin took stock, Stalin became increasingly angry and told Churchill that if the British did not want Russia to receive reparations they should say so. Churchill denied this vigorously: His doubts, he said were over what would prove feasible and his government had sent him a telegram (which he read) expressing these doubts very forcefully.

The Americans tended to side with the Russians. Stettinius, the new Secretary of State, thought the Russian figure of $20 billion 'reasonable'. Although Roosevelt did not commit himself to the figure, his acceptance of it 'as a basis of discussion' gave the Russians some cause for assuming that deliveries from current production would not be opposed, and that the scale which they had suggested for such deliveries might have American support. Their quiescence if not acquiescence was to be the source of much later recrimination.

[24] For the 'Protocol', see *Malta and Yalta*, pp. 982–3.

British Policy Takes Shape

In the months before the Reparations Commission began its meetings – for it did not meet until nearly the end of June – the UK was at last obliged to make up its mind what policy on reparations it intended to pursue. The first paper on the subject to reach the Cabinet was circulated by the Chancellor of the Exchequer within a month of the Yalta conference.[25]

It began with a series of negatives, starting with the 'first charge' principle. The UK must *not* incur any expense arising out of the supply of 'permitted imports' into Germany, whilst Germany was simultaneously expected to make reparation deliveries, either of a once-for-all or of a continuing character. Payment for relief and other imported supplies was a first charge on Germany's export earnings; and the value of *any* goods removed should be paid for so long as export earnings were insufficient for that purpose.

Other negative principles followed. No occupying power should be expected to make deliveries of reparations beyond what it judged to be within the capacity of its zone; no once-for-all deliveries should be made from any zone without the agreement of the occupying power that there was no risk of creating conditions contrary to its administrative interests; permitted imports should be enough to provide the Germans with the necessary means of subsistence and no more.

What ran through the Chancellor's paper was the fear of adding to the liabilities of the UK when these were already so enormous, and ending up overdependent financially on the USA. It seemed unlikely that Germany would be able to make current deliveries of reparations on any substantial scale for five years after the war and, it was implied, any attempt to extract them would be at Britain's expense. After five years things might be different, and in the meantime reparations should be limited almost entirely to once-for-all deliveries and labour services. The paper looked kindly on the latter, which it seemed willing to exempt from the first charge principle, but it wanted to make sure that they were properly entered in the reparations account.[26] This reflected a continuing intellectual effort to find common ground with the Russians whom it was hoped to 'wean away' from their extravagant demands at Yalta.

---

[25] 'Reparations', Memorandum by the Chancellor of the Exchequer, 7 March 1945, WP(45)146, in PRO CAB 66/63.
[26] Keynes hoped, mistakenly, to get closer to the Russian total by including a figure for labour services. At £40 per head, 4 million workers would in ten years provide services worth $6.4 billion or two-thirds of the Russian total (PRO T 236/255). The Russians had mentioned 4 million workers at Teheran.

The Chancellor – or Keynes who wrote most of the paper – deluded himself. Its whole temper was at the opposite pole from Russian plans. In spite of its talk of a bare minimum subsistence level and of reparations 'as large as possible' (subject to the various provisos), the argument of the paper implied an effort to get Germany going again in the interests of European and British economic recovery. There was a danger of 'social convulsion' if considerations of economic security were pushed too far. Dismemberment was another danger. It was fundamentally incompatible with reparations; and if it went beyond the loss of territory to Poland and Russia it would meet with growing resistance and provide a rallying cry for dangerous elements. If Germany was to pay her way in the world and have some prospect of even a minimum standard of living, the totality of her resources would have to be brought in, without dismemberment.

No discussion in the coalition Cabinet of the Chancellor's paper ever took place. Arrangements were made for the preparation of draft instructions to the British representative on the Allied Reparations Commission. But these instructions, too, although duly prepared, were never considered by the Coalition Cabinet. Thus it is not too much to say that, from beginning to end, the members of the Coalition Government never met in Cabinet to agree on a reparations policy of any kind.

Discussions did take place, however, on the Ministerial Committee on Reparations, appointed in April 1945 to consider what line should be taken by the British delegation to the forthcoming meeting in Moscow of the Allied Reparations Commission. The Committee was chaired by Anderson, and included Cherwell as well as Bevin and Dalton. At the only meeting of the Committee before the break-up of the Coalition Government, the Foreign Office was represented by Law, while Duncan (Minister of Supply) and Llewellyn (Minister of Food) also attended.[27]

A paper was prepared in the course of April 1945 by a group of officials who set out the questions on which ministerial guidance was required.[28] To each question the officials indicated their own tentative response, which, in general, ministers endorsed at their meeting on 3 May. A report was then prepared, but not circulated at once to the Cabinet. It was made the basis of draft instructions which also remained for a time in limbo. Both documents finally reached the Cabinet on 5 June, by which time the Labour members had withdrawn.[29]

[27] RM(45) 1st Meeting, 3 May 1945, in PRO CAB 98/59.
[28] 'Reparations; report by a group of officials', RM(45) 1, 1 May 1945, in PRO CAB 98/59.

The instructions ('the Views of the United Kingdom Government on a Detailed Plan for the Exaction of Reparations from Germany') formed the basis of British policy at the Moscow conference and subsequently at Potsdam. Keynes found them 'almost sensible' and commented on a draft 'this is a paper we can one day publish without shame.'[30] It started from the proposition that security was more important than reparation. As the group of officials put it: 'German industry should not be reconstructed beyond the minimum point required to enable her [i.e., Germany] to pay for essential imports.' This implied that no provision should be made for deliveries of finished manufactures in reparations from current production. Since the UK had no use for reparations in this form – except in the first two years, when there was no hope of receiving them – this was a proposition readily acceptable to the British Government but less likely to appeal to the Soviets. Officials also pointed out, no doubt with one eye on Cherwell, that the proposition derived added support from the need for a large expansion in British exports in order to cope with the heavy burden of overseas debt incurred during the war. If the reparations settlement helped to establish Germany as a supplier of manufactures to British export markets, it would create a vested interest in claimant countries in favour of the development of competing German industries, thereby seriously aggravating British balance of payments difficulties.

When the draft instructions echoing this reflection came eventually before the Conservative Cabinet on 11 June, Cherwell called for a more pointed and emphatic declaration of principle. There should be an explicit statement that the capture of Germany's pre-war export trade was the main advantage to be derived by the UK from reparations.[31]

This line of argument had already been strongly attacked by officials. S. D. Waley of the Overseas Finance Division of the Treasury could see no reason to suppose that the impoverishment of Germany would confer any benefit on the UK. If the prosperity of the USA was likely to be the greatest single contribution to the UK's post-war balance of payments, why should the prosperity of

---

[29] They formed Annexes to a memorandum on reparations circulated by the Chancellor on 5 June 1945 (CP(45)16) and discussed by the Cabinet on 11 June 1945 (CM(45)7, in PRO CAB 65/53). The directive to the delegation, as amended after Cabinet discussion, is annexed to RM(45) 2nd Meeting, in PRO CAB 98/59.

[30] Keynes to Playfair, 10 June 1945, in PRO T236/258.

[31] 'British Exports, German Industry and Reparations', Memorandum by the Paymaster General, WP(45)224, 7 April 1945, in PRO CAB 66/64; and CM(45)7, 11 June 1945 in PRO CAB 65/53.

Germany have a different effect? The logical conclusion of Cherwell's argument was that it would help the British balance of payments if every other manufacturing country ceased to manufacture.[32]

Ministers offered Cherwell little support. Some attacked the whole idea and others its avowal. It was one thing to set out to destroy Germany's war potential and find incidental advantage in the prospect of capturing a substantial part of her export trade, but quite another to suppress German competition deliberately. To do so would cause other claimants, when their expectations of reparations were disappointed, to lay the blame on Britain. Nor was it a policy likely to enjoy popular support for long. Already in the USA it was under attack as immoral and impractical.

The outcome of this part of the discussion was that the Cabinet agreed not to relate reparations policy to an effort to destroy Germany's trade. Since other expressions of view came to the surface from time to time, it is important to emphasize that this was the only occasion on which ministers discussed the matter in Cabinet before Labour took office in July. There is no evidence that commercial considerations exercised a decisive influence on British reparations policy in 1945.

What eventually was retained in the directive was an instruction to ask for a limitation of reparations from current production to a specified list of items consisting mainly or predominantly of raw materials and semi-manufactured goods. Coal. potash, timber, cement and bricks were mentioned and, if there were strong pressure, steel might be added; prefabricated houses and their components would also be acceptable.[33]

Nothing much came of all this since no provision of any kind for reparations from current production was ever agreed internationally. The delegation to Moscow was successful in securing agreement to the principle that 'long run payment of reparations in the form of manufactured products shall be restricted to a minimum', and the principle was blessed along with others at Potsdam.[34] But it found no place in the final agreement and dropped out of sight.

A second important element in the directive was the first charge principle. This took two forms. The first laid it down that 'the full requirements of the Allied forces of occupation and the essential

---

[32] Waley to Playfair and Bridges, undated, in PRO T236/255.

[33] CM(45)7, 11 June 1945, in PRO CAB 65/53.

[34] The principle, preceded by the words, 'in order to avoid building up German industrial capacity and disturbing the long-term stability of the economies of the United Nations', was one of eight discussed below (pp. 81–2) and reproduced in Butler and Pelly (1984), p. 225.

minimum requirements of the German population should be a first charge on German assets and German production.'[35] From this it followed that there should be a common minimum standard for the level of consumption of the civil population throughout Germany, the Commander in each zone being left to give detailed application to the principle. In its second form the principle required that payment for any relief and other supplies from abroad that had been approved by the occupying powers should be a first charge on deliveries made to other countries by Germany as a whole. This meant that all exports from Germany would have to be paid for until there was a surplus in the balance of payments that could be taken in reparations. The principle, moreover, should be applied, not zone by zone (since this would be unfair to the Western powers, occupying the main deficiency area) but to Germany as a whole. Both as exporter and importer, and in the interchange of goods between zones, Germany must be treated as a single economic unit. The directive recognized, however, that it might not be easy to give effect to the first charge principle, as some of the Americans proposed, in relation to once-for-all deliveries (e.g. of dismantled equipment), still less to labour services rendered by prisoners of war and others.

Of the three categories of reparations envisaged at Yalta, once-for-all deliveries were to be made within the first two years, as already agreed, even if the programme had to be left uncompleted. The purpose of such deliveries was to destroy Germany's war potential, but they should not be confined to assets important from the point of view of economic security. Reparations from current production were not to begin until those two years were over – at least were not to be made without payment – and they were to continue for ten years with provision for reconsideration after five. The impressment of labour, the third category, was to be undertaken by the Allied Control Commission and completed quickly with no replacements after the first wave.[36] Impressment was not to be confined to prisoners of war and active Nazis, but was to be subject to a declaration by any country using such labour that minimum standards of treatment would be observed, for example, in relation

[35] Annex I to 'Reparations', Memorandum by the Chancellor of the Exchequer, 5 June 1945, CP(45)16, in PRO CAB 66/66.

[36] The Ministerial Committee on Reparations contemplated impressment 'for a relatively short period such as five years' and the termination of impressment six months from the end of hostilities. The UK would be unwise to participate and should think rather of continuing to use prisoners of war. RM(45) 1st Meeting, 3 May 1945, in PRO CAB 98/59.

to pay, food, etc. The declaration was to be purely voluntary: the delegation should disclaim any responsibility on the part of the British Government for its enforcement.

Subject to these conditions, reparations should be as high as possible. The Russian figure of $20 billion, however, was dismissed by the Chancellor as 'far too high'. Nor was he prepared at that stage to accept unconditionally that Russia should receive 50 per cent, or any specific percentage, of the total. No global total should be fixed; it would be wrong to do so when so little was known of the state of the German economy, and when no final decisions had been taken on dismemberment, Germany's post-war frontiers, economic security measures, the scale of population transfers, and many other matters. There should also be no finality in any percentages agreed except as part of a general reparations settlement.

The Prime Minister expressed strong agreement with all this at the meeting of Cabinet on 11 June. Although the crux of the negotiations in Moscow seemed likely to be the fixing of a total amount of reparations from Germany, he attached particular importance to the avoidance of any such commitment.[37] 'No opportunity should be lost', he is reported as saying, 'of bringing home to the Russian representatives the dangers and difficulties of exacting reparations. We should give the Russians the benefit of the experience which we have gained in these matters after the last war.'

One way of inflating the total and bringing it nearer to the kind of total that the Russians wished to announce (no doubt for the benefit of their public) would be to include an estimate of the value of labour services. These had not been included in the Yalta total and it is most improbable that this was an oversight: the Russians intended to make their own arangements for slave labour, as for war booty, without negotiation or prior agreement. Keynes had demonstrated, however, that if the Russians carried our their reported intention to employ 4 million Germans for, say, ten years in the USSR, the value of the services they would receive, over and above the cost of maintenance, could reach a total of $6.4 billion (taking £40 per head per annum), or two-thirds of their claim to $10 billion.[38] Ministers grasped at this straw and, although doubtful whether it would be possible to find an agreed basis for valuing labour services, invited the delegation to press for their inclusion in principle. When

[37] CM(45)7, 11 June 1945, in PRO CAB 65/53. By this time the Coalition Government had broken up and there were no Labour ministers.
[38] PRO T236/255. Maisky repeated the figure of 4 million workers at the Moscow Conference (Playfair, 'Note on negotiations', 16 July 1945, in PRO T236/262; Document No. 165 in Butler and Pelly, 1984).

the delegation sought to do so, they were opposed by the Americans and allowed the matter to drop.

The instructions to the delegation were not such as to hold out much prospect of agreement in Moscow. On what seemed the key issue of a fixed total for German reparations, the tactics to be followed were to agree in principle on the need for such a total and to couple this with an explanation of the reasons why it could be not be settled at the outset. Discussion should be postponed until the forms that reparations might take, and the ways in which they would be valued, distributed and shared, had first been considered. It was not at all clear what the delegation was to do – except stonewall – in the event of the Russians sticking to the position they had taken up at Yalta. Churchill, indeed, showed no anxiety to reach agreement. 'The object of the Moscow conference' he summed up, 'was to explore the complex technical aspects of the reparations problem.'[39]

It was some time before the delegation was able to leave. One reason for the delay was the difficulty of finding an acceptable head of the delegation: it was not until 27 May that the Government was able to announce the appointment of the Solicitor-General, Sir Walter Monckton, to lead the team. A second reason was a dispute over whether France should be allowed to participate. This was pressed by the UK, although the French held views rather different from theirs, arguing in the Economic Advisory Commission that restitution should take precedence over reparations and that restitution should cover the replacement of items removed by the Germans.[40] The Russians were opposed to the inclusion of France, whose part in the war Stalin consistently derided, and suggested the addition of Poland and Yugoslavia as a blocking move. The leader of the American delegation, Edwin Pauley, offered no support for the British proposal, and was, indeed, determined to avoid any suspicion of 'ganging up' with the British. Thus when the steering committee began its work on 19 June, only the three main powers were represented, with Maisky, Monckton and Pauley leading the three delegations.

Before the delegation left, Mark Turner (who represented the Foreign Office) listed its main objectives as follows:

1 to avoid final decisions;
2 first charge principle;
3 no global figures to be agreed.

The first and last of these objectives, both of them negative, were

[39] CM(45)7, 11 June 1945.
[40] Baggaley (1980) p. 380.

achieved. The second, positive, objective was not, although a watered-down version was ultimately accepted at Potsdam. The UK and the USA both attached great importance to the first charge principle, but they did not, at this stage, interpret it in quite the same way. The US delegation (unlike the State Department) held that the principle should apply to all exports from Germany, including once-for-all deliveries. The UK, on the other hand, foresaw practical difficulties if, as seemed likely, Germany was in external deficit over the first two years of the occupation. It was indeed these difficulties that made it desirable to rule out current deliveries during that period. But what of deliveries of capital equipment? On the American delegation's interpretation, recipient countries would be acting as underwriters who could be called upon to put cash on deposit for what they received in reparations, so long as German resources were insufficient to pay for essential imports. Since the USA would be the largest supplier of imports and the smallest claimant of reparations, the cash deposit would be in dollars; and the British doubted whether European countries would run the risk of having to part with dollars for second-hand German equipment.[41]

Preliminary calculations by Turner suggested that even if German imports and exports were in balance there would still be a large dollar bill to be met – perhaps $500 million over the first three years. Three-quarters of German imports would cost dollars when dollars were hard to find. Some of Turner's arithmetic, however, was far too optimistic. For example, he thought it possible to limit imports of food and tobacco in the third year of occupation to RM 300–350 million (compared with RM 1,500 million written into the Reparations Plan in 1946), and for the German balance of payments to be in surplus by 1947–8 to the tune of $400–$500 million, so that current deliveries might then be on that scale.[42]

Provisionally he put British reparations demands at £550 million and the British share in the global total at 25 per cent, the Russian at 40 per cent, leaving 15 per cent for the other allies. If one took these figures literally, they would imply an expectation of £2,200 million in total, or nearly $9 billion. It is unlikely that the Foreign Office, or the British Government, would ever have supported so high a figure.

Nevertheless the delegation took with them estimates of what might be available in equipment surplus to peace-time requirements that reached a total of about $9 billion (but only $6.5 billion at a

[41] 'Payment for German Imports', Note by Mark Turner, CR/P41, 12 June 1945, in PRO T236/258.
[42] 'German Exports and Imports', Note by Mark Turner, CR/P42, 12 June 1945, in PRO T236/258.

more realistic rate of exchange).[43] Of this total, $3.5 billion represented armaments factories, $3.1 billion capacity in industries that were to be entirely eliminated under the British proposals and $2.8 billion plant to be removed from industries that were to be restricted (apparently by about 60 per cent on average). A later version of these estimates divided the total between the Russian and Western zones and showed a split in the ratio 45:55.[44] Curiously enough, the total reached by the British was well above the Russian proposal for the same group of industries when submitted at Potsdam ($4.3–4.9 billion), and somewhat higher also than American estimates.[45]

The Reparations Commission

The delegation to Moscow under Walter Monckton duly set out on 18 June – more than four months after Yalta. They had quite lengthy official documents to guide them (including the papers on economic security and dismantling) but remarkably little in the way of ministerial decisions.[46]

The Americans were in no better a position. After Roosevelt's death an entirely new group had been appointed under Edwin Pauley, an ambitious oil magnate with little knowledge of previous studies of policy towards Germany and a firm but misplaced confidence in his capacity to negotiate on equal terms with the Russians. While the State Department was persuading the Foreign Office to delay the departure of the British representatives until the participation of the French had been pressed on the Russians, Pauley impatiently set out for Moscow a week ahead of the British delegation.[47]

Except in three respects, the instructions that Pauley took with him were not very different from those issued to the British delegation. The

[43] 'Note on capital plant values' by W. P. Johnson, in PRO T236/262.
[44] Note by W. P. Johnson, 28 July 1945, in PRO T236/265. In these calculations Greater Berlin was included in the Russian zone. The capacity remaining in the metal, engineering and chemical industries covered by the calculations would be $2.4 billion out of an assumed total (with no allowance for war damage) of $11.6 billion. Russian removals would amount to $4.2 billion and Western removals to $5.0 billion.
[45] For the Russian figures see above, p. 67 n18; the Americans worked on a figure of $2 billion for the British zone alone, implying a total for Germany of about $6 billion (FRUS, 1945, Vol.II, p. 892).
[46] Above, p. 60.
[47] Penrose (1953), p. 277; Baggaley (1980), p. 429. Pauley met British officials on his way through London on 22 and 23 May before touring the American zone of Germany. He claimed that Eden had concurred in the change of policy but Eden denied this.

three exceptions related to the German standard of living (which was not to be higher than in any neighbouring Allied country but 'a minimum subsistence standard'), the use of German labour (only those convicted as war criminals should be required to perform compulsory labour services outside Germany) and interim deliveries of capital equipment in advance of an agreed reparations plan (largely, no doubt, from the Ruhr and the sole bargaining weapon the British had). If it was found necessary to agree to 'recurring' reparations over a period of years, these should be as small as possible in relation to once-for-all deliveries and should be primarily in the form of raw materials and natural resources, not manufactured products.[48]

It had been expected that the Russians would take an early opportunity of tabling a detailed reparations plan as a basis for discussion. This they failed to do in meeting after meeting before the delegates moved on to Potsdam on 14 July for the conference there. The Russians reiterated their demand for a total of $20 billion, and clearly hoped for agreement on some fixed total expressed in money without going into too much detail as to its composition. From their point of view, reparations up to the agreed limit should have first claim on German resources, while the German standard of living and the German balance of payments adjusted themselves as residuals. If $20 billion were too high a figure, the Russians were not averse to some lower total – in conversation Maisky mentioned $12 billion as conceivable – but once fixed, it should be the point of departure for planning the German (and perhaps also the Russian) economy. It would be easier and more advantageous to reach international agreement at an early stage; and if a bargain had to be struck, what else but an aggregate in terms of money could form the subject of such a bargain?[50]

Neither the Americans nor the British were willing to agree to a fixed total. The State Department, it is true, thought that a figure should be negotiated, suggesting a total of $12–14 billion.[51] But Pauley was anxious not to name a figure, or to repudiate openly the total agreed upon at Yalta 'as a basis for discussion', and preferred to open the negotiations by tabling a list of eight principles to govern the post-war treatment of Germany. This approach seems to have puzzled the Russians; and since they found no disposition to settle the total to be removed they were uncertain how to proceed.

---

[48] IPCOG 2/1, approved by the President on 18 May 1945.
[49]. Playfair, 'Note on the negotiations', 16 July 1945, in PRO T236/262.
[50] Baggaley (1980), pp. 441–2.
[51] Ibid., p. 445.

Presumably, as Waley commented later, the Russians 'had decided that they would get a better bargain by producing their plan at the Potsdam Conference.'[52] From the British point of view, the absence of a plan, although robbing the conference of purpose and interest, was no bad thing. It would make it possible to wait for the participation of the French in the work of the Commission and for the Control Council to get to work in Berlin and survey the situation and prospects in Germany before final decisions were reached.

The one issue on which definite progress was made was the share-out of reparations. The Soviets claimed for themselves the half they had suggested at Yalta, but wanted a further share for their Eastern European allies. More surprisingly, Pauley insisted on a share equal to that of the British, while making it plain that this was not to meet American needs but to compensate for the outlays that America would be making to help the liberated countries. The claim horrified the British who were only too conscious of their own need for help in rebuilding their economy. The Chancellor 'saw no reason why the United States any more than the United Kingdom should claim excessive reparations merely in order to be philanthropic', and wanted to contest the American claim. Other ministers, particularly Lyttelton, thought that this would be unwise and it was agreed that the balance of advantage lay in accepting equality of treatment 'providing that you make it clear that our agreement is based on broad and general considerations of Anglo-American relations.'[53] In the end the UK and the USA were allocated 22 per cent each, with the USSR taking the balance of 56 per cent. The claims of other countries were to be met by a proportional reduction in these shares up to a limit likely to be 10 per cent in all; that is the percentages (net of these claims) would work out roughly at 50:20:20:10.

Much of the conference was taken up with discussion of Pauley's eight principles. These were designed to broaden the discussion and provide guidance for the quadripartite administration of the German economy, with reparations emerging as a kind of by-product of the guidance. In this way they provided an alternative route to the determination of a total figure, but a route that could be followed only after all the necessary information was available. To most of the principles there was little opposition but two in particular gave rise

[52] 'German Reparations', Note by S. D. Waley, 4 August 1945, in PRO T236/264.
[53] RM(45)3M, 9 July 1945, in PRO CAB 98/59. The Ministerial Committee on Reparations had been reconstituted on 11 June to include Anderson, Cherwell, Lyttelton, Sir Arthur Salter and Mabane (Minister of State at the Foreign Office). Eden, when he heard of the Committee's decision to give way was furious, demanding to know why neither he nor the Prime Minister was consulted (Butler and Pelly, 1984, p. 164).

to controversy. The first of these introduced the principle that Germany should be allowed to enjoy a standard of living not exceeding the average of other European countries (excluding the UK and the USSR): the second was the first charge principle.

The first of these, in one form or another, had cropped up frequently in war-time proposals. Sometimes the standard of comparison was in terms of Germany's neighbours, sometimes Europe as a whole, sometimes 'comparable categories of the population in liberated territories'.[54] Rarely was it the standard of living in the USSR.[55] Such comparisons seemed reasonable in principle; but how large a reduction did they imply in practice? Waley suggested in Moscow that it would be as large as 40 per cent, Radice in London thought 30 per cent, and Maisky put it at 25 per cent.[56] The argument continued in Berlin over the winter of 1945–6. Even a 40 per cent reduction was a great deal better than the 'subsistence' that Morgenthau and the others had contemplated. But there was no assurance that after reparations removals the standard of living would be pressing against the European average: it was a maximum, not a minimum, that was specified. Moreover the Russians made it clear from the start that, in their view, reparations came first and that the German standard of living would have to give way if it conflicted with reparations requirements. The principle was therefore agreed to by the British delegation, anxious to ensure an adequate supply of food, 'with some foreboding'; and the Treasury warned that the Russians might seek to use it 'to drive the reparations plan beyond the limits of common sense'.[57]

The first charge principle we have already met. In Pauley's principle number 8 it read: 'the necessary means must be provided for payment for imports approved . . . before reparation deliveries are made from current production or from stocks of goods.' As is clear from this formulation, the principle was applicable only to deliveries from current production.

At first the principle seemed to have been accepted without challenge, but at the final meeting on 13 July Maisky rejected it. His argumentation was casuistical to a degree. No food imports should be allowed after the next six months or so. If there were any difficulty in paying for imports then imports should be cut. Since

[54] Draft Report of the Ministerial Committee on Reparations, para. 27, RM(45)4, 18 May 1945, in PRO CAB 98/59.
[55] Roosevelt at Yalta did not want to see a higher standard of living in Germany than in Russia (WP(45)157 in PRO CAB 66/63).
[56] For Waley and Maisky, see minutes of seventh meeting of Steering Committee on 6 July 1945, in PRO T236/262; for Radice see his note in the same file.
[57] Playfair, 'Note on the negotiations', 16 July 1945, in PRO T236/262.

food imports were nil, the cut could not fall on food imports. There could therefore be no question of starvation resulting. Maisky's other arguments were no better. To apply the principle would be a political error, in his view, because it would give the liberated countries the impression that German needs had priority over their own. Why exacting payment for German exports should create such an impression while the spectacle of large imports into Germany of grain paid for by the Western allies would not, he did not explain. Maisky's final suggestion was that necessary supplies for Germany should be provided by UNRAA (i.e. by the USA and the UK), or that supplying countries (again, the USA and the UK) should add the bill to their reparation claims.[58] This carried no conviction with Pauley who had come to Moscow determined to ensure that the USA would not again have to foot the bill for German reparations. Still less did Maisky's suggestions appeal to the UK.

At a later stage, in the Potsdam negotiations, the enthusiasm of the Americans for the first charge principle ebbed away. If it found its way at almost the last moment into the Agreement (in a qualified form) this was entirely because of the efforts of Bevin.[59]

A third issue was interim removals of reparations. The idea, as put forward by the Russians, had capital equipment in mind. In this form it was anathema to the British, although they would not have objected had the proposal been confined to raw materials and consumer goods of the kind urgently needed in the liberated countries. Capital goods were another matter altogether. 'The one negotiating weapon which we have'. Monckton told Eden, 'is that the Russians want to remove capital goods from the Western zones. If we allow them to do so before agreement is reached on a reparation plan, the Russians will have no motive to reach agreement and the negotiations will drag on forever.'[60]

The proposal first came before the Steering Commiittee at its sixth meeting on 5 July. Maisky pointed out that it had been agreed to limit Germany's metallurgical industry to what was needed for a reduced level of internal consumption, together with a small allowance for exports. Factories built specifically for the supply of armaments were to be totally eliminated. There would therefore be no lack of plants for immediate disposal. A committee of three should be set up in Berlin with instructions to list the plants that

---

[58] Eleventh Meeting of Steering Committee, 13 July 1945, in PRO T236/264.

[59] Memorandum by Sir D. Waley, 2 August 1945, Document No. 600, in Butler and Pelly (1984) p. 1257.

[60] Monckton to Eden, 15 July 1945, in PRO T236/262. The note was drafted by Waley.

could be removed and allot them to claimants. The Reparations Commission could agree in a week on a list of industries to be included and the limits up to which removals would be permitted.[61]

Monckton said that he would ask for instructions from his government. How did the proposal fit into a general reparations plan (of which there was still no sign)? Was it possible to embark on such a scheme with no agreement on what constituted booty or on how restitution was to be treated? How was it intended to deal with the French, who were members of the Allied Control Commission, a four-power body that proceeded by unanimous decision and was under no obligation to accept instructions from the tripartite Allied Reparations Commission? What about the accountancy?

Four days later, at the ninth meeting, Monckton reported that his government was not prepared to begin reparation deliveries of capital goods (they might think differently of deliveries from current production) in advance of an agreed reparations plan. Any interim deliveries would have to be paid for in cash and in 'acceptable currencies', subject to a refund on final accounting. It would not be necessary to settle everything before interim deliveries began, but at least, as he repeated two days later at the final meeting, there should be 'the outlines of a plan'. He also insisted once again on the need to agree on a definition of booty.

All this came as 'a very unpleasant surprise' to the Russians. Maisky said it was a very serious matter for the USSR; and Saburov, who stood higher in the party hierarchy and took a leading part in subsequent Russian policy, was equally disappointed. The Russians were counting on early delivery of German equipment from the Ruhr and this meant not just agreement on interim deliveries, but high priority, just below the needs of the occupying power, for transport facilities, including shipping. As for current deliveries, what the Russians wanted was not imported coal but the mining machinery that would allow them to produce their own coal.[62]

The issue was left undecided in Moscow, but with the conclusion of a reparations agreement at Potsdam, provision was made for advance deliveries as recorded in section III, para.7 of the Agreement

Thus the Moscow negotiations had made little progress when the delegations moved on to Potsdam for the opening of the conference there on 17 July. No final agreement had been reached on all of

---

[61] The minutes of the sixth and later meetings are in PRO T236/264. There had been a long break in the negotiations before the sixth meeting until Pauley sent an exasperated letter to Maisky demanding a resumption.

[62] Saburov at ninth meeting of Steering Committee, 9 July 1945, in PRO T236/264.

Pauley's eight principles, or on interim deliveries, or on definitions of reparation, restitution and war booty, or on the way in which other powers were to be brought into the final arrangements. The total to be taken in reparations remained obscure. It was to be in Berlin, not Moscow, that the Allies would reach agreement, or the appearance of agreement, on a reparations settlement. And with that Agreement the Reparations Commission was to become virtually redundant.

The Potsdam Conference

In the months after the Yalta Conference, as the war drew to an end, relations between the Allies deteriorated sharply. The causes of that deterioration are not our concern since they had to do with Soviet activities in Eastern Europe and Soviet fears and suspicions of a deal between the Western powers and the German armed forces. But the deterioration itself, and the accentuation of distrust that went with it, coloured the subsequent negotiations. The Potsdam Conference marked an important stage in the dissolution of the war-time alliance and its replacement by the Cold War.

It was at Potsdam that argument between the Allies over reparations came to a head and for the first time international agreement was reached on what was to be done. It was an agreement that reflected Western doubts as to Soviet intentions. In what state of mind the Russians themselves approached the negotiations is not altogether clear. It is just conceivable, but highly unlikely, that they were still unaware of the abandonment of the Morgenthau proposals and of the change in American views since Yalta. If so, it does not say much for their diplomacy; they can have been in no doubt after Yalta (still more after the discussions in the Reparations Commission in Moscow) that they would encounter opposition to a total sum fixed in advance. Their haste to remove all they could from Berlin before giving access to their Allies strongly suggests an expectation of stiff negotiations ahead rather than – as has sometimes been suggested – a natural presumption that they could count on Allied approval.

Poland, not reparations, was the most contentious business of the conference. The two issues, however, were closely linked. The further west the Polish frontier was drawn, the larger would be the loss of agricultural land to Germany and the greater the difficulty of ensuring adequate food for a population swollen by refugees from the east. Unless the surplus of food (and fuel) within the 1937 frontiers of Germany remained available to the Germans within these frontiers, Germany would need to retain more industry and build up larger markets in the West. The conference would have failed, Churchill maintained, if Poland were allowed to become a fifth occupying power without any arrangements for sharing the food produced equally over the whole German population. The proposed transfer of 25 per cent of Germany's arable land to Poland, and the expulsion of 8–9 million Germans that would accompany it, were on much too big a scale. When Stalin argued that it was even more important to settle the question of coal and steel from the Ruhr, Churchill replied that Russia could not enjoy the right to dispose unconditionally of all supplies in the Russian zone and to the east of it, and share simultaneously in the products from other zones. There the matter rested until near the end of the Conference, by which time Churchill and Eden had left and their places had been taken by Attlee (who had attended the earlier sessions of the Conference) and Bevin, the new Foreign Secretary.

The negotiations on reparations fell into two parts. In the Economic Sub-Committee there was a replay, with some additional material, of the earlier discussions in Moscow. Then, half-way through the Conference, a deal began to take shape – although it was not finalized until almost the last moment.

The Americans brought with them to Potsdam a statement of political and economic principles to govern the future treatment of Germany. The political principles passed into the Potsdam Agreement virtually intact. Of the economic principles – which overlapped with those tabled by Pauley at the outset of the Moscow negotiations – three gave rise to debate.[63]

The first of these was the proposition that Germany should be treated as a single economic unit. To this Molotov initially refused to give unqualified support. He argued instead for a modification giving the Control Council power to rule in detail on the extent to which Germany could be treated as an economic unit for particular purposes. Next day, however, he withdrew his objection.[64] In return he asked for the withdrawal of another principle to which he took exception: the principle that each zone of occupation (and the

---

[63] The first seven of Pauley's eight principles were endorsed by the Economic Sub-Committee but did not find their way into the Agreement in that form. Some were dropped and some were incorporated in the revised version brought by the Delegation. Among those dropped was the principle that 'long run payment of reparations in the form of manufactured products shall be restricted to a minimum' (Butler and Pelly (1984), Document No. 116). The eighth and final principle – the first charge principle – continued to be opposed by the Russians.

[64] Sixth Meeting of Foreign Secretaries, 23 July 1945 (Butler and Pelly, 1984, Document No. 233).

Greater Berlin area) should so far as possible draw its supplies from the areas in Germany on which it had drawn before the war.

This principle was clearly designed to provide chapter and verse for efforts to revive trade between the zones, including the flow of foodstuffs from the Eastern to the Western zones. The British and Americans had been much disturbed, when the Russians allowed allied troops into the zones assigned to them in Berlin, to find that Marshall Zhukov simultaneously cut off supplies of food and fuel to the Western sectors, leaving it to the occupying powers to bring in (and pay for) supplies from the West instead of from the adjacent territory to the East. Molotov, however, insisted that it was no use thinking back to the pre-war structure of trade and asking for access to traditional sources. There had been big, irreversible changes, including the changes in Germany's Eastern frontier; and it should be left to the Control Council to review in detail what sources must now be tapped in the light of these changes. In the end the Americans concluded that the principle was too weak a prop to safeguard inter-zonal trade flows, and abandoned it for a deal on reparations that seemed to offer a better guarantee.

This left the third point of disagreement – the first charge principle. When the Foreign Ministers came to deal with this on 23 July, Molotov, suggested a new formula. Instead of settling which was to have priority, reparations or approved imports, let any shortfall in foreign exchange earnings be divided equally between the two. If, for example, coal production fell 10 per cent below target, then allocations of coal for reparations, export and home consumption should each be cut by 10 per cent. This suggestion, which seemed fair to Molotov, seemed muddled to Eden and Byrnes. If exports were cut, who would meet the deficit in the balance of payments? And if the basis of the reparations plan was an agreed level of consumption well below the pre-war level, how could that be depressed still further without overturning the plan?

The matter was referred to a Plenary Session of the Conference and agreement was reached at what was virtually the last meeting on 1 August. Neither the British nor the American version of the principle was accepted and the language used avoided the words 'first charge'. But the three propositions to which the British attached most importance were all, in the end, included in the Agreement:

1   Germany was to be treated as an economic unit;
2   Germany was to be left sufficient resources to make her self-supporting;

3 export earnings were to be 'available in the first place' for use in paying for approved imports.

The provision as to the German standard of living agreed in Moscow found its way into the Agreement in a rather involuted form. According to Feis, the original clause proposed by the Americans spoke of the production of goods and services 'essential to prevent starvation, disease or civil unrest'.[65] But at the Economic Sub-Committee this was judged to leave too open a discretion to zone commanders who could use the clause to keep open almost any factory they chose. The language was then changed to 'essential to maintain in Germany average living standards not exceeding the average of the standards of living of Eupopean countries (the United Kingdom and the Soviet Union excluded)'.

The Reparations Deal

The economic principles agreed at Potsdam, around which so much argument subsequently revolved, made no mention of reparations, this was the subject of an almost entirely separate deal recorded in another section of the Potsdam Agreement. The idea behind the deal was that it would prove very difficult in practice to levy reparations on a uniform basis from all four zones, and that it would be simpler if each occupying power took reparations from its own zone. It was an idea that had occurred independently to the British and the Americans. Waley had suggested that such an arrangement might be necessary before leaving for the Moscow Conference; and at the Conference the proposal had been broached by Pauley.[66] Now at Potsdam it was put forward by Byrnes at a meeting with Molotov on 23 July, and brought up again by Clayton at a meeting with Maisky and Monckton next day.[67]

What lay behind the proposal was the evidence that Russia was systematically stripping her zone of everything she could move.[68] Allied troops had not been allowed into Berlin until the end of June,

[65] Feis (1960) p. 248.
[66] O'Rorke to Waley, 13 June 1945 in PRO T236/258. Waley thought that it might prove inevitable that the Russians had 'freedom to take what they liked from their zone, in which case we should try to prevent them taking anything from the Western zones.' The idea had been in circulation in Washington well before the end of May (McCombe to Carter, 25 May 1945, in PRO 236/257). When it reached the Treasury in London it was greeted at first with some scepticism.
[67] Butler and Pelly (1984), Documents No. 240 and 266.
[68] Baggaley (1980), pp. 524–9.

and when admitted to their sectors of the city, had found that much of the factory equipment had been removed, even from plants making civilian goods or in American ownership. When the American reparations delegation, including Harriman and Pauley, toured the American sector on 27 July, they returned 'so worked up about this that they found difficulty in discussing the matter coherently.'[69] There was no way of checking what the Russians had taken and no likelihood that they would be able to supply a comprehensive and trustworthy account of it. The signs were that access to their zone and, still more, trade with it, would be severely restricted. Some members of the delegation, notably Harriman and Pauley, drew the conclusion that there was simply no prospect of quadripartite control of Germany as a single economic unit.

The proposed deal had the additional advantage, from the point of view of the USA and the UK that it made it unnecessary to name any figure for total reparations. The Americans had had second thoughts since Yalta and both countries were now anxious to avoid a commitment to a fixed total which later information might show to be too high. In that event, they would be obliged either to acquiesce in an intolerable depression in the German standard of living, and perhaps a slide towards Communism as the state's grip on the economy tightened, or to assume the burden of supporting the Germans out of additional imports. If, however, the Russians drew only on their own zone, or were promised only a percentage from the Western zones, there would be no need to agree on some absolute minimum such as the Russians were anxious to announce. There would also be no need to reach agreement on such tricky matters as the definition of restitution and booty.[70]

The submission by Maisky on 21 July of an unexpectedly wide definition of war booty, which appeared to cover 'everything of any sort which [the USSR] had already removed', was another element behind the American proposal.[71] The definition might suit Russia's book; but it appeared to allow the Western Allies also to take anything they wanted as war booty, thus making agreement on reparations superfluous. When this was pointed out, the Russians hastily produced a new definition. The episode confirmed the suspicions of those who feared that Russia intended to take all she could as booty from her own zone and come back for a full share in reparations from the Western zones.

When taxed by Byrnes, the American Secretary of State, with

[69] Turner to Playfair, 28 July 1945, in PRO T236/265; FRUS, 1945, Vol.II, pp. 889–92.
[70] Feis (1980), p. 255.

large-scale removals from the Russian zone, Molotov admitted that 'perhaps 300 million dollars worth' had been taken and offered to reduce the Russian claim by 1,000 million, or perhaps even 2,000 million, dollars, that is, by several times as much as had been taken. He qualified this later, however, by making the offer dependent on the inclusion in the Russian total of 2,000–3,000 million dollars worth of equipment from the Ruhr.[72]

The American proposal assumed that Russia was already in control of half of pre-war Germany, including the area administered by Poland, so that Russia could obtain the full share to which she was entitled without any supplementation from the Western zones. Russia and Poland had also the benefit of the total wealth of the areas ceded to them, and not just the assets in categories scheduled as reparation deliveries. The Russians disputed these assumptions. The movable wealth of their zone was less than one-third of the total, according to Varga. The territory under Polish administration accounted for a further 16 per cent of Germany's wealth within the 1937 frontiers (not 20 per cent as the Americans maintained). But was it intended, Molotov enquired, to take reparations from this territory before handing it over to Poland? That had not been suggested at Yalta. To which Byrnes replied that, if the territory were excluded, what was now available for reparation purposes had contracted by 20 per cent since Yalta, apart from further war damage and destruction. Eden also pointed out that the Russians seemed now to be suggesting that part of German territory should be exempted from reparation.[73]

It was clear that the Russians would not be satisfied without some share in reparations from the Western zones. When the proposal was discussed in more detail, Saburov laid stress on the wholesale destruction that made Russia so anxious for equipment from the Ruhr. In south Russia 80 per cent of the steel industry had been destroyed, and in other industries heavy machinery and plant had suffered equally. Russia was unable to restore her industries without the kind of assistance that could only be provided from the Rhineland. But the heart of German's war potential lay in the iron and steel and heavy engineering industries in that area and the assistance Russia needed should automatically become available as these industries were dismantled.[74]

[71] 'German Reparations', Note by Waley, 4 August 1945, in PRO T236/264.
[72] Informal meeting of Foreign Secretaries, 23 July 1945, Document No 240, in Butler and Pelly (1984).
[73] Ibid.
[74] Meeting on German Reparations, 24 July 1945, Document No. 266, in Butler and Pelly (1984).

The Russians had at last circulated their 'reparations plan', which did little more than repeat their proposals at Yalta, supplemented by a table itemizing the components of the total $10 billion for once-for-all removals, and indicating the commodities to be included in annual deliveries in kind.[75] The 'plan' was received with some indignation by Monckton, who found it 'inconceivable' that he should be asked to comment and present alternative figures at one day's notice and without any explanation of how the Russian figures were arrived at, after waiting for it for nearly four weeks in Moscow. Pauley, for his part, declined to accept the plan or treat it as a basis for discussion.[76] It was completely ignored in the Russian explanation of the basis of their claim to $3 billion in reparations from the Western zones.

Their explanation was as follows. Russia, they said, was unlikely to obtain more than $2 billion in once-for-all deliveries from her zone: this in spite of the fact that 35 per cent of German industry was admitted to be located there, which would seem to imply that $3.5 billion of once-for-all deliveries out of a total of $10 billion should be available. The implication was countered by the argument that far more of the heavy industry from which reparations would be taken was in the Western zones. But if Russia was to receive half the total of $10 billion, she would be $3 billion short and this was the measure of what the West should give her. This line of argument presumed that $10 billion was the 'right' total for once-for-all deliveries. As Monckton pointed out, however, the Russian 'plan' reached a total for Germany as a whole of only $6–7 billion ($4.5 billion, he might have added, if removals were to be from heavy industry only). On their own showing, the chances of removing $10 billion in capital equipment from Germany were remote and their claim to $3 billion from the Western zones correspondingly suspect.

To this critique the Russians made no response. It might have been expected that if they took seriously a limit of $2 billion for once-for-all deliveries from their own zone, they would revise their proposal for a total of $10 billion and make an offsetting, upward, adjustment to their proposal for a like total from current production. But the discussion proceeded with hardly any reference to current deliveries and the package deal made no provision for such deliveries. The Russians seemed more intent on getting equipment with which to resume manufacturing than to activate German

[75] See above, p. 67 n18. The total for equipment of all kinds came to only $6–7 billion at 1938 prices, plus 15 per cent, and nearly one-third of this was from 'peaceful' industries like building and textiles.
[76] Butler and Pelly (1984), Document No. 266.

production of manufactured goods for their use; the Western powers attached more importance to economic security than to the receipt of reparations; and the UK in particular had no wish to encourage German exports of manufactures more than necessary. Although all thought of current deliveries had not been abandoned it was not for a further year that the issue was revived.[77]

When Byrnes first indicated to the Russians what the Americans had in mind – immediately after he had repudiated any supposed agreement to a total of 20 billion dollars – Molotov appears to have assumed that the Americans still wished to specify a total and were initiating a bargain with some lower figure in mind. He was prepared to abate the Russian claim to 10 billion dollars, provided he could count on 3 billion dollars from the Western zones.[78] The matter was persued the following evening at a meeting between the three delegations but thereafter there was a lull before discussions were resumed.

The Revised Package

The impasse that had been reached produced a further proposal from Byrnes. He seems at first to have expected that by allowing the Russians a share in equipment from the Western zones he could induce them in return to continue to supply food and coal from the former German territory under their (and Polish) control.[79] Later, when he saw Eden on 25 July, just before the election results were announced – and Eden's departure from office – he suggested that the Russians might be offered equipment from the Ruhr in two parts, half as reparations and half against delivery of food and coal from the Russian zone and Polish-administered territory. The offer would be in a proportion, say half, of the total amount of equipment surplus to peace-time requirements and no figure by value would be quoted. On Byrnes's assumption that the industrial equipment in the Ruhr was worth $4 billion and that half of this was 'surplus', the proposition implied that the Russians would receive $500 million in 'free' reparations and $500 million against payment. Eden was non-committal but expressed some scepticism as to the chances of

[77] Waley was still talking of 'deliveries of coal, potash, timber, etc., out of current production' on 4 August, that is after the conclusion of the Conference (PRO T236/264).
[78] Informal meeting of Foreign Ministers on 23 July at 4 p.m. (Butler and Pelly, Document No. 240).
[79] Memorandum by Waley, 2 August 1945, Document No. 600, in Butler and Pelly (1984).

receiving $500 million in food, coal, and raw materials from the Soviet zone except over a period of several years. If the Russians ceased to do everything reasonable about sending supplies, the UK would feel free to suspend deliveries of equipment.[80]

At Eden's request, Monckton flew back to London on 26 July to acquaint the Chancellor, as Chairman of the Ministerial Committee, with the details of the American plan. It was Anderson's last day in office. He was persuaded by Monckton (along with Keynes) to accept the American proposals, and two days later Dalton, the new Chancellor, also signified his agreement.[81] This was subject to three conditions: (1) an agreed, satisfactory programme of reparations; (2) acceptance of the first charge principle; and (3) agreement that Germany should be treated as a single economic unit.

All of these conditions were ultimately accepted, although, as Waley noted, ther were those in the American delegation who regarded them as quite unrealistic. Pauley, for example, thought that the Russians would do as they liked in their own zone and had no business to interfere with what was done in the Western zones; that the first charge principle which the Americans had once urged so passionately would merely serve to tie their hands; and that the Russian zone would inevitably be treated as a separate economic unit.[82]

No agreement was in sight when Attlee and Bevin arrived on Saturday 28 July. The following day, with the conference drawing to an end, Byrnes put to Molotov (Stalin was alleged to have a cold) the various elements in his revised package. He was prepared to trade acceptance of the Western frontier sought by the Poles for Russian agreement to his reparations plan. Initially he suggested the Eastern Neisse as the new frontier but in the end, after talking to Attlee and Bevin, the Americans made a last concession and improved their offer so as to include German territory up to the *Western* Neisse.

Byrnes had met with little enthusiasm, much less agreement, from the British to his proposals. Ministers had no objection in principle to the offer of equipment from the Ruhr. But they were bound to feel some uneasiness at bargaining between the Americans and the Russians over the only card that they might be able to play. They were reluctant also to agree unconditionally to the proposed Western frontier of Poland, and hoped for some guarantee of free elections, freedom of the press, free access for newspaper corres-

[80] PRO T236/263.
[81] *Walter Monckton* by Lord Birkenhead (1969) p. 212; Butler and Pelly (1984) p. 956.
[82] Memorandum by Waley, Document No. 600, Butler and Pelly (1984).

pondents, and so on. But they were in a weak position since they were new to the international scene, unable to carry much weight with the Americans and unlikely to find much backing at home from their own supporters if they took up an intransigent position.

What was most disliked by British officials was the idea of swapping reparations from the Western zones for food and fuel from the Soviet zone.[83] The Americans could see no other way of ensuring a flow of goods to the West from the territory under Russian or Polish control. The British saw things differently. 'Some of us feel', wrote Waley just afer the Conference, 'that the system of swaps is so utterly wrong that we should refuse to be party to it.'[84] Behind the American proposals lay 'a defeatist view that the Russian zone would be administered as a separate unit with a lower standard of living and few facilities for interchange of goods with other parts of Germany'.[85] If a line was drawn 'across the middle of Europe, so that there is a frontier with Russia on one side and the Western powers on the other side, this has an importance far transcending reparations.'[86] In the Foreign Office and the Treasury these objections were voiced not just once but over and over again: the proposed swaps smacked of an exchange between two separate countries. As Eady put it: 'the plan is probably a decisive step towards the separation of Germany into a Western Area and an Eastern Area under Russia.'[87] Acceptance of the proposal must be coupled with an understanding that there would be no departure from paragraph 13 of the Economic Principles, which provided that during the period of occupation Germany should be treated as a single economic unit.[88] There would have to be common policies, with a common currency, central bank, budget, system of taxation, and above all import and export programmes for Germany as a whole. Why these should be easier to agree about than a common

---

[83] Both sides were qute clear that what was intended was that payment should be made in goods from former German territory, not from the USSR. At the meeting on 24 July, for example, Maisky included in a summary of the American plan his understanding that 'industrial plant and equipment from the Ruhr might be exchanged for agricultural and other products *from the Soviet zone*' (italics added).

[84] Waley to Eady, 31 July 1945 in Document No. 485, Butler and Pelly (1984), p. 1051.

[85] Waley at staff conference with Prime Minister and Foreign Secretary, 31 July 1945, in Document No. 486, Butler and Pelly (1984) p. 1053.

[86] Waley to Eady, 31 July 1945, in Document No. 485, Butler and Pelly (1984) p. 1050.

[87] Eady to Padmore (i.e. to the new Chancellor, Dalton) 26 July 1945, in PRO T236/263.

[88] Waley, Note on German Reparations, 31 July 1945, Document No. 491, in Butler and Pelly (1984) p. 1068; Eady to Padmore, 26 July 1945, in PRO T236/263.

reparations policy was left unexplained.

As if these objections were not enough, the Treasury also pointed to the likely reactions of the French, who had taken no part in the Potsdam negotiations and had strong views about the future of the Ruhr and the Rhineland. They would 'hate to see plant taken out of the Ruhr for the benefit of Russia because of a side deal about which they were not consulted'.[89] This apart, Britain had no interest in withholding equipment from the Russians since there would be an ample supply, given the wide margin between existing capacity and the probable requirements. What concerned them was that they should not throw away their strongest bargaining counter when it might be used to arrive at a settlement in which they had some confidence.

Bevin decided, however, to call it a day. It would be best, he suggested, 'to try to settle the reparations problem on the general lines of the American plan, but to pursue the question of treating Germany as an economic unit in separate discussions on the exchange of supplies between the various areas of Germany. He drew comfort from the Russian proposals on 30 July for central administrative institutions for foreign trade, industry, finance, transport and communications, since these appeared to indicate a willingness to treat Germany as an economic whole.[90]

When first approached, Molotov raised no objection in principle to the reparations part of the proposed deal, but wanted to know how much capital equipment Russia would get from the Ruhr. He was not satisfied with the offer of a proportion of what would become available: He wanted a definite amount, by value or by weight. He also wanted to know how much would be 'free' and how much would be in exchange for goods from the Eastern zone.

At lunch with Molotov on 30 July, Byrnes made a more specific offer, to which the British had still to agree. Russia would receive 15 per cent of what was available from the Ruhr without payment, and a further 25 per cent against deliveries of goods. Discussion continued at a meeting of Foreign Secretaries in the afternoon when Molotov made a succession of higher bids including a firm minimum of $800 million, or 2 million tons of equipment. He also enquired how the total amount available was to be decided, arguing for a joint determination on a quadripartite basis either by the Control Council or the Reparations Commission.[91]

A final decision was left to the 'Big Three', meeting in plenary

[89] PRO T236/264.
[90] Staff conference with Prime Minister and Foreign Secretary, 31 July 1945, Document No. 486 in Butler and Pelly (1984).

session on the second last day of the Conference, 31 July. Stalin, Truman and Bevin completed a deal that promised the USSR 25 per cent of the reparations taken from the Western zones, 10 per cent without payment and 15 per cent against deliveries from the Eastern areas. This compared with an initial offer by Bevin of only 10 per cent in all. The steps by which final agreement was reached are of little interest now. But so far as they threw light on the Soviet position or on subsequent disputes, some are worth recalling.

First of all, there was a stage at which the Russians sought a make-weight in German assets other than capital equipment. They wanted 500 million dollars' worth of shares in industrial and transport undertakings in the Western zones, 30 per cent of German foreign investments and 30 per cent of German gold in Allied hands.[92] These additional claims, which clearly reflected a Soviet wish for participation in the control of German industry in parallel with the control they were busy acquiring in the east, were rejected outright by Byrnes. Stalin, however, made it a condition of their withdrawal that Russia should have a higher percentage of the equipment available.

A second issue related to deliveries from current production. These formed no part of the final deal but remained in the mind of the Russians to the very end. At the plenary session on 31 July Stalin repeated a claim, tabled by the Soviet delegation the previous day, for current deliveries over the ten years following the capitulation.[93] He did not name any figure for these deliveries; but the earlier submission on 30 July asked for 8 billion dollars over ten years, with a Russian share of 50 per cent, or 4 billion dollars. This claim related, not to the Western zones, but Germany as a whole on the basis of a general plan to be worked out by the Allied Commission on Reparations.[94]

Russian pressure for a general plan was a third feature of the negotiations. Molotov had not been content with the offer of a percentage of an unknown total and wanted to be satisfied that Russia had a hand in deciding how much could be taken in reparations. The minimum he could accept was 800 million dollars' worth of equipment, not from the Ruhr only but from the Western zones. Byrnes could give no assurance of any fixed total when his own experts were not in agreement on an estimate. 'His Soviet friends', he said 'must accept the US Delegation's statement in good

[91] Tenth meeting of Foreign Secretaries, 30 July 1945, Document No. 469 in Butler and Pelly (1984).
[92] Butler and Pelly (1984) p. 1075.
[93] Ibid., p. 1074.
[94] Ibid., p. 1014.

faith that the economy of Germany would be carried out in accordance with the uniform principles laid down by all the four Powers.' The agreement to hand over a certain percentage 'said all that it was possible to say if quarrels and misunderstandings at a later date were to be avoided.'[95] Byrnes and Bevin both agreed that how much could be made available in reparations should be decided by the Control Council or the Reparations Commission, with a right of veto by the zone commander. This still did not satisfy Molotov who stuck to his demand for a minimum figure, in tons if not in dollars. But at the plenary meeting next day Stalin accepted a settlement in terms of percentages, provided the Control Council determined the total available and provided also that there was a time-limit (fixed at six months from 2 August) for the process of determination.[96]

It was the insistence by the Russians on participation in the process of deciding what could be taken in reparations that shaped the subsequent negotiations in Berlin over a reparations plan. There was no good reason, except Soviet distrust, why the plan had to be a quadripartite affair. Nobody imagined that it would affect what was taken from the Soviet zone. Nobody could be sure that it would ever be possible to establish how much survived in that zone. Russian participation was neither necessary nor compatible with a determinate solution. Its purpose apart from the Russian desire for a share in the control of the Ruhr, was to ensure that as much as possible was made available in reparations; but in the end it proved counter-productive and issued in a plan that discredited the whole affair.

The unseemly haggling by which agreement was reached did not bode well for four-power control of Germany. For those unfamiliar with Soviet bargaining it cast a vivid light on the difficulty of arriving at, and then operating, common policies such as the Potsdam Agreement envisaged. The trade in percentages of totals that were themselves unknown was to become familiar in the level of industry negotiations that followed, when even the population of Germany was settled by bargaining across the table; and so too was the alternation between unyielding attitudes and sudden changes of front that characterized Russian methods of negotiation.

With the Americans still talking of pulling out of Europe within two years and half-disposed, none the less, to divide the world with the Russians, the prospect confronting Attlee and Bevin was a daunting one. They were likely to be left face to face with the Russians, bearing crippling debts that imposed on the UK a burden not very different from that which the Russians sought to impose on

[95] Ibid., p. 1022.
[96] Ibid., p. 1075.

Germany. In a state of virtual bankruptcy, they would become the sole barrier to Russian expansionism and were already marked out as such by the Russians themselves.

The Potsdam Agreement was incomplete, unrealistic and ambiguous. The clauses governing reparations proved to be contradictory and obscure, the subject of long wrangles over an entire winter and issuing in a plan that did not last long and had no enduring effect. The Agreement named no total for what Germany was to pay and left for later settlement the level of industry she was to be allowed. Neither at Potsdam nor at any later stage was it possible to say how much in reparations corresponded to the formula on which agreement had been reached – not even after the conclusion of the level of industry discussions. The Agreement implied that no reparations would be taken – at least in the Western zones – from current production (an assumption carried over into the Reparations Plan), left Russia free to take what reparations she pleased from her own zone, and yet promised uniformity of treatment for all parts of Germany. It required Germany to be treated during the period of occupation as a single economic unit when the Western powers had little or no access to the Eastern zone and the Russians showed no disposition to keep the Control Council informed of what went on there.

5

From Potsdam to the Reparations Plan

'It seems monstrous that we should first de-industrialise and thus bankrupt the Ruhr to please Russia and then hand over the territory, or at any rate the industries, to an international body to please France, but that we alone should remain responsible for feeding the place. . . . Our present policy towards Germany, by which we have become involved in paying her large reparations, might rank as the craziest ever – if one did not remember last time.'

Keynes on 'The Overseas Deficit', 8 February 1946

Potsdam had settled how reparations from the Western zones were to be divided. It had also laid it down that the amount to be taken in reparations must be fixed within six months at most, that is by 2 February 1946. But one had to search through the Agreement for guidance on how the amount and character of the 'industrial capital equipment' to be removed should be calculated.

Confusingly enough, such general principles as there were did not appear in the section dealing with reparations but in the section entitled 'Economic Principles to Govern the Treatment of Germany in the Initial Control Period'. One clause began:

Payment of reparations should leave enough resources to enable the German people to subsist without external assistance. (section III, para. 19).

A second clause read:

Production of metals, chemicals, machinery and other items that are directly necessary to a war economy shall be rigidly controlled and restricted to Germany's approved post-war peace-time needs to meet the objectives stated in paragraph 15. Productive capacity not needed for permitted production shall be removed in accordance with the Reparations Plan recommended by the Allied Commission on Reparations . . . or if not removed, shall be destroyed. (section III, para. 11).

This clause had to be read in conjunction with the relevant part of paragraph 15, which read:

Allied controls shall be imposed upon the German economy but only to the extent necessary:
(b)   To assure the production and maintenance of goods and services required to meet the needs of the occupying forces and displaced persons in Germany and essential to maintain in Germany average living standards not exceeding the average of standards of living of European countries. (European countries means all European countries excluding the United Kingdom and the Union of Soviet Socialist Republics.)

It is not easy to interpret this rigmarole unambiguously. But it appears to mean that reparations should be confined to a limited group of industries, including metals, engineering and chemicals, and that enough equipment should be left in those industries to let Germany enjoy, through her own efforts, a standard of living comparable with the rest of Europe. The Reparations Plan to be drawn up would not be a plan for the future of the German economy but would be designed to show how the equipment remaining after payment of reparations was capable of supporting a standard of living comparable with the European average, and with a level of exports sufficient to pay for imports into Germany at that standard of living. In preparing a plan it would be necessary to work out what such a standard of living implied in terms of levels of output from the various German industries and compare with those levels the surviving industrial capacity in Germany. The excess capacity revealed by such a comparison could then be translated into actual industrial plants and removed in reparations.

All this, however complicated, might seem in principle fairly straightforward. But it left plenty of room for disagreement. What *was* the average European standard of living? What date in the past was to be taken for comparison? To what date in the future did the German standard of living refer? Would a comparison of past and future yield similar results? Would the Russians really be content to see the German standard of living higher than their own?

Other, larger, questions lay behind these. How did the removal of industrial equipment lower a country's standard of living except by creating unemployment? With millions of refugees crowding into the Western zones, would they not need more industry rather than less? What if the Russians maintained, as they did, that whatever happened to 'peaceful' industries, the restricted industries must at all costs not exceed the European average? And what if a plan for the whole of Germany turned out to be built on sand because each zone went its own way, so that capacity in one zone was not interchangeable with capacity in another? Could one really reckon in such circumstances on uniformity in the standard of living in each zone and freedom of movement for persons and goods between them? The Russians were already far from forthcoming about data for their zone, but the plan covered that zone as well as the others so it was likely to contain a large question mark unless things changed radically. Finally, since the Russians started with definite expectations as to what the Plan would yield in reparations there might be difficulty in agreeing on a plan that was likely to yield less than they hoped.

There was also some uncertainty about the mechanics of preparing a Reparations Plan. The Potsdam Agreement referred to 'the Reparations Plan recommended by the Allied Commission on Reparations' and to the 'policies fixed by the Allied Commission'. But after a short, fruitless meeting in August, renewed early in September, the Commission faded out. From the middle of September, when the Russians finally agreed to the change, the duty of preparing a Reparations Plan fell on the Allied Control Council in Berlin.[1]

Even before this was decided the Americans were ready with a draft. Professor Calvin Hoover of Duke University, with the help of a small group of economists, had prepared a tentative report by 10 September after a month's intensive study in Berlin. This was circulated to the other delegations 'as a basis for quadripartite consideration in determining the level of industry necessary'. Quadripartite negotiations began on 18 September in the Level of Industry Committee, set up by the Allied Control Council, and ended on 28 March 1946 when a Reparations Plan was finally issued, nearly two months after the date fixed at Potsdam.

[1] The move had been proposed in July while the Commission was still in Moscow and was strongly resisted by the Russians. After the American delegation had left Moscow on 15 August the USSR accepted a French proposal (rejected at an earlier stage) that the Russians should prepare their own plan and hold a meeting in Moscow to consider it. The Commission duly reassembled on 3 September and met again on 6 September but no Russian plan was forthcoming (Pauley Report to the President). The Russians finally submitted a plan to the Level of Industry Committee in Berlin at the beginning of February 1946.

Meanwhile, there had been a pause after the Potsdam Conference before British ministers gave further thought to the future of Germany. Throughout the winter they had many other major issues to occupy them and Germany seemed to pose no problems of compelling urgency. They were content for the most part to leave German affairs to their representatives in the Control Commission under the direction of a junior minister, Mr J. B. Hynd, Chancellor of the Duchy of Lancaster, of whom little was heard before or after his year in office. Bevin concentrated more on *political* issues such as future control over the Ruhr and the Saar than on *economic* issues such as reparations and the future level of industry in Germany. Thus, in Berlin, the quadripartite negotiations on the level of German industry called for by the Potsdam agreement proceeded with virtually no guidance from London. In the House of Commons no debate on Germany took place before 18 March 1946. Very little about the negotiations appeared in the press except after – many days after – the absurd and ambiguous decision on the level of the steel industry at the end of December 1945.

The first issue to come before ministers was reparations labour. A Cabinet sub-committee, set up in August to instruct the UK delegation to the Allied Reparations Commission (which had returned from Potsdam to Moscow), held its first and only meeting on 10 September with Dalton in the chair. The committee was told that according to Pauley, the US member of the Allied Reparations Commission, no reparations labour should be recruited except from established war criminals.[2] This was 'quite unacceptable'. Recruitment, the committee thought, should be limited to prisoners of war in Allied hands, of whom the UK held 209,000, over half of them at work. These were needed in agriculture, and possibly also for work on the roads, but some might be made available to France where the Government was aiming to employ 1.7 million reparation workers at full French rates of pay. In the UK, *German* rates of pay would apply and workers would be credited in Germany with any shortfall below British rates, including family allowances. Only work of reconstruction and repair was to be undertaken, not normal productive work, although an exception was made for agriculture. German coal miners were to be exempt from impressment and so too was other labour needed to support a minimum level of production in Germany. The Minister of Labour proposed that German authorities

[2] Only one meeting of the sub-committee was held. It was appointed on 17 August 1945 to give instructions to the UK Delegation to the Allied Reparations Commission and did not, as originally appointed, include the Minister of Labour (ORC(R)45 and 46, in PRO CAB 134/602).

(unspecified) should be responsible for the selection and maintenance of a supply of reparation workers throughout the period for which they were required.

Prisoners of war were protected by the Geneva Convention and this raised problems. For one thing the Russians had not signed the Convention and had not gone further than to recognize 'certain obligations as regards treatment of prisoners of war'. They certainly did not propose to pay current rates of wages since that would have reduced the reparations element in such labour. The UK itself was not prepared to allow international supervision of conditions of work, pending the substitution of civilian labour for prisoners of war. There was not the least likelihood that Russia would. On the contrary, the Russians maintained strict secrecy over the scale on which German labour was employed in Russia, how it got there, what it did and on what terms and under what conditions it worked. The work done by forced labour in the uranium mines in Saxony, where total employment was thought to have reached 250,000 by the early 1950s, was equally shrouded in secrecy.[3]

A few days after the meeting on reparations labour came the first Cabinet discussion of Germany's economic future by the incoming Government. This took place at its third meeting on 13 September 1945. Bevin, as chairman of the ORC (Overseas Reconstruction Committee), had circulated a paper on the industrial disarmament of Germany.[4] Much of this was a repetition of earlier papers considered by the Conservative Government in June. It reiterated that Germany was to be disarmed indefinitely and prohibited from maintaining plant for the manufacture of arms and munitions; that Rhineland–Westphalia would remain part of the country; and that the military occupation of Germany would last for not less than ten years so as to allow changes in her industrial structure 'to become permanently established' (as if there were any permanence in industrial structure).

The Cabinet approved a draft statement of policy on industrial disarmament, endorsing the measures proposed before Potsdam.[5] Other measures affecting precision and optical instruments, radio, synthetic rubber and light metals had still to be examined – some

[3] 'The Economic Situation in East Germany', IR 6415 (National Archives, Washington), 28 April 1953. See also R. Slusser (1953). In January 1948 General Sokolovsky assured the Control Council in Berlin that 'the Soviet Union had never recruited the labour of German prisoners of war nor did it intend to do so' (CONL(48)1, 20 January 1948, in PRO FO 1005/375).
[4] 'Industrial Disarmament of Germany', Memorandum by the Chairman of ORC, CP(45)160, 10 September 1945, in PRO CAB 129/2.
[5] See above, p. 74.

were still being examined in Whitehall the following spring when the Americans and Russians had already accepted the Reparations Plan. A study was also to be put in hand of economic and trade aspects of the measures taken, from the point of view of British exports and the balance of payments.

What seemed like an afterthought threw doubt on the whole approach. 'Any programme of industrial disarmament', it was pointed out, 'may be put out of date by the progress of scientific knowledge and industrial applications. In a few years' time war potential may be based on quite different industries from those mentioned above.'

The Cabinet was undeterred by this acknowledgement of the existence of atomic and hydrogen bombs and accepted the proposals. Nevertheless some pertinent questions were raised. Was not some restoration of Germany's industrial potential indispensable if there was to be any hope of maintaining order in the country? The British might find the Ruhr bankrupt and be faced with a starving population. Was it possible in those circumstances to count on popular support over the next ten years for the drastic steps proposed? These doubts did not dissuade the rest of the Cabinet, especially as they had Bevin's assurance that the proposals were 'essentially interim in character and did not prejudice the ultimate issue', a very dubious assertion. The existing policy was approved without amendment.

Over the winter a number of modifications to the original proposals were accepted by ministers. On 25 January 1946 the Overseas Reconstruction Committee agreed that plants making synthetic oil and rubber, nitrogenous fertilizers, and similar products should be allowed to continue production for the time being or be restored so as to allow production to be resumed. It was also agreed that Germany should not be held down permanently to the European average but allowed to recover, subject only to limits on the output of war-important industries.[6]

Meanwhile negotiations were in progress in Berlin. Much of the discussion in the early stages followed lines foreshadowed in the Hoover Report. This estimated that Germany had enjoyed a standard of living about one-third higher than the rest of Europe on the average of the pre-war years 1930–8; so that, if those years were taken as representative, a reduction of 25 per cent or so could be made without bringing the German standard of living below the European average. Such a reduction, again using 1930–8 as a measure, meant setting a standard equal to that in the year 1932; and the pattern of that year, making allowances for distortions

[6] ORC(46)2M, 25 January 1946, in PRO CAB 134/596.

caused by acute depression, could be used as a guide to the levels of production and consumption that should prevail in future. On the other hand, it was assumed that, allowing for war damage, industrial capacity would be at the 1938 level, leaving an ample margin for reparations.[7]

Three of Hoover's conclusions are of particular interest. First, he allowed for the production of 7.8 million tons of steel, of which 800,000 tons was for export. Next, he based food requirements on 2,600 calories per person per day, with imports of food and feeding stuffs costing RM 2,300 million (at 1936 prices) and accounting for well over half the total value of imports. But, thirdly, he ended up with a level of exports insufficient to cover imports and leaving nothing at all for occupation costs. His Report therefore failed to meet one of the fundamental conditions from which it had started. Nevertheless it was to have a major influence on subsequent efforts to base a reparations plan on the Potsdam Agreement.

The Hoover Report was not published; but such parts as did appear had a very hostile reception in the United States, the left-wing press being particularly violent in its attacks. Opinion there still took a tender view of Russian susceptibilities and was disposed to regard the report as condemned *ipso facto* by the displeasure and suspicion that it was said to have aroused among the Russians. Significantly, it was the figure for steel (wrongly reported as 10 million tons) that set off the strongest denunciations.[8]

Meanwhile the British were preparing their own report and had completed a draft by the beginning of November. This was largely the work of Austin Robinson and Donald MacDougall and seems to have been treated in London as for all practical purposes *the* British plan. The Economic Advisory Panel in Berlin, which they had headed before their return to London in November, did however continue work on the draft, and on Cabinet instructions circulated a shortened and revised text to the Americans, French and Russians when the level of the steel industry was about to be decided.[9] All three of these delegations subsequently circulated their own plans, the Russians last of all on 5 February 1946.[10]

---

[7] Ratchford and Ross (1947) pp. 78–80. Since capacity was in fact substantially higher than in 1938 the margin was correspondingly larger than Hoover assumed.

[8] Ibid., pp. 82–3.

[9] The first British plan is in PRO CAB FO942/527. It was circulated in Whitehall but not shown to the other delegations in Berlin. The second plan does not appear to have been circulated in Whitehall but *was* distributed to the other delegations, after a frantic rush to get it ready, on 31 December 1945. There is a copy in PRO CAB 134/595.

[10] No copy of any of these plans seems to be available in the Public Record Office.

The British plan was prepared in the firm belief that it was a mistake to try to settle the level of any one industry without first examining how it fitted in with the other parts of the jigsaw making up the German economy. How else could one judge whether a limit on the output of, say, the steel industry would prejudice Germany's chances of becoming self-supporting at an average European standard of living? Thus it was necessary to form a complete picture, with hypothetical levels in each industry, those making consumer goods as well as those making capital equipment, and to vary the levels until they yielded the right standard of living and balance of payments, before formulating a plan giving effect to the Potsdam Agreement.

In principle this was accepted by the experts in the Western delegations. The Russians, however, hankered after a simpler approach. They took the view that the level of *each* industry should be held to the European average or, at least for industries with high war potential like steel, that it ought to be, if anything, appreciably less. It was not so easy as it might seem to find convincing reasons why under the Potsdam Agreement it must be perceptibly *greater*. At one point in the negotiations this issue was referred to the Co-ordinating Committee, the highest quadripartite court of appeal, immediately below the Control Council, using electric generating capacity as an illustration. But no decision on the principle was ever taken. Instead of discussing the principle, the Committee decided instead to proceed at once to settle the future (maximum) level of the steel industry. General Clay had made up his mind that steel was the heart of the matter (a widespread view but nonetheless illusory) and that a decision on steel must be taken before his turn as chairman of the Committee came to an end on 31 December.

By the time this was known, the Cabinet was on holiday and the Foreign Secretary in Moscow. The leading British officials in Berlin, including General Robertson and Sir Percy Mills, had gone to London for Christmas confident that no decisions of any importance would be taken in their absence. The only British representative available was General Telfer, summoned urgently from the zone with no previous knowledge of the matters in dispute. In these circumstances, in the forlorn belief that the principle thus blatantly ignored (of relating the level for any one industry to a general plan) might still be rescued and reasserted, the authorities in London gave instructions for the immediate circulation of the British plan (then unfinished) in support of its view of the appropriate level of production for steel.

At the meeting, however, nobody paid the slightest attention to the British plan. The discussion was entirely about steel and the decision taken made no reference to anything else. Initially there was a wide spread between the figure of 9 million tons used in the preparation of the British plan and the proposal of the Russians to limit capacity to 4.6 million tons, with the American and French figures of 7.8 million tons and 7 million tons closer to the British than to the Russian level.[11] General Telfer was briefed to regard 8 million tons as the lowest figure to which he should, in the last resort, agree. But by the end of the meeting he had accepted 7.5 million tons as the limit of the capacity to be retained and 5.8 million tons as the permitted level of output. To make matters worse, the other delegations took capacity to mean theoretical or rated capacity, which in normal circumstances might be expected to produce rather less, and were mystified why the British made such a large allowance for the divergence between rated capacity and normal output. The misunderstanding took some time to emerge and produced much unnecessary acrimony. Sir Percy Mills brazened it out successfully so that the final plan specified both 7.5 million tons of steel capacity and 5.8 million tons as the production ceiling. But the episode did no good to the reputation of the British in Berlin.

It seems to have been Clay's idea that if agreement could be reached on steel all other differences would be quickly or even automatically resolved. Such a view bore little relation to reality. Steel happened to monopolize attention at the highest levels as the primary material for the manufacture of armaments and the symbol of an industrial civilization (although energy in its various forms is far more important). It was practically the sole example of a wide difference between British and American views, and may, for that reason, have acquired special prominence in Clay's thinking, even if this made it the weakest ground to choose for a debate between the Western Allies and the USSR. The presence in Berlin of a number of American steel men – notably Wysor of Jones and Laughlin – who hoped to boast on their return to the USA that they had settled the future of the German steel industry, may also have played some part. But whatever Clay's motives and expectations, the decision on steel did not bring agreement between the Allies on a reparations plan perceptibly nearer.

---

[11] It will be remembered that the British Cabinet favoured a level of 11.5 million tons. In the first draft of the British plan a figure of 9 million tons was used; the figure first put forward in the quadripartite discussions was 10.5 million tons (including 1.5 million tons for exports); the revised draft reverted to 9 million tons since it was quite clear that none of the other delegations would accept 10.5 million tons and very doubtful if they would even contemplate 9 million tons.

In January 1946, with the six months from 2 August that the Potsdam Agreement allowed for agreement to be reached already in sight, there was still disagreement on the whole range of major industries, steel alone excepted. As a rule and on the average the British figures were about twice those advanced by the Soviet delegation. One of the most extreme examples was building construction and repair, where the Russians were proposing a level of RM 375 million compared with a pre-war figure of RM 8,500 million and a British proposal of about RM 10,000 million.[12] For coalmining the difference was between 50–60 million tons and 140 million tons, and for electric power between 22 billion kWh and 37 kWh. These differences reflected differences in the proposed levels of the consuming industries and, still more (in the case of electric power), the stress laid by the British on the need to economize on imports by using indigenous resources (e.g. for the production of synthetic fibres).

Some of the levels proposed by the USSR were little greater than, or even below, the current rate of consumption in a devastated Germany. In October 1945, for example, Germany's consumption of electric power was at an annual rate of 20 billion kWh, not far from the 22 billion kWh which the USSR proposed for 1949. The consumption of oil and oil products was running at about 2 million tons per annum when the USSR was proposing a figure, first of 1.8 million tons and then of 2.1 million tons.

Progress of the Negotiations

The haggling over steel was typical of the way in which negotiations between the four powers were conducted. Levels for other industries were fixed in a bargaining process without any attempt to investigate the repercussions on other industries and so check that exports would still have a reasonable chance of balancing imports. Reassuring noises were made from time to time by the generals and other distinguished figures engaged in the bidding. But their reassurances were of the most general kind and bespoke a great depth of ignorance of the magnitudes involved and their interconnections. No set of figures less resembled a plan than the hotchpotch resulting from the Dutch auction in Berlin.

If, for example, on 31 December 1945, the British plan showed imports and exports in balance at RM 3,000 million each, they could not still be in balance after all the reductions in the level of industry

---

[12] All figures in Reichsmarks in this chapter are at 1936 prices.

made after 31 December. It was not really possible to argue with conviction that the original British plan gave effect to the Potsdam Agreement and that the new Reparations Plan did so too. There was room for *some* difference of opinion over how to interpret the provisions of the Agreement but the changes that had been introduced went far beyond that. The only legitimate defence of the Plan was that it preserved the semblance of alliance, or at least avoided an outright break with Russia.

But even this was an illusion, for the Russians were themselves following a course that made collision almost inevitable. They were already conducting the affairs of their zone in a way which made it seem unimaginable that there would ever be agreement between the four powers on a merger of the four occupation zones. Equally, the French were thwarting all attempts to achieve economic unity, demanding to be given the Saar and to have the Ruhr and Rhineland split off from Germany and brought under international control.

How the Plans Took Shape

The original idea seems to have been that a quadripartite committee would consider how effect should be given to the decisions at Potsdam and prepare an agreed plan similar to that submitted by Hoover.[13] Members of the British, American and French delegations engaged in this task had earlier agreed to pool information and to try to work as far as possible along the same lines. Since there was no desire to leave the Russians out, the British then proposed, in one of the Berlin committees, that liaison officers should be appointed by each of the Allies to assist in communicating information. Instead, however, it was decided to set up a Technical Staff made up of representatives of each country, and this very rapidly became the quadripartite committee where battle commenced. Exchanging information and comparing notes gave place to efforts to reach agreement on basic assumptions (for example, as to the size of the population to be expected), ground rules (what standard of living, in what notional year, was to be used in calculations) and, inevitably, levels for individual industries. The disagreements in the Technical Staff, which soon began to pile up, were passed on to the Level of Industry Committee, its disagreements to the next highest committee in the hierarchy, the Economic Directorate, and from there,

[13] Cf. *The Papers of General Lucius D. Clay* (1974) Vol. I, p. 65: 'the Economic Directorate has also appointed a quadripartite Level of Industry Board which will attempt to agree on a report somewhat similar to that of Dr Hoover's board.'

given the usual situation of continuing disagreement, to the Co-ordinating Committee and eventually the Control Council.[14]

It was agreed at the start, the Russians dissenting, to take consumption levels first and work back to the implied requirements for raw materials and capital equipment. Concentration on the consumer goods industries also made it possible to assess the contribution those industries could make to exports and what would have to be made up by exports from the capital goods industries. The Russians, however, saw little point in spending time on industries whose output they had no intention of limiting and wanted to go direct to the capital goods industries.

The difficulties of reaching agreement were compounded by the lack of normal secretarial and statistical services and by repeated changes in the early months in the expert staff fielded by the Soviet delegation. It was not until mid-November that their 'first division' team arrived in Berlin and promptly repudiated the tentative agreements on working assumptions that had been reached at meetings of the Technical Staff.

The Four Plans

Each delegation, beginning with the British, tabled a plan summarizing its proposals. The most elaborate was the American, circulated at the end of January, almost a month after the British one. The Russian plan followed on 5 February (i.e. three days after the Potsdam time-limit for quadripartite agreement). The French had been quicker off the mark and their memorandum, headed 'Commercial balance corresponding to the future level of German industry', was dated 13 January. This consisted, however, of only a couple of pages of text and a statistical appendix based largely on American and British material. It will be observed that the British plan was circulated before the decision on steel while the others were able to take that decision into account. No British plan incorporating the low permitted level of steel production was ever produced.

The plans were *ipso facto* an acknowledgement of the fact that one could not proceed by working out the European average for each industry in turn and then calculating how much capacity in excess of that remained for reparations. It had to be shown, as the heading to the French plan emphasized, that Germany could be self-supporting

[14] An account of the early stages of the negotiations is given in a lengthy report by Donald MacDougall 'Some random notes on the reparations discussions in Berlin, September–November 1945', 29 November 1945, in PRO T 230/75.

through the use of what was left: the Potsdam Agreement made specific provision for the retention in Germany of 'enough resources to enable the German people to subsist without external assistance' (section III, para. 19). There was also the question, although the Agreement did not touch on it, of how output was to be reduced to the average European level without causing heavy unemployment: some demonstration was necessary that the Germans would still be able to find jobs. Another, but separate, issue was whether the average European level was to be interpreted as a floor or a ceiling: whether the whole purpose was to decide what could be removed in reparations or whether the levels agreed, industry by industry, were to be policed as maxima even after all surplus capacity had been removed as reparations. Thus there had to be a plan, if only to demonstrate consistency with external balance and, if possible, with adequate opportunities of employment. There was also an underlying ambiguity in the word 'plan': was it simply a demonstration of consistency or a plan of action?

Whatever it was, it was bound to involve some highly elaborate calculations. It amounted to an input-output exercise before input-output analysis had been developed. First there had to be a statistical dossier for the past, against which to measure the changes to be made in the future, in order to comply with the Potsdam formula. It was convenient to pick as a base a census year for which all the magnitudes required were available: population, employment, exports and imports in the aggregate and in detail; and, for each of the main industries and products, output, home consumption, exports, imports, raw material inputs, labour requirements etc. The last census year was 1936 and the figures were in the *Statistisches Jahrbuch* for that year so that they were not too difficult to find if you had a copy; the British were lucky enough to have procured one – but only one. All the magnitudes had then to be converted to match the frontiers of the new Germany, shorn of a quarter of its pre-war territory. European averages had also to be worked out, at least for income and consumption per head. After that came the need to decide what limitations should be held to in the name of security; how far and how fast other industries might expand in the future; and what further adjustments might be required if Germany was to be self-supporting and if the plan was to be self-consistent. Making the necessary forecasts, and fitting them together so as to strike a balance between the objectives agreed upon at Potsdam, was a chancy, imprecise business that left ample scope for argument. Far from being a mechanical interpretation of a simple prescription, the various plans were bound to reflect all the heroic assumptions and simplifications necessary to their preparation and all the hopes and hates, notions and nostrums of their authors.

The Standard of Living

The first question to be settled was how big the reduction in the German standard of living should be: it was important to reach agreement on that fundamental issue. Hoover, in his preliminary study, had assumed that the rest of Europe would regain the pre-war standard of living in from three to five years – by, say, 1949. He suggested also that it would be reasonable to take the years 1930 to 1938 as a measure of pre-war levels. The reduction to be made in German living standards, to bring them down the average European level in those years, would have taken Germany all the way back to 1932; that is, to the bottom of the pre-war slump. British experts reached a similar conclusion by a different route, involving a comparison with the 15 years before the war when the rest of Europe was 30 per cent behind; they then established that the same margin separated 1938 and 1932. But they went on to point out that, quite apart from any hesitations they might have about reproducing the conditions of 1932, the production levels of that year were insufficient to maintain the contemporary standard of living, which was eked out by using up durable equipment and stocks of consumption goods without full replacement or making good the current wear and tear. Thus provision ought to be made for levels of production rather higher than in 1932.

At first there had been no dissent from this way of proceeding, although no outright agreement was ever recorded in the minutes. But when the new Russian team arrived in November they disclaimed the working assumption of a 25–30 per cent cut. They argued that a fifteen-year comparison had little justification and claimed that immediately before the war – a more relevant comparison – per capita income in Germany was 60 per cent higher than in the rest of Europe (other delegations put the margin of difference at 40 per cent). In their view, the cut in the standard of living should be one of 40 per cent, not 30 per cent, below the level in 1938. The issue was never explicitly resolved in Berlin. Instead, the two principal items of food and clothing were singled out for direct comparison.

Population

A second issue on which it was important to reach agreement was the size of the population of post-war Germany. It was impossible to avoid using *some* figure, whether one was making per capita comparisons or trying to foresee the export-import balance or the likelihood of extensive unemployment. The higher the population the greater the strain on Germany's balance of payments, if only because food production would not expand much in response to the growth of population and because food imports would therefore have to make up the difference between a swollen demand and an inelastic supply. Food imports would have to be paid for; a greater industrial output and a larger industrial capacity would be required in order to furnish the necessary exports; and the margin available for reparations would be *pro tanto* diminished. The importance of this argument will be apparent from an example. If, through a miscalculation, Germany's post-war population turned out to be 10 per cent greater than was expected and food consumption was underestimated to the same degree, the whole of this additional food might have to be imported. Assuming that it had been expected that Germany would draw, say, 10 per cent of her food requirements from abroad, she would find herself instead obliged to import 20 per cent of the total. A large slice of her imports would increase, not by the 10 per cent of the miscalculation, but by 100 per cent.

Allowance in the population figure had to be made for war casualties, the inflow into the Rump of millions of German refugees, and the return of large numbers of prisoners of war. The British and Americans started from independent estimates of just under 70 million, the French from a figure of 67 million, and the Russians from 60 million, subsequently raised to 65.7 million and then lowered again to 65 million. On the proposal of the American representative in the Level of Industry Committee a compromise was accepted – the first of many – that halved the difference between a *minimum* figure of 68 million, on which the three Western members were willing to agree, and the Soviet estimate of 65 million. The resulting total of 66.5 million was regarded by the representatives from the West as demonstrably too low, while the Russians were equally insistent that it was too high.

Late in November, the new Russian team sought to re-open the whole issue, arguing for a figure of 62 million. They felt strongly on the matter, and said that they had fresh information. This turned out to be a new figure for German war casualties; and although it was about three times the true figure,[15] it would have been a matter of some delicacy, if not actually a slur on the Red Army, to set about convincing them of this. Fortunately, the results of a preliminary

---

[15] Three quite independent methods of calculation point to a total of about 3 million for German war casualties on all fronts; the Russian estimate was 9 million.

census, which had just been given quadripartite endorsement, showed that two months previously the population of Germany was already over 65 million. The British and Americans sent in a hot fire of statistics to show that their previous estimates had been too low; and in the end the Russians were content to fall back to the comparative safety of 66.5 million, while the other delegations entered a still larger question mark against the 'working assumption'.

In the final negotiations in March the population issue surfaced once more, first in the Co-ordinating Committee and then in the Council. The British and the Americans wanted to provide for adjustments in the level of industry if it turned out that the assumed population of 66.5 million was too low. The move was blocked by the Russians who dismissed such fears as unfounded and, more surprisingly, by the French whose plan in January had taken it as 'certain' that the German population would be in the neighbourhood of 71 – 72 million. The French representative, General Koeltz, argued that the provision for food imports in the final plan was sufficient to cover such an eventuality – in flat contradiction of the view taken earlier by his own experts.

Unemployment

A major issue, which received rather little attention until the British plan was tabled, was unemployment. More than half the text of the British document was devoted to a consideration of employment prospects. A tentative manpower budget estimated the working population in 1949 at 31.3 million. This left a surplus of 2.5 million unemployed, the majority of them women. After further work, which took account of the decisions on the level to be permitted in the various industries, this estimate was doubled. The new estimate, however, was not communicated to other delegations. One reason for the revision was that, in the interests of realism, it was based on a population estimate of 70 million, not 66.5 million, the higher figure being consistent, while the lower was not, with the rest of the British calculations. This gave a working population of 32 million compared with 34.3 million before the war in the Old Reich: the fall was likely to be in men (about 2.7 million or 12.5 per cent) with a slight increase in women. On the other hand, there would be no more than about 27 million jobs, leaving 5 million workers unemployed, most of them, on the new calculation, men.

There was no chance that agriculture would absorb more labour. On the contrary, a fall of a million or so was to be expected, given the contraction in farmland by a quarter. Employment in the armed forces would cease, and in industry (excluding building and handicrafts) over 40 per cent of the jobs might disappear. There might be some occupations in which employment in Rump Germany expanded to the level in the Old Reich, but only one of any importance that might expand more – building, building repairs and clearing out the ruins. Even in building there was obviously some limit to expansion. It was assumed that, somehow, the work could be financed and that 75 per cent more building workers would be employed than had survived the war.

The Russians were at first inclined to dismiss the danger of unemployment as a failure of social organization, but they later admitted that they had paid insufficient regard to the problem. According to one of their experts, they did not expect a working population of more than 26 million and they were reckoning on a *fall* in productivity by about 25 per cent. They had no reason, therefore, to anticipate heavy unemployment. Rarely has so much unemployment been explained away so quickly.

The Russians took the view that if the Allies stood together and unemployment reached, say, 1 million, their united experience should be sufficient to find a way out. The matter should be dealt with empirically without taking fright in advance from dangers which the British were exaggerating.

Yet, in the British zone in particular, structural unemployment on a large scale could hardly be avoided. In some places the withdrawal of plant would be on such a scale that they would be overtaken by catastrophe not unlike that familiar in the depressed areas of Britain in pre-war days. Workers in the service industries would find their livelihood disappearing as the main income-creating industries in the area themselves disappeared. Where plant survived, there might still be a whole variety of bottlenecks limiting employment, and workers might be in the wrong places, or occupations, or age-groups, so that surpluses and shortages continued to co-exist.

There was also the problem of how the labour market could be adapted to the low levels of output projected. In principle, it would be possible to make the most of a limited stock of equipment by organizing a six-hour day in the industries affected and running four shifts a day. But apart from the technical difficulties in doing so there would be financial difficulties. Could one assume that if industrial production was 20 per cent lower than in 1936 real incomes would also be 20 per cent lower? How did one bring about the changes in *relative* wages that were likely to be necessary in order to redistribute labour between different industries and occupations?

These were not questions much discussed in Berlin. But had there been less statistical diplomacy and more real planning it would have been necessary to think hard about the whole problem of employment and unemployment, wages and hours of labour.

The Balance of Payments

What many people took to be the nub of the matter was the balance of payments. All the plans submitted paid lip service to the need to balance Germany's external accounts by the agreed reference year, 1949. But they did so at different levels of trade, on different assumptions as to what constituted balance, and with wide differences in respect of particular items. In the plans as submitted to the Level of Industry Committee even the three Western Allies were by no means in agreement. The figures are shown in table 5.1.

It might seem as if there was at least fair agreement on export possibilities. But even there, the disagreements were of some importance. The French were unwilling to allow the export of pharmaceutical products and potash (which other countries put at about RM 200 million) but made up most of this by crediting

Table 5.1 Balance of payments plans, 31 January 1946[a]
(millions of 1936 RM)

		UK	USA	France	USSR	Total agreed in 1946	Actual 1935	Hoover Report
Imports	Initial	2990	2858	2875	1500			
	31.1.1946	3186	3094	2949	2027	3000	4338	4128
Exports	Initial	3145	2900	3157	2410			
	31.1.1946	3185	3015	3097	2797	3000	4335	3967
Balance of trade	Initial	+135	+42	+282	+910			
	31.1.1946	−1	−79	+148	+770	−	−3	−159
Change of balance		−156	−121	−134	−140			

[a] The British estimate also took credit for a favourable balance on invisibles of RM 55 million, compared with a deficit in 1935 of RM 100 million.
Source: Cairncross to Turner, 2 February 1946.

Germany with much larger exports of coal (60 million tons compared with about 45 million tons). In the British view, none of these differences had much to do with security: all of them reflected French commercial interests. The Russians made no provision for exports of chemical products (other than pharmaceuticals) or (for some obscure reason) sawn timber. But they had no hesitation in entering estimates for other commodities similar to those of Britain and America, although they proposed to restrict production of those commodities far more heavily.

The differences on the import side were larger and more numerous. Roughly half the imports in the plans of the Western powers consisted of foodstuffs, with complete agreement on a figure of RM 1,400–1,500 million. The Russians, however, thought RM 600 million enough and reached a correspondingly lower total of RM 2,000 million. On the other hand, they had higher estimates than any other delegation for fertilizers (with the UK more or less in agreement, and the USA and France far below) and for textile fibres (with the UK at the other extreme).

The trade surplus in the plans varied between RM 57 million in the US plan and RM 800 million in the Russian. This was intended in the Russian case to cover occupation costs and any deficit on invisibles. The British, in their first draft, had allowed RM 500 million for occupation costs but had cut this later to RM 200 million. The French had a slightly higher figure for their surplus which they too assumed would go to meet occupation costs.

It is most unlikely that any of these figures was derived from an explicit assessment of probable occupation costs. They were simply residuals left over in the process of trying to fit together the prescribed level of industry and the requirement that Germany should be self-supporting. As bargaining proceeded they were gradually eliminated, as concessions to the views of other delegations made it necessary to add to imports or to take from exports until nothing was left for occupation costs or to cover contingencies that might weaken the balance of payments still more, such as an underestimation of future population.

The American figures provided a good illustration of how easily the surplus could be made to vanish. The original Hoover Report based itself firmly on the clause in the Potsdam Agreement requiring capacity to be left to meet the needs of the occupying forces; and, when the earliest trade balance sheet concocted showed a deficit, the figures were revised so as to leave more industrial capacity and permit larger exports. A second revision for the same purpose yielded a surplus big enough to meet the half of occupation costs assumed to require a transfer across the exchanges, the other half falling on goods and services supplied in Germany. Then, when still more revisions to meet technical objections wiped out the projected export surplus, the American plan, as circulated in January, took a different line. Now it was argued that no plant should be left in Germany specifically to pay for occupation costs: either the cost of goods required by the occupation forces and involving the use of local resources, or the foreign exchange costs incurred by the occupation forces and absorbing the proceeds of exports. Instead, occupation costs incurred in Germany would be a charge on German resources, delaying the attainment of the permitted standard of living; and externally incurred occupation costs would be a first charge on any excess of exports over imports at the permitted standard of living. Thus the earlier principle was replaced by a diametrically opposite one so as to accommodate failure to square the circle by showing how a trade surplus might plausibly emerge at the level of industry permissible under the Potsdam Agreement.

In the end, the final quadripartite plan showed an exact balance between imports and exports at RM 3,000 million for each. Curiously enough, this meant the acceptance of a higher figure for imports than any of the four draft plans had proposed. The figure for imports, however, was to be a maximum. Occupation costs figured only in a highly involved clause which seemed to mean that export proceeds could be drawn upon to meet occupation costs to the extent that approved imports of food and fodder fell short of RM 1,500 million. The clause originated with the Americans and was the means of bringing to an end an apparently interminable wrangle over the future diet and the future level of agricultural output to be assumed in the reparations plan.

Food

Food was one of the key items both in the balance of payments and in the standard of living debates. The agricultural experts in the Western delegations were emphatic that agricultural recovery in Germany would be slow and protracted. It would take a long time to rebuild the livestock population – indeed it was bound to fall further to begin with – and in the meantime crop yields would suffer through lack of natural fertilizers and equipment. The most that could be hoped for, even with such applications of chemical fertilizers as Germany could afford, was that yields might reach 90 per cent of the pre-war level by 1949, and it might be up to 15 years before they were back to normal. This view, which proved to be much too gloomy, was strongly challenged by the Russians who claimed, quite correctly as events proved, that with sufficient equipment and fertilizers, crop yields could be restored by 1949.[16]

It was common ground that, whatever the level of output, there would have to be a shift in the crops raised towards potatoes and cereals and away from livestock products. The shift corresponded to a necessary shift in the German diet, reflecting the fall in living standards. At the early meetings of the Level of Industry Committee and its Technical Staff it had been agreed to work on the basis of a cut in calorie consumption of about 10 per cent of the pre-war level, to 2,700 a day, and to assume changes in diet to give effect to this cut equivalent to a reduction of about 20 per cent in cost. These assumptions, when taken in conjunction with the assessment of the outlook for agricultural production by Western experts, yielded an estimate for imports of food of RM 1,500 million. These estimates were not challenged at that stage and it seemed as if the issues raised by food and agriculture could be dismissed from further consideration.

Not a bit of it. The Russians had never formally accepted the estimate of crop yields. It became clear also that the new team were assuming a population of only 62 million, a calorie consumption of only 2,500 a day, and a level of imports of only RM 500 million, one-third of the figure adopted by the Western delegations. There followed a long, long series of meetings, usually with food experts in attendance, at which the disagreements were gone over in the utmost detail. It was at one of those meetings that the average size of a Balkan hen's eggs was hotly debated. At another, it was pointed out by Professor Ratchford, the chief American expert, that the diet proposed by the Russians would require the average German to consume nearly two and a half times as many potatoes as the inhabitants of the rest of Europe, and that it would be difficult to absorb so much starch without extra fat to season it.

At the beginning of February the disagreements were as great as ever. There were three points of difference, each of roughly equal importance in terms of their impact on imports. The first was diet, where the three Western countries were allowing for a higher consumption of meat and fats than the Soviet; the second was the disagreement over future yields; and the third had to do with the rate of increase of the animal population, which was much faster in the Soviet than in other calculations. There seemed no way of resolving

---

[16] Estimates quoted by Mendershausen (*Two Post-War Recoveries of the German Economy*, p. 8) put the output of plant foods in 1949–50 at 106 per cent of the 1935–39 level and the output of all foods at 93 per cent. By 1950–1 these figures were 116 and 103 per cent respectively and improved further in the years following.

the dispute in the Level of Industry Committee, and it weas agreed to pass it to the Economic Directorate.

To everyone's surprise, agreement was reached in the Directorate. At the meeting on 15 February, only one week after the submission of the Russian plan, the Russians accepted a formula very close to the American position: capacity would be left sufficient to produce RM 3,000 million of exports and cover Germany's domestic requirements under the Potsdam Agreement; but not more than RM 1,500 million could be used to pay for imports of food and fodder, and if less was spent for that purpose the difference would go to meet the costs of occupation and imports of services.

Engineering and Chemicals

This was the beginning of a series of compromises at meetings of the Economic Directorate. Mechanical engineering was discussed on 20 February, on the basis of each delegation's proposal for the percentage reduction to be made in each of the main branches of the industry in comparison with the value of sales in 1938. It was agreed to group the various branches under three headings: heavy engineering, light engineering and machine tools. Agreement on machine tools was held up because the French were unwilling to permit the manufacture of *any* machine tools. Provisional agreement was reached on heavy engineering after a very long battle, but the Soviet delegate clearly felt that he had gone too far unless bigger concessions were made in light engineering to the Soviet view and he was unwilling to commit himself firmly. The issue was therefore referred to the Co-ordinating Committee. There, final agreement was reached on a basis that implied a reduction averaging 40 per cent in the output of the mechanical engineering industry as a whole in comparison with 1938. In this case, as in later ones, the compromise did not rest on any economic logic but lay a little above half-way between the Russian proposals and those of the three Western Allies.

Two days later it was the turn of chemicals. Here again a threefold division was made, between: basic chemicals and fertilizers; a group of particular importance in the German balance of payments including pharmaceuticals, dyestuffs and synthetic textiles; and a miscellaneous group of end-products covering soap, paint, plastics and many other products. These groups were obviously related to one another since basic chemicals are an input in the manufacture of finished chemical products. But in the negotiations in the Economic Directorate, and later in the Co-ordinating Committee, no account was taken of these interconnections, much to the annoyance of the experts from the Industry Committee who insisted afterwards that, if basic chemicals were held to 40 per cent of the 1936 level of production, the user industries could hardly be expected to reach 70 per cent of the 1936 level.

The Economic Directorate was again unable to reach final agreement although the differences were greatly narrowed. On basic chemicals the Russians came up from 19 per cent to the agreed figure of 40 per cent and made a further concession in agreeing that production of synthetic ammonia (for nitrogenous fertilizers) should continue for the time being. On the user industries in the third group they came up from about 45 per cent to 70 per cent and for soap and cosmetics were actually above the other countries. (The Soviet expert remarked that he did not want his country to be accused of advocating that the Germans should be left in a dirty condition.) Since the British figures for these two groups had originally been 48 per cent and 80 per cent respectively, there was no doubt who was making the bigger concessions.

The main difficulty was to reach agreement on the second group. The French persisted in opposing any export of pharmaceuticals in excess of RM 50 million on the grounds that the German sales organizations for these products acted as a fifth column and intelligence organization in the countries supplied. They and the Russians were willing to withdraw their opposition in principle to the export of dyestuffs but again the French wanted to set narrow limits to such exports. In addition, the USSR still regarded the production of synthetic fibres with suspicion, although willing to permit production up to the 1936 level – far below what the other countries were suggesting in the interests of economizing on imports of natural fibres.

Concluding Negotiations

By this time it was clear that the Russians were going all out for agreement and, as it was their turn to be in the chair in March, it was reasonable to conclude that a settlement was in sight. Four of the major issues – steel, food, engineering and chemicals – had already been thrashed out, even if some limited elements were still outstanding. The Level of Industry Committee seemed to be in limbo. It was left to the Technical Staff to prepare and simplify the outstanding issues for consideration by the Economic Directorate.

By the end of February the only things still to be settled were the three chemical items in dispute – pharmaceuticals, dyestuffs and synthetic textiles – and three others – cement, electric power and machine tools. A meeting of the Co-ordinating Committee was held on 7 March to resolve the disagreements on these six items. The meeting began unpromisingly with a renewed disagreement on each in turn. As before, the French wanted to limit the export of pharmaceuticals on security grounds, and the production of dyestuffs for less specific reasons, while the Russians were strongly opposed to a high level of production of synthetic textiles because the sulphuric acid needed for the purpose could be diverted at any time to the production of explosives. The French were also unwilling to allow machine-tool production to exceed 8 per cent of the 1938 level, while the other three delegations had settled on 12.5 per cent.

Thus, at what proved to be the decisive meeting, the Russian anxiety for a settlement did not prevent them from continuing to bargain tenaciously. But it was not only the Russians who held out for lower levels of industry. The French, whose participation throughout the winter had had little or no influence on the negotiations except over coal, had now become the main obstacle to agreement on three of the six items still in dispute: pharmaceuticals, dyestuffs and machine tools. The Russians were in disagreement on three others: electric power, synthetic textiles and cement, backed in the case of cement by the French.

Cement might seem an unlikely candidate for inclusion under the heading 'war potential industries'. But the Russians were particularly anxious to take cement plants in reparations.[17] In January Kaganovich had coined the slogan 'Cement means the Five Year Plan', and the first Russian proposal had envisaged a reduction in German cement-making capacity from 14.7 million tons to 3 million tons so as to allow most of the capacity to be taken in reparations. Later this figure was doubled.

The Russian chairman, General Sokolovsky, expressed astonishment that the British delegation should wish to leave in Germany capacity for a greater production of cement than in their own country and was supported by General Koeltz, speaking for France, who thought it contrary to the spirit of Potsdam that Germany should be able to use her extensive cement capacity to engage in reconstruction at a much faster rate than other European countries. She had got along with brick and plaster before the war. These building materials had the advantage of requiring more manpower than cement and so contributing to a reduction in unemployment. It was in vain that General Robertson pointed to the need to use more

[17] See below, p. 205.

cement when the output of steel was heavily curtailed, and to the desirability of avoiding upper limits on the building industry when the level of unemployment would inevitably be high. Even when Clay applied the rule of four, averaging the four proposed levels for cement, and suggested a compromise at 10.7 million tons, Sokolovsky was unable to agree to leave more than half the existing capacity of 14.7 million tons.

Synthetic textiles seemed equally unlikely as a candidate for restriction. Similar motives may have been at work but the ostensible objection was to the high level of sulphuric acid required, sulphuric acid being, in Sokolovsky's view, the stuff from which bombs were made. He went on at some length on the link between an ample supply of this material and the damage his country had suffered from the bombs and shells in which it was used. It was not easy to see how this justified restricting the output of rayon, which was the subject under debate. Sulphuric acid, like many raw materials, had a multitude of uses. But was it right to limit peaceful uses because of possible diversion to other uses in war, particularly in a world that kept finding new and more powerful weapons of destruction?

Electricity generating capacity, which was just as important to a peace-time economy as steel, was the last item to be settled. It too, was desperately needed in Russia and the Eastern zone had already been stripped of much of its plant. Agreement on generating capacity of 11 million kWh had in fact been reached in the Technical Staff early in November, the British proposing 13 million kWh but falling in later with the other three delegations. This surprisingly unanimous recommendation was referred to the Level of Industry Committee, only to meet with objections from the Soviet member, who first suggested 7.3 million kWh and some time afterwards substituted a fresh proposal for a capacity of 4.6 million kWh. The usual series of discussions ended in the usual deadlock, although agreement had nearly been reached in the Economic Directorate on a British proposal to retain 9.5 million kWh of installed capacity (compared with 15 million kWh in 1936).

The discussion in the Co-ordinating Committee was confused by references first to hydro-electric power and later to stand-by power equipment installed in industrial plants. Although both of these were included in the figures under discussion, Sokolovsky was under the impression that stand-by plant was not. This may have contributed to his reluctance to accept a higher level of installed capacity than 8 million kWh.

After registering six successive disagreements, Sokolovsky proposed to refer them all to the Control Council; that is, to the same group of Generals, wearing different hats. He would have to inform the Council that the deadline set at Potsdam had not been met although the Soviet delegation, conscious of the unfavourable effect of delay on world opinion, had made large concessions and done everything that could be expected of it in the hope of reaching agreement.

When he was about to adjourn the meeting, Clay came forward with a proposal to apply the rule of four to the various issues submitted to the Committee. Koeltz asked for time to consult his Government and this set Sokolovsky off again. Six months had passed and there was still no agreed plan. Of the items in the plan before the Committee, 90 per cent exceeded the average European standard. Some of the concessions made by the Soviet delegation were even in contradiction of decisions taken at Potsdam. It was not possible for him to agree to the expansion of branches of industry which constituted war potential and for that reason he could not accept the whole of Clay's formula.

He was again about to adjourn when Clay persisted, urging that when there was agreement on 99.5 per cent of the plan, the Committee should be able to resolve differences amounting to a mere 0.5 per cent. Sokolovsky reiterated his earlier contentions and seemed bent on rejecting Clay's proposals. But he ended by accepting in full those that applied to the three chemical items and raising his offer on cement and electrical power. Clay made no objection to the offer of 8 million tons of cement capacity (as against his compromise suggestion of 9.2 million tons) but stuck out for 9 million kWh of electric generating capacity (as against 9.2 million kWh in his compromise and an offer from Sokolovsky of 8.5 million kWh). He was also willing to apply the rule of four to machine-tool production and settle with the French for 11.4 per cent of the 1938 level instead of 12.5 per cent.

Clay's proposals went to the Control Council for final agreement, with the Russians reserving their position on electric power and the French entering reservations on pharmaceuticals and dyestuffs (and adding last-minute riders on the need to import less food and export more coal after 1949), while the British insisted that the plan would have to be modified if the census figures revealed a population in excess of 66.5 million.

On the day following the Co-ordinating Committee's meeting on 7 March, the Control Council met to discuss the situation and accepted the Co-ordinating Committee's report, subject to confirmation at a later meeting. Sokolovsky withdrew the Soviet reservation on electric power after attempting to reach agreement on 8.75 million kWh and the way was clear for agreement on the plan as a whole. The British and French asked for time to consult their Governments and it was not until the meeting of the Council on 26 March that final approval was given. From then on it was capacity, not levels of industry, that took the stage; and, as later became clear, there was just as much disagreement about capacity as there was about levels of industry. By the end of March the Russians were arguing that capacity must be defined and measured on the basis of double-shift working.

Reparations from 'Peaceful' Industries

The change from levels of industry to their implications for reparations had already begun with a dispute in the Economic Directorate on 5 March over the title of the report that was in preparation. Was it to be called simply 'The Reparations Plan' or should it be 'The Level of the Post-war German Economy'? The Americans insisted that any figures relating to 'peaceful' industries were not binding on the Germans but an indication of outputs that were both feasible and consistent with external balance and an average European standard of living. Even if capacity exceeded the suggested level of output, 'there should be no removal of capital equipment as reparations from the light consumer-goods industries necessary to sustain a peace-time economy'. So they had argued in their plan, submitted in January, but the contention had gone unnoticed.

Throughout the whole of the negotiations, different delegations had quite different conceptions of what they were doing. The Russians regarded the Plan as a plan, not just as a piece of intellectual scaffolding for the purpose of setting limits to what could be taken in reparations. When a level was agreed for any industry at a quadripartite committee, that level indicated a limit which a future German Government should respect whether reparations were removed or not. The Russians could hardly believe their ears when they heard General Draper, Mills's opposite number in the American delegation, give unambiguous expression to the American view for the first time in the debate over the title of the report. Draper, however, insisted that figures for agreed levels of production in 'peaceful' industries should be treated as estimates, not limitations.

It was easier to settle the title than the issue of substance. Sir Percy Mills's suggestion that the report should be called 'The Plan for Reparations and the Level of Post-war German Economy' was accepted and preserved a nice ambiguity. The removal of reparations from peaceful industries was the subject of lengthy debate, first in the Economic Directorate, then at the Co-ordinating Committee two days later, at the Allied Control Council next day, and again after the Plan had been agreed by governments, at a meeting of the Economic Directorate to edit the final text on 27 March. On the last occasion the Soviet delegate drew attention to the US reservation which still appeared in the text (and again in a footnote), pointing out that he could not issue a document making public a disagreement among the four Allies in the middle of an agreed Plan. He suggested the deletion of the reservation. The ensuing debate produced no agreement and it was not until the next day (28 March), already scheduled for the publication of the document, that General Clay accepted a French amendment that virtually conceded the American position.[18]

On the issue of substance the French sided with the Russians; and the British, at first doubtful of the American proposition, ended by supporting it. It was a curious episode, especially after the long negotiations that had gone before. The Potsdam Agreement had asked for primary emphasis to be given to the development of agriculture and peaceful domestic industries; and this could legitimately be construed as freeing all such industries from any limitation. But nothing in the Agreement specifically ruled out reparations from peaceful industries with excess capacity. The Americans regarded the two propositions – no limitation of output, no reparations – as identical. In practice this might well be so; but it was not so in principle.

In any event, what precisely was a 'peaceful' industry as distinct from an industry with war potential? As every economist knows, these distinctions hold only at the margin and tend to disappear as output shrinks, even in an apparently innocuous industry. It may not be fatal to lose half the output of nails; but the time comes when the shortage begins to pinch and first the shoe and then the battle is lost. There is no fixed military hierarchy in which industries can be graded independently of the state of the military art and the availability of substitutes. There were, no doubt, some industries or plants that had no value except for military purposes and some that were genuinely of critical importance in war. But with these few exceptions it was all a matter of degree, even if it was accepted that war potential was a function of industrial structure.

---

[18] A full account of this episode appears in B.U. Ratchford and W. D. Ross, *Berlin Reparations Assignment: Round One of the German Peace Settlement* (1947).

British Acceptance of the Reparations Plan

When the Allied Control Council met on 8 March 1946, the Reparations Plan was accepted by the American and Russian representatives (Clay and Sokolovsky). As we have seen, a final decision was deferred until the British and French Governments had been consulted. A meeting of British ministers was held on 15 March to consider the position on the basis of a paper on the 'Level of Industry' by the Chancellor of the Duchy of Lancaster (J. B. Hynd), and two papers by the Foreign Secretary on 'The Future of Germany and the Ruhr' and 'The Saar Territory'.[19]

It cannot be said that the key paper on 'The Level of Industry' did justice to the issues at stake. In particular it did not bring out that the use of the word 'Plan' was a misnomer, since the levels of industry to which ministers were asked to agree were neither consistent nor coherent. They were the outcome of a bargaining process in which each decision ws unrelated to the others and the resulting jumble could not be assumed to make any sense whatever. Nobody could say what the German standard of living would work out at, or whether Germany would achieve a level of exports sufficient to pay for the imports required at that level, or how many Germans would be unemployed. There was no real agreement even on the size of the German population. There was open disagreement whether reparations could be taken from the so-called peaceful industries. And, of course, no one knew how much industrial capacity remained in Germany, least of all in the Soviet zone. The figures agreed touched reality only where they implied an upper limit to some particular industry's permited output and freedom to remove as reparations any capacity in excess of that limit. But the combination of figures agreed did not add up to anything that could be described as a 'plan'.

It was quite true, as ministers were told, that 'nearly always Russian concessions have been substantially greater than those of the other three powers'.[20] But this had not been true until a few weeks before; in the earlier bargaining process, the Russians had felt free to withdraw agreement and try again for a figure midway between the outcome of some earlier compromise and their own original figure, so approaching that figure asymptotically. No doubt this was only common practice in Russian negotiations. But the Western delegations found it hard to reconcile with the idea of

---

[19] The first of these papers (Gen. 121/3) is dated 12 March, and the other two (Gen. 121/1 and Gen. 121/2) 11 March. They are in PRO CAB 130/9.
[20] Gen. 121/3.

drawing up a plan to satisfy the various requirements of the Potsdam Agreement.

Thus when ministers were told that 'in the view of the British Delegation the plan represents neither a drastic nor a generous interpretation of the Potsdam Agreement but one that can be considered to be fair',[21] they were being offered a rather odd judgement which would not have been widely shared in Berlin, least of all by those who prepared the British plan.

Even at this late stage departments in Whitehall were still pressing for more severe limitations on German industry. The Ministry of Supply and Aircraft Production was asking for a prohibition of the manufacture of watches and most other precision instruments, partly no doubt in the interests of the newly established British watch and clock industry, partly because of the importance in the Second World War of capacity to make fuses and precision instruments. The dyestuffs industry was said to be basing its plans on the complete elimination of the German industry and making representations against the retention of even a limited amount of capacity. It was, however, much too late to seek to modify the plan and nothing came of these representations.[22]

Ministers had no choice but to accept the plan or reject it. In the circumstances rejection was out of the question. It would have been difficult enough to repudiate what had already been agreed in Berlin; virtually impossible when the Americans and Russians had already accepted the plan; and politically out of the question to break off negotiations, as rejection would almost certainly have involved. Although British public opinion had moved a long way, it was certainly not pro-German and there would have been consternation in a large section of the Labour Party if the Government had appeared to be denying reparations promised earlier to the Russians.

All that the Government could do was to communicate its reservations to the Control Council without writing them into the plan. The conditions which it attached to its acceptance and their bearing on the Plan are discussed in chapter 7.

[21] Ibid.
[22] Ibid.

6

The Reparations Plan:
an Assessment

If Four should join to shape a Plan
For taking all the loot they can
While leaving to a Fifth enough
Of all the necessary stuff
To just maintain but not exceed
The average of Europe's need
(Always excepting from the sum,
What may appear a trifle rum,
The Bear and Lion as extremes
Beyond the reach of Europe's dreams). . . .

Snatches

The Reparations Plan was given final approval and published on 28 March 1946. It distinguished between three types of industry: those that were forbidden and would be eliminated completely although not, in every case, at once; those, like building, that would be free to develop within the limits of available resources; and those that would be subject to a ceiling imposed by the Allies (assumed to apply to the year 1949). Rather confusingly, the third group also included those 'peaceful industries' like textiles and coal over which there had been such a battle, and it was only in the footnote introduced on 27 March, at the very last minute, that it was made clear that the levels shown for those industries were not fixed at all but could be exceeded unless the Control Council decided otherwise.

Prohibited Industries

The Allies regarded industrial disarmament as a necessary step to wiping out Germany's war potential, irrespective of any contribution to reparations that might result. Industrial disarmament did not mean, however, that only industries making munitions and nothing but munitions would be prohibited. With remarkably little discussion, a long list of industries not normally thought of as contributing markedly to war potential was scheduled for closure. The list started with 'arms, ammunition and implements of war', continued with sea-going ships and aircraft, military or otherwise, and then added 14 other industries: synthetic oil and gasoline, synthetic rubber and synthetic ammonia; aluminium, magnesium, beryllium and vanadium; ball-bearings, heavy machine tools and heavy tractors; radioactive materials, radio transmitting equipment, hydrogen peroxide above 50 per cent strength, and specific war chemicals and gases. Three of these – synthetic oil and gasoline, synthetic rubber and ball-bearings – were to be permitted until they could be replaced by imports for which there was enough foreign exchange. The production of a fourth, synthetic ammonia, was subject to a similar provision and was to be limited to Germany's peace-time requirements.

Restricted Industries

While reparations were likely to come mainly from the first group of industries they could also be removed from those whose output was to be restricted, to the extent that capacity exceeded the permitted level. The Potsdam Agreement had not specified the industries to be restricted beyond a general reference to 'production of metals, chemicals, machinery, and other items that are directly necessary to a war economy'. The British plan in November singled out steel, machine tools, locomotives and heavy vehicles for special mention. But, by the time agreement was reached in March, non-ferrous metals, basic chemicals, dyestuffs, pharmaceuticals, synthetic fibres, and various engineering products had all been added. Even at the end, it was not very clear whether the levels specified were to be treated as fixed ceilings that could not be exceeded or whether they merely provided a measure of what plant must be retained and what could be taken in reparations. The language used in the final document is generally 'there will be retained' a stated percentage of 1938 capacity; but for non-ferrous metals the formulation is more peremptory: 'the annual consumption of non-ferrous metals . . . is fixed at the following quantities'.

Unrestricted Industries

The final document carries no heading 'unrestricted industries' but, as already indicated, includes two lists that might warrant this heading. First, there are seven industries for which no attempt was made to agree on a level, of which 'building and building materials (excluding cement)' is much the most important, the others including a wide range of industries from potash to furniture, glass and ceramics. Then there are the industries for which the agreed levels were intended as estimates only: coal, textiles, rubber, paper, boots and shoes, and agricultural machinery other than tractors.

The Final Picture

For all of the industries included in the final document, only the barest details were given. The information published related

Table 6·1   Level of German industry in 1936 and 1949
(as measured by net value added in Rm of 1936 value)

	1936 RM billion	1949 RM billion	Ratio of 1949 to 1936 %
Mining	2.24	1.8	80
Metallurgy and metal working	4.98	2.4	48
Engineering	5.88	3.35	57
Chemicals	2.79	1.7	60
Textiles	3.59	3.0	83
Food Processing	3.59	2.9	80
Paper and pulp	1.46	1.0	67
Woodworking	1.04	1.25	125
Electricity	1,49	1.2	80
Miscellaneous (glass, ceramics, leather and gas)	1.63	1.4	86
Total	28.69	20.0	70
Building and building materials	5.50	7.5	136
Grand Total	34.19	27.5	80

Source: 'The Reparations Plan and the Future Level of Industry in Germany', unpublished official report by A. K. Cairncross, April 1946.

exclusively to production and provided no general picture of the way in which the different elements fitted together. Perhaps this was just as well, since in some industries (chemicals is only one example) the negotiated levels could probably *not* be made to fit together. More important, no indication was given of the assumed *aggregates* for production and consumption or of the assumed *components* of the export and import totals. It may be useful, therefore, to conclude this chapter with some indication of the British view of these matters as I set it down at the time.

The projected reduction in the level of output is shown in table 6.1. The biggest reduction was in the steel and metal industries with engineering and chemicals not much less. On the other hand, the building and building materials industry was to be greatly expanded and would account for some 27 per cent of total industrial production compared with about 16 per cent in 1936. Excluding the building industry, the cut in comparison with 1936 would be 30 per cent; including the building industry, the cut would be reduced to 20 per cent.

Turning to consumption, the reduction implied in the Plan was estimated to be of the order of 25 per cent. But this was a hypothetical

Table 6·2 Food consumption[a]

	Pre-war Germany	Rest of Europe	Post-war Germany
Cereals and pulses (flour equivalent)	114	151	136
Potatoes	176	109	225
Vegetables	49	60	80
Fruit	37	30	25
Fish	13	7	12
Eggs	7	6	4
Milk	125	94	90
Cheese	5	4	4
Sugar	23	16	20
Meat	46	28	32
Pure fat	22	11.2	13
Beer, wine and spirits	64	76	
Coffee and tea	2.7	1.9	
Tobacco	1.9	1.2	1.2

[a] kg per head, per annum.
Source: 'The Reparations Plan and the Future Level of Industry in Germany'.

calculation based on what might be provided, not on what consumers would want. The change in diet would be nothing less than revolutionary (see table 6.2), with meat consumption lower than for over 50 years and fats reduced almost as drastically (although in each case to a level above the pre-war European average). If the only way of making consumers economize on food to such an extent – equal to a saving of about 20 per cent – was to resort to a cut in money incomes it was unlikely that a fall of 25 per cent would be enough: some form of rationing might also be required. The shortage of imported textile materials was also likely to compel stringent rationing of clothing.

Thus, what seemed to underlie the agreed levels for the post-war German economy was not just a drastic fall in living standards and a

Table 6·3   German imports 1936–1949

	Imports: c.i.f. cost[a]	
	1936	*Estimated 1949*
1 Food and feeding stuffs, occupation costs, etc.	1,485	1,500
2 Nitrogenous fertilizers	11	250[b]
3 Phosphates	40	115
4 Textile fibres	728	360
5 Non-ferrous metals, scrap and alloys metallic ores	467	150
6 Liquid fuels and lubricants	171	100
7 Hides and skins	140	100
8 Technical oils and fats	54	55
9 Ball- and roller-bearings	–	35
10 Rubber	66	30
11 Chemical raw materials	58	25
12 Wood	248	20
13 Raw fur pelts	37	15
14 Rosin, copal, shellac	21	15
15 Other items	692	230[c]
	4,218	3,000

[a] RM millions of 1936 value.
[b] On assumption of eventual suppression of synthetic ammonia process.
[c] Including wood pulp, motor vehicles, heavy forgings, etc.
Source: 'The Reparations Plan and the Future Level of German Industry'.

comprehensive change in spending patterns but a series of structural adjustments in order to make the best use of the available resources, especially the use of imported materials and of manpower. Reliance on market forces to accomplish these adjustments was no more likely to prove effective than similar reliance on market forces to bring about the speedy transformation of a peace-time economy to a war economy. On the other hand, to leave behind an economy in which control and compulsion continued to be indispensable and pervasive was not perhaps the best way to set about rebuilding a disarmed and peaceful Germany.

Table 6·4   German exports 1936–1949

	Exports: c.i.f. cost[a]	
	1936	*Estimated 1949*
1 Coal and coke	386	450
2 Potash and other mineral products	69	105
3 Iron and steel products and engineering, other than electrical and transport	1,440	250
4 Non-ferrous metal products	300	75
5 Optical and precision instruments	138	120
6 Bicycles, motorcycles and vehicles	172	30
7 Electrical equipment	269	130
8 Textiles		500
9 Apparel	} 514	60
10 Books, stationery and paper goods	105	120
11 Paper and cardboard	108	70
12 Wooden goods (including furniture)	30	85
13 Stones and clays	44	50
14 Ceramics and glass and glassware	119	150
15 Leather goods	86	100
16 Chemical products	574	250
17 Chemico-technical products	87	30
18 Toys and musical instruments	65	75
19 Beer, wine and spirits	18	20
20 Electric power	–	80
21 Miscellaneous (including wood)	244	250
	4,768	3,000

[a] RM millions of 1936 value.
Source: 'The Reparations Plan and the Future Level of German Industry'.

Tables 6.3 and 6.4, giving the imports and exports that were assumed to balance at RM 3,000 million, show some of the upheavals expected. Food, feeding stuffs and fertilizers would absorb nearly two-thirds of export earnings. Imports of textile fibres would be cut in half and non-ferrous metals to one-third. Other raw materials like rubber and chemicals would undergo similar reductions and wood imports would virtually cease. Exports, too, would be much less than before the war, chiefly because the metal and engineering group, which had supplied about 40 per cent of total exports in 1936, could not expect to furnish even one-fifth as much in 1949. Textiles and clothing, in spite of the shortage of imported fibre, would have to take the lead in exports along with an expansion in coal, potash and various consumer goods.

Tables 6.3 and 6.4 are interesting as statistical pyramids. They were constructed through long laborious days by toilers in different delegations and different divisions within each delegation. But once put in position they served no purpose except as relics of past effort. Things took a course very different from what had been sketched. The world of 1949 bore little resemblance to the Plan for that year, which had occupied four delegations in Berlin throughout an entire winter. In the years between, production never reached even the low limits of capacity envisaged in the Reparations Plan.

British Views of the Reparations Plan

What view ministers took of the Reparations Plan it is not possible to say. The reservations on which they insisted bespeak little enthusiasm and grave hesitations. In Berlin the hesitations were even stronger: the undercurrent of feeling was one of increasing irritation over Russian behaviour in Germany and a corresponding welling-up of pro-German sentiment.

In a report to the British Government soon after final acceptance of the Plan ('The Reparations Plan and the Future Level of Industry in Germany'), I recorded a personal assessment, the concluding section of which ran as follows:

A   The Plan in Retrospect

86   The Reparations Plan is a compromise between widely different interpretations of the Potsdam Agreement. The British and American delegations have laid more emphasis on those provisions in the Agreement that look towards a revived and self-supporting Germany;

the Soviet delegation, with memories of the powerful war machine by which their country was ravaged only a little time ago, have made industrial disarmament and the restriction of heavy industry their first consideration.

87   No plan could ignore the preoccupation of the Western Powers with Germany's balance of payments and the financial burdens that they may be called upon to assume. Equally, no plan could ignore Russia's insistence on the danger of a rapid revival of German strength and her desire to have time to put herself in a state of defence against any possible attack from the west. Six years were sufficient for Hitler's preparations for war; and the levels of industry agreed to for 1949 are higher on the average than those of 1933. The Soviet felt that they were accepting a plan that left in Germany much more equipment than Germany was disposed to leave in Russia. They believed, and still do believe, that the amount left behind is more than ample to provide for a standard of living comparable with the rest of Europe and that the amount does less than justice to Russia's need for reparations. On the other hand, the British and Americans, surveying the destruction and dislocation throughout their zones, the neglect and disrepair of industrial equipment, the food crisis and the wholesale slaughter of livestock, were naturally somewhat alarmed at the possible removal of large quantities of serviceable equipment such as was suited to the manufacture of exports. The prospect of a Germany that could not pay her way was much more alarming to the British Treasury, struggling with the food bill for the Ruhr, than to the Soviet, with no need to import food and no lack of opportunity to take direct delivery of manufactured goods in settlement of any deficit. To Britain and America, the removal of equipment in reparations was as likely to do injury by putting off the day when exports and imports balance, as to bring a commercial advantage by suppressing German competitors; to Russia, reparations meant a plain addition to the stock of industrial capital just when it might be of most value in carrying out the latest Five Year Plan.

88.   The prospect of unemployment in Germany suggests a similar contrast. The Western Allies, accustomed to a high level of industry, are conscious of the risks of unemployment this involves; the upheavals of deindustrialisation, on a scale unparalleled in history, are bound to leave behind structural unemployment on a large scale. The Soviet know only the upheavals of industrialisation; and with these there generally goes a chronic shortage of manpower. While the Soviet think that the danger of unemployment has been exaggerated and that the question is merely one of social organisation, the Western Powers, with their different background, are extremely sensitive to the danger and afraid of the impetus that unemployment might give to a revival of Fascism.

89   It was only with the utmost difficulty and after prolonged negotiations that interests and views so conflicting were reconciled in

a single plan. There is indeed such a delicate balance, that what to one side seems leniency strained to the danger point, seems to the other to put recovery in jeopardy without help from outside.

90　The Reparations Plan must be seen in a wider context than the future of Germany alone. At the end of the last war, Lord Keynes familiarised us with the truth, which experience is now reiterating, that Germany was the hub of the entire European economy and that upon her prosperity the prosperity of Europe in large measure depends. So far as the Reparations Plan involves a policy of destroying capital equipment and letting industrial skill rot, the price will be paid not merely by Germany but by the rest of Europe as well. The metallurgical industries of Germany provided the exports with which Europe bought food from overseas, and contributed to the industrialisation of the Central European and Balkan States. Her engineering industries furnished the equipment out of which the industries of these countries grew. Metals and engineering were the mainspring of industrial growth as well as the driving power behind Germany's war machine and without their revival, the whole level of industry in Europe would tend to sink in comparison with pre-war years.

91　It will be natural in the next few years to lay Germany's disabilities at the door of the Reparations Plan. It is apparent, however, that Germany's present difficulties and those that will face her for some time, spring not from any limitations imposed by the withdrawal of industrial plant nor from the prohibitions imposed by the Reparations Plan, but from the circumstances of her defeat; the bombing of her towns, factories and transport system and the loss of a large tract of agricultural land contributing in normal times about a fifth of the total food supply of the country. Even within the Reparations Plan the major disabilities are likely to be those associated with the suppression of war potential industries and the removal of plant from armament factories that might otherwise have been redeployed for peaceful purposes. The power of recovery of German industry could not in any circumstances have been rapid and it will be some years before the equipment which will be left to maintain Germany's peace economy is fully assimilated.

92　Given that the Plan is primarily an instrument for measuring what can be removed in reparations and not a fixed basis for the future planning of the German peace-time economy, the measure of the harshness or otherwise of the Plan is obviously the amount of plant that will be removed from Germany in consequence of agreement upon it. Yet no one knows whether that amount will be large or small. We do not know what proportion of the total capacity to be retained will be in the British Zone nor how that compares with the capacity which has survived there. In other words, we are not in a position to judge the amount of reparations that will be removed from the British Zone under the Plan nor how industrial recovery will be retarded and limited.

93   It is obviously of the first importance that a study should be made as soon as possible of the effects of the Plan on the British Zone. Such a survey should be directed not only to establishing what will be removed but also to reviewing what can be done with what is left as a contribution to the overall levels of industry for Germany contained in the Plan. In such a study it will be necessary to consider what modifications in the Plan would be called for if the Zone were face to face with continuing unemployment on a large scale, localised in certain areas such as the Ruhr.

94   Faced with the prospect of a surplus of labour and a shortage of equipment, we may have to adopt many highly unorthodox schemes to make the fullest use of manpower in ways that will add to the net output of the country. It may be necessary to reduce hours of work without alteration in hourly rates of wages; or to operate factories at the current rate of wages and dispose of the product at prices that do not cover costs but limit the burden that would otherwise fall on the State in unemployment relief.

95   The tractability of unemployment in post-war Germany will depend largely on psychological factors. It will depend, for example, on the enthusiasm with which workers seek new jobs and the ingenuity and enterprise with which employers build up new industries; it will depend also on the self-discipline with which the Germans accept a reduction in real incomes, a shortage of consumer goods and of proper shelter, and government intervention to dilute and direct labour. It will not be easy to accept all those, without some grand object in view, in a mood free from truculence and xenophobia, at the hands of any government, however strong and authoritative.

96   It is an obvious corollary of this line of thought that the future government of Germany will not readily acquire a democratic colour. A government which is faced with heavy unemployment, a potentially adverse balance of payments and an acute shortage of raw materials will require to assume powers of direction and control such as are normally associated with a war-time economy. Where the margin between life and death is so narrow, the temptation to stifle criticism in the interest of unity and to narrow choice in order to promote efficiency will be very strong. The lower the level of industrial activity, the less rapidly will Germany gravitate either towards the west, with which her industrial links will be feebler, or towards democracy, which will appear more of a luxury.

97   Against this must be set the supreme importance of reaching an Anglo-Russian accord on one of the chief outstanding differences between the two countries. The Reparations Plan offers some prospect to the Soviet that they will be able to recover more rapidly than our defeated but still formidable enemy.

98   From this point of view it is right to recognise that great concessions have been made by the Soviet in agreeing to the levels of

industry in the Plan and that if the British view is fearful of the repercussions of the Plan on Germany's balance of payments and of the financial burdens that we may be called upon to assume, Russia is equally fearful of a Germany that might recover as rapidly from the levels of 1949 as she did from the not very different levels of 1932.

B   Modifications to the Plan

99   The Reparations Plan is based on three fundamental assumptions, none of which may yet prove to be sound –

(1) that Germany is treated as a unitary system;
(2) that Germany's western frontier remains unaltered;
(3) that the population of Germany will be 66.5 millions.

100   If any of these assumptions proves mistaken it will be necessary to modify the Plan. The chief modification will be to the level of the steel industry since without some change in the steel industry other modifications would be either nugatory or ineffective. It is the steel industry which could make the largest single contribution to improving Germany's balance of payments and it is the steel industry which will be the main subject of reparations removals from the British Zone.

101   The only other important modifications that might be made would be in withdrawals of machine tools and electric generating capacity. It is likely that the British Zone will require ultimately to surrender approximately 500,000 machine tools in reparations. It will, however, prove extremely difficult administratively to find and earmark the surplus machine tools, and long before all of them have been removed we should know whether modifications to the Plan are necessary. The same applies to electric power. It will take some time to arrange for the removal of generating capacity in excess of 9 million kW; and it should be possible, therefore, to provide the additional capacity which would be required if any general upward revision took place in levels of industry within the next twelve months.

102   Finally, there are a number of industries which are due for eventual suppression but which are to be retained until such time as Germany can obtain and pay for the necessary imports. Here too there is an obvious possibility of revision.

C   Ultimate Controls

103   No agreement has yet been reached on the ultimate controls to be exercised over German industry. The American view inclines towards few or no ceilings to production in any industry and distinguishes between the levels of industry established for the purposes of the Reparations Plan and the ultimate levels to which Germany should be allowed to climb. It is probable that the Soviet regard the levels of industry for 1949 as those of a peace-time German economy to be modified only when necessary and to operate as effective limitations on production. There is as yet no clear British

view on the methods by which continuing control is to be exercised over German industry after reparations withdrawals are complete. It is, however, natural to assume that these controls will be limited in number and will generally take the form of outright prohibitions so as to keep within manageable dimensions the number of British controllers and inspectors needed to police Germany.

What this amounted to was that, unless we were willing to fall out with the Russians, we had better make the best of a bad job. After the long wrangles in Berlin we seemed unlikely to win agreement to a plan that provided for a materially higher level of production; the decision on steel had put paid to any such idea. As for reparations, a substantial part of these would come from the prohibited industries, most of which the Cabinet had agreed to prohibit as far back as September. Moreover, if the plan was now regarded as too harsh this was because public opinion had changed over the winter and was beginning to accept views which the British delegation in Berlin had held (and expressed) from the start.

We could in fact take some credit that we had helped to withstand pressure from all the other delegations for far stiffer terms. The Americans had never been completely free of the shadow of Morgenthau, with his utterly unrealistic vision of a pastoralized Germany; the Russians regarded the agreement as dangerously lenient; the French had pushed for some very idiosyncratic restrictions and were even now urging dismemberment, in flat contradiction of one of the key principles on which the plan was based.

Germany, said the Plan, was to be treated 'as a single economic unit'. But the Russians were already working their will on their own zone and there seemed little prospect that food would flow from it to the Western zones as the Plan required. The French, who had not been allowed to take part in the discussions at Potsdam, had entered reservations from the start and made it clear in September 1945, at the London meeting of the Council of Foreign Ministers, that their representative on the Control Council would insist on the separation of the Rhineland and the Ruhr area from Germany and veto any decision that would prejudice such a separation. Throughout the winter of 1945–6 France resisted the setting up of central agencies of government, agitated for the internationalization of the Rhineland/Ruhr and ran affairs in their own zone with an eye to the eventual annexation of the Saar. These conditions were hardly propitious for a plan that made no reference to zones of occupation and assumed that all four zones would unite and function as a single country.

For the British zone in particular the prospect was bleak if no such unity could be achieved. It was from the British zone that the heaviest removals of plant in reparations would occur; and it was the British zone that would have the greatest difficulty in balancing its accounts so as to pay for the large imports of food it would inevitably require. Uncertainty over its industrial future would prolong the zone's dependence on the charity of the occupying power, which faced the prospect of conniving at large-scale removals of plant for the benefit of other countries while it continued to foot the bill for imports of food.

It was the failure of Russia and France to accept the need to treat Germany as a single economic unit that drove Clay on 4 May 1946, little more than a month after the publication of the Reparations Plan, to suspend deliveries of reparations from the American zone; and it was the heavy dollar drain in payment for imports of grain to the British zone that induced Britain to unite her zone with the Americans in 1947 and join in launching the Federal Republic of Germany two years later.

Clay's action in May did not by itself destroy the Level of Industry Plan; but by implying that there was no hope of fulfilling one of the preconditions of the Plan it struck at its foundations. By the time the American zone was united first with the British in the Bizone and then with the French to form the Federal Republic, it had become impossible to hold to the Plan and the limits were raised as they were approached. Equally, it became patently absurd, once the industrial recovery of Germany was an acknowledged aim of policy, to remove equipment needed for that recovery: all the more once the Marshall Plan was in operation and the inconsistency of pouring in new resources at one end of Germany and removing or dismantling them at the other was too striking to be ignored.

The Russian attitude made it natural to ask what would happen if the Plan were put into effect in the Western zones alone. Would they be self-supporting at the levels proposed? Would the German population in those zones remain so cowed as the years went by that they would raise no violent protests against the continuing removal of the means to a better life? It would be many years before all the dismantling and packing was completed, and during that time things would not stand still. Industrial output, still far below the proposed levels, would expand and bump up against capacity limits that were quite artificial since they could be relieved at once by relaxing the restrictions in the Reparations Plan. Unemployment would be heavy, perhaps very heavy, and still increasing. Meanwhile, Europe would be crying out for the very goods Germany was held back from producing. European recovery would be delayed by fear of what Germany might one day do. But might not that fear prove misconceived? What Germany might do, if treated in the way proposed, was to make common cause with Russia and help to build up a Communist bloc far more powerful and aggressive than Russia alone or with the whole of eastern Europe in her 'camp'.

On the horizon was yet another doubt. The Russians had been removing capital equipment on a large scale from Germany for the past year and had begun to doubt whether it was really worth while. They had learnt that it was one thing to move Russian factories beyond the Urals, complete with management and skilled mechanics looking after their own plant, but quite a different matter to send squads to do a hurried job of dismantling unfamiliar equipment in a foreign country.[1] By the middle of 1946 they were alive to the greater convenience of deliveries from current production, and to the propaganda value in the Eastern zone of switching from one form of reparations that threatened employment to another that ensured it. It was not long before the Russians began to think of a similar switch in reparations from the Western zones. Molotov took up the idea, pressing it on Byrnes and Bevin in Paris in the summer of 1946. Within a few months of the adoption of the Reparations Plan the Russians had abandoned it in their own minds, more resolutely even than their allies, and were unsaying many of the extravagant declarations of a year before.

If this was to be the outcome, was the Reparations Plan not doubly a waste of time? It was based on the hypothesis of a united Germany which never came about; and it was equally based on the hypothesis that reparations should be taken exclusively from capital equipment when the country most in need of reparations was about to abandon the hypothesis.

That the Plan itself was utterly unrealistic seems obvious enough in retrospect. We have seen Germany recover until her industrial production is three times as high as Britain's – far higher relatively than before or during the war – and this without benefit of the Russian zone. The German standard of living is not merely above the average European level, but far exceeds the British. Even before 1949, German production was increasing by leaps and bounds: in 1948 alone by over 50 per cent. Before the end of 1949 industrial production had surpassed the level of 1936 instead of being 20 per cent below it. Unemployment, although high by post-war standards, was no more than 1.5 million by 1950 in the Federal Republic, far below the level expected if the Plan had been implemented.

---

[1] See below, chapter 9. For a different view, see Antony C. Sutton (1973), Vol. 3, chapter 2.

These achievements were not much affected by the Reparations Plan. Reparations do not appear to have exercised any significant check on expansion at any time. As the restrictions imposed were relaxed, the industrial structure reappeared in much the shape that it had taken before the war. Exports of machinery, transport equipment and electrical machinery, instead of forming a contracting proportion of the total, were just under half in 1952 compared with 28 per cent in 1936.[2] The procrustean grip of the balance of payments, which had distorted the projected pattern of industry, was prised loose by the Marshall Plan. In the early post-war years Britain and America poured in food, for which no payment was received. Each year until 1952 Germany's current account remained in deficit, and by the end of 1953 a total of over $3,600 million had been received in aid from the USA alone since 1946.[3]

Were the Level of Industry negotiations, then, an irrelevance? Did the struggles to secure agreement, the agonizing over concessions, the meticulous examination of their long-run consequences, serve no purpose whatever? Some historians seem to think so.[4] They suggest that Clay was anxious for an agreement merely as a preliminary to facing the Russians and the French with the more immediate problem of treating Germany as a single economic unit. 'Concessions' such as the steel settlement were really no concessions at all when steel production was far below the level agreed and there was every likelihood that the level would later be reviewed. Clay, it is claimed, was taking the long view and could afford to add a few more absurdities to a plan that was already heading for obsolescence.

That may seem a plausible view in 1986. It does not accord with my own impressions in 1946. It is true that in the final stages in March Clay played an important role in removing the last differences. But it was the Russians as much as the Americans who were by that time anxious to settle quickly. Earlier, the American position had been more complex and they showed every sign of attaching real importance to the levels agreed in the Plan. Certainly in December, when the negotiations had been in progress for months, American officials in Berlin did not appear to find much in common between Clay's attitude and that expressed in the Directive that had just been issued by the State Department. Whatever appeared in that Directive or in their plan, there was never any suggestion that the levels agreed could be disregarded because of some larger disagree-

---

[2] Mendershausen (1955) p. 103 n.

[3] Ibid., p. 103.

[4] For example, Backer (1971) pp. 76–9: 'Was it wise to fight too long about figures that might soon become meaningless?'

ment just round the corner. When disagreement deepened, the Reparations Plan was not discarded but amended, and amended after a struggle.

The really significant question is how anxious the various Allies were to agree with one another. The Plan, if taken seriously, showed that they could agree. If there were other, more important matters, on which they could *not* agree, then agreement on the Plan might matter little. But to give priority to reaching agreement on the Plan solely in order to bring into the open other disagreements was not, in the circumstances, a very attractive strategy. For if these disagreements were in turn resolved the Allies should be stuck with a plan that was more damaging than it need have been. And if they were not resolved, the effort to reach agreement on the Plan would have been to no avail and might even seem hypocritical. The Western Allies would be open to the accusation of collaborating freely to give substance to the mistaken notions of the Potsdam Agreement.

Yet the Plan was not altogether a waste of time. The negotiations over the winter months had given time for opinion in the West to reconsider what was happening in Germany and how it would affect the rest of Europe. There had also been time to take more careful stock of Soviet policy and actions and to observe the resurrection of ideological warfare. Nobody was satisfied with the Plan when it was produced, but that was quite as much because they had had time to change their minds as to what they wanted as because of the defects of the Plan itself. Above all the quadripartite negotiations were a conclusive demonstration that four-power operation of a regime covering the whole of Germany simply would not work.

As in all political affairs, one has to start from what is possible or can be made possible. It might have been better to recognize earlier that no accommodation was possible between the views of the USSR and the Western Allies. This would have allowed encouragement to be given to German industrial recovery right from the start. But it would have meant falling out with Russia when opinion in the west would have found it unthinkable that such a thing should occur over the treatment of Germany. It would also have damaged relations with Russia far more even than they were; some effort had to be made to demonstrate the reasonableness of Allied intentions. In any event German recovery was bound to be slow at first, whatever the relations between the Powers. If in these circumstances negotiations were persisted in, there was little chance that the Russians could be brought to accept a different kind of plan. It is true that they exploited every indication of weakness and indecision but when faced with firm opposition they were willing to give ground. They would probably not have given way appreciably more than they did.

Perhaps the mistake was to set so much store by agreement. Would it have mattered if each country had held to its own plan and each zone had gone its own way in 1946? The Russians would not have felt that they had been fooled into making concessions for no real purpose, since the agreed plan was never put into effect and there was no real meeting of minds on the future of the German economy. It is not at all obvious that the course of events would have been very different but we should have been spared the self-deceptions that allowed a succession of diplomatic hagglings to be passed off as a consistent plan.

One other possibility would have been to switch from a plan to dismantle German industry and make surplus plant available in reparations to a plan to reactivate the remaining capacity and pay reparations from current production. Such a scheme had proved unsuccessful after the First World War when Germany had been left to find markets abroad in countries that had no wish to intensify German competition. Now she would have been asked to supply countries that were not highly industrialized and would have had far less difficulty in absorbing German manufactures: The rapid recovery of industry in the Russian zone showed how such a transfer could at least ensure employment for the local population, even if they enjoyed little of the benefit in imports. But such a solution had been pretty well ruled out at Potsdam. The Western Allies insisted that the first call on anything earned from exports must be payment for necessary imports. The Americans also suspected that some of what was paid out to German workers in the Russian zone came from the printing press and was ultimately exchanged against dollars, so that it was the American Treasury that footed the bill for the manufactures shipped to Russia.

Neither in 1945–6 nor later were reparations from current production acceptable to the Western Allies. That being so, there was no escape from an effort to supply reparations through dismantling; and since that was neither a sustainable policy in face of the revulsion it created, nor compatible with a programme of industrial recovery to make Germany self-supporting and no longer dependent on external aid, the Reparations Plan could be at best a makeshift that would itself soon be dismantled.

7

After the Reparations Plan

We shall all be brought to recognize, in the next few years, that the industrial recovery of Germany must involve a progressive raising of the levels of industry which the Plan sets out. The Russian anxiety is that this should not take place more rapidly than their own recovery, so that they can keep pace with the potential menace of a Germany restored to its pre-war strength by a more or less sympathetic Anglo-Saxon combination.

Cairncross to Bader, 23 February 1946

British ministers attached three conditions to their acceptance of the Reparations Plan. They reserved the right to review the agreed levels of industry if:

1 Germany were not treated as an economic whole, or if there were a change in frontiers or a decision against centralized administration;
2 the population was greater than 66.5 million;
3 a financial burden rested on the occupying powers; that is, exports were insufficient to pay for imports.

In putting forward these stipulations, Bevin made two observations of some later importance. He told his colleagues that he thought that British net expenditure in Germany could be reduced in two years' time from £80 million a year to £25 million a year – a surprising and, as it proved, radical misjudgement. In addition, this lower rate of expenditure might, in his view, be met by reparations deliveries from current production. Thus in accepting the Plan, Bevin had not in his own mind abandoned altogether the idea of reparations from current production.[1]

Britain was alone in making her acceptance of the Plan subject to specific conditions. But the first and third of the conditions were not new, since they formed part of the Potsdam Agreement; the USA attached just as much importance as Britain to the first and almost as much to the third. It was only the second condition, as to the size of the population, that had any real novelty. This condition could not be put to the test until a census was taken on 29 October 1946. This yielded a total of 64.9 million – less than in the Reparations Plan – but a later census in September 1950 was much higher at 69.1 million, possibly because of errors in the first census but mainly because of the return of prisoners of war and a continuing inflow of refugees. Since the Plan was supposed to relate to 1949, not 1946, the right comparison is between the figure of 66.5 million on which the Plan was based and an estimate of about 68 million derived from the two censuses.[2] Thus the Plan did underestimate the population, but not by as much as the British and Americans maintained.

In the long squabble over reparations from 1946 onwards, what dominated the discussion was the failure to treat Germany as a single economic unit and the deficit in the balance of payments of the American and British zones, which had to be met by the occupying powers; that is, the first and third of the Cabinet's conditions.

The division of Germany into zones was not of itself fatal to the economic unit of the country. It had been conceived and accepted as a matter of convenience to the occupying powers, chiefly with the object of keeping apart the various armies of occupation, not as a way of carving up the German economy and introducing obstacles to the free movement of men and goods.[3] It was not surprising that there should be no uniformity of treatment between the different zones, nor was it necessarily to be deplored when so much emphasis had been placed on the need for decentralization and increased powers at the local level. The Potsdam Agreement said quite clearly, however, that there *was* to be 'uniformity of treatment of the German population throughout Germany' and that, although there

[1] CM(46)25, 18 March 1946, in PRO CAB 128/5. At the end of July Bevin predicted exactly the same reduction in the net cost of the British zone 'in two or three years' time' if the British and American zones were merged (CM(46)73, 25 July 1946).
[2] These figures are from the *Statistisches Jahrbuch für die Bundesrepublik Deutschland*. General Clay quotes an official estimate of 67.9 million for 1 January 1949 (*Decision in Germany, 1952*, p. 318), and this seems consistent with the figures given above for 1946 and 1950.
[3] British ministers were, however, 'perfectly aware that the short-term plan might turn out to be the basis of a more permanent settlement' (Burridge, 1981, p. 576).

was to be no central German Government for the time being, a number of central administrative departments should be established, headed by state secretaries and under the direction of the Control Council, 'particularly in the fields of finance, transport, communication, foreign trade and industry'.[4]

All efforts to secure agreement to a central German economic administration during the winter of 1945–6 were unavailing. There were two main reasons for this.

First, the French made it clear from the beginning that they did not accept this provision of an Agreement to which they were not themselves party. They wanted to ensure that Germany was sufficiently weakened through the detachment and military occupation of the Ruhr and the Rhineland, and the annexation of the Saar. Before setting up central agencies they also sought to secure for themselves continuing access to German coal supplies on favourable terms, intending to build in France the heavy industry denied to Germany. But they had other motives. When the American Ambassador in Paris told Bidault (the French Prime Minister) in December 1945 that the USA intended to stand by the Potsdam Agreement on centralized administrative agencies and 'with great reluctance' would go ahead with allowing such agencies to operate in the other three zones if France stood out, Bidault repeated 'what he and de Gaulle have so often said before, that they are convinced that the setting up of centralized administrative agencies in Germany will inevitably lead to the eventual setting up of a Soviet-dominated central government in Germany'.[5]

Next, the Russians, although agreeing in principle with the setting up of central agencies, took shelter behind the French and adopted policies inconsistent with the principle.[6] They would have been quite happy to see the agencies already set up in their own zone operate on a country-wide scale, but they had no intention of surrendering the administration of their zone to freely elected German authorities with a different political programme. They had not proved at all communicative about what was going on in their zone. No information had been provided on removals of plant and equipment (much of it claimed as war booty, not reparations) from Berlin and the Eastern zone in spite of a promise in September 1945 to supply

[4] Potsdam Agreement, section IIIA (Political Principles), paras 2 and 3.
[5] Byrnes to Caffery, 6 December 1945 and Caffery to Byrnes, 8 December 1945, in FRUS, Vol. III, p. 916. A year later, Bedell Smith, the US Ambassador in Moscow was cabling the Secretary of State that 'I realize now French fears of centralization were not entirely unfounded' (Telegram No. 33, 7 January 1947).
[6] Minute by M. Franklin in C4662, 27 April 1946, in PRO FO 371/55424.

it; and there had been no mixed commissions inspecting plants in the Soviet zone in spite of Soviet agreement in principle to admit them.[7] It was difficult, therefore, to work out how much plant should be left in the Western zones and how much could be removed in reparations without destroying the chances of a reunited Germany becoming self-supporting at an early date.

It was no answer to this that Russia had been given a free hand in the Potsdam Agreement to take reparations from her zone. Other, contradictory, provisions of the Agreement required uniformity of treatment, and the treatment of Germany as a single economic unit. It would have been more to the point to insist on a speeding up of deliveries from the Western zones, as indeed Molotov did at successive meetings of the Council of Foreign Ministers. But there were practical difficulties in large-scale removals of plant, as the Russians had good reason to know from their own experience. The Western Allies claimed to be exerting pressure to speed things up.[8] In any event, by the time a substantial flow of used equipment could have been got under way the Russians themselves were coming round to the view that deliveries from current production were preferable.

Current deliveries, however, raised in an even more acute form the allied issue of economic unity. If goods produced in one zone were exported without payment, as reparations, other zones could complain that they were denied either the goods themselves or command over the resources employed. There was no provision in the Potsdam Agreement for the retention of resources to make deliveries from current production, and both the Agreement and the Reparations Plan of March 1946 made no mention of such deliveries. The Western Allies were particularly sensitive to the issue when they were having to pay hundreds of millions of dollars to feed the Germans while foodstuffs were removed from the Eastern zone as reparations. It was precisely at this point that reparations and the export-import balance intersected, and the intersection marked the spot where the absence of economic unity was felt most deeply.

[7] Letter from Vyshinski to American Ambassador on 16 September 1945 in *Report on German Reparations to the President of the United States* by E. W. Pauley and I. Lubin. Nine months later Bevin told the House of Commons that 'we cannot accept the position that the Soviet zone is an exclusive place while our zone is wide open for inspection, and we are subject to accusations for which there is not the slightest foundation'. (H. of C. Debates, 4 June 1946, Vol. 423, col. 1853).

[8] See, for example, minutes of 55th meeting of the Co-ordinating Committee, 6 May 1946, in PRO FO371/55425. General Robertson had doubled the number of men employed on the first list of plants and expedited the work. The first list was unaffected by Clay's suspension of further dismantling in May (below, pp. 154–5).

The cost to the British Exchequer of feeding the Germans was a particularly sore spot. Dalton never tired of declaring that Britain was paying reparations to the Germans when she could ill afford the dollars. At the end of May 1946 he told the Cabinet that since VE Day the United Kingdom had received in all less than £2 million from German exports and reparations deliveries.[9] This was all that could be set against an expenditure expected to reach £131 million, exclusive of occupation costs, by the end of 1946. The Control Office estimated that £49 million would be received in export proceeds during the current year, but neither Dalton nor his advisers could take such an estimate seriously. On the other hand, the bill for imports into the British zone in 1946 was expected to reach £91 million (of which £59 million would go on food alone) and a further £10 million would be needed to cover the external costs of civil administration. To this had to be added external military occupation costs, which were put at £100 million in 1946–7.[10] By November the estimate for imports had been revised upwards to about £125 million while the estimate for exports was a little lower at not much over £40 million. On this showing, the United Kingdom looked like having to extend credit to Germany to the tune of nearly £200 million for 1946. In dollars alone, the Chancellor expected to have to find $160 million for the British zone in the financial year 1946–7.

The fundamental issue, however, was political not economic. The West might rebel at the idea of paying reparations once again instead of receiving them; but they were far more interested in avoiding the establishment of a Communist regime in Germany. Similarly, the Russians regarded the most important objective of the military occupation of Germany as the 'democratization' of the country, not some change in the standard of living or even the exaction of reparations.[11] By 'democratization' they meant the establishment of a regime patterned largely on their own, with the control of the levers of economic and social power in reliable hands. There was to be no restoration of the old order: its pillars were to be removed for good and all and its institutions restructured as the only real guarantee against renewed German aggression.[12]

[9] 'The Cost of the British Zone in Germany', CP(46)218, 4 June 1946, in PRO CAB 129/10. Of the total amount, £750,000 represented deliveries of scrap, £100,000 machine tools removed as reparations and £90,000 exports, mainly of coal.
[10] This was the figure used in the November discussions in Washington. See PRO CAB 130/14, 'Anglo-American Discussions on Germany'.
[11] Sokolovsky, speaking at the meeting of the Co-ordinating Committee on 1 February 1946.
[12] Sandford (1983) p. 81.

There were those who saw the inconsistency of Western and Eastern political aims and concluded that there was no solution except in a division between West and East: central economic agencies were a mirage. The former Soviet Foreign Minister, Litvinov, for example, thought it obvious by June 1946 that, since each side wanted a unified Germany under its control, Germany would be broken up into two parts.[13] To those who thought in this way there was no real possibility of unifying the German economy.

This would have been even more apparent had the Western Allies taken stock of the changes in progress in the Soviet zone. From Potsdam onwards, the Soviet zone followed a path that diverged increasingly from the path taken by the other zones. The economy was bound more and more tightly to the Soviet economy. Trade, which had been overwhelmingly with the West and above all with the rest of Germany, became almost exclusively directed to the East, especially the Soviet Union.[14] The Communists in the central agencies set up in the zone resisted all pressures for closer interzonal co-operation that might compromise their plans and were strongly against allowing 'economic unity' to bring about an easing of trade between zones.[15] Ulbricht, the leader of the Party, insisted that any move to joint food supply must be conditional on land reform 'operating according to a unified, democratic agricultural plan . . .'.[16]

When production planning in a rather primitive form was introduced in the Soviet zone in the final quarter of 1945, the plans were naturally submitted for approval to the Soviet authorities and, as time went on, to Gosplan in Moscow. As the plans made increasing provision for deliveries of reparations from current production, they were geared into Soviet planning arrangements. In such circumstances, whatever might be said to the Control Council in Berlin, there was no real prospect of allowing trade to flow freely between the Soviet and Western zones.[17]

The year 1946 was one of increasingly vituperative attacks by the Russians on the Western Allies and their conduct of affairs in Germany.[18] Such attacks became an almost regular feature of the

[13] FRUS 1946, Vol. VI, pp. 763–5. Similar views were expressed by Americans such as Kennan and Murphy, and by various Foreign Office officials.
[14] ECE *Quarterly Bulletin*, Third Quarter, 1949, p. 26.
[15] Sandford (1983) p. 183.
[16] Ibid.
[17] V. Rudolph, 'The Administrative Organisation of Soviet Control, 1945–8', in R. Slusser (ed.) (1953).
[18] 'Soviet propaganda throughout the year remained consistently hostile to Britain' ('Annual Report on Soviet Union 1946'), Peterson to Bevin, 5 June 1947, in PRO FO371/66433.

meetings of the Control Council in Berlin and the Council of Foreign Ministers in Moscow, Paris, London and New York. The charges made had usually little or no foundation but were given full publicity in the Russian-controlled press, where no denials were likely to appear. They took colour from Soviet ideology by denouncing the Western powers as imperialists, warmongers, protectors of monopolies and trusts, and given to exploitation. But they almost certainly derived from the expansionist policies of the Zhdanov faction, which had gained the upper hand in the Soviet power struggle in 1946–7.[19]

That the Russians made reparations a major bone of contention was not, however, fortuitous. If the countries of Western Europe needed American help to sustain and speed their recovery, how much more did Soviet Russia after her appalling losses, human and material. From the Eastern zone she was deriving just such help. No wonder she resented the demand that it should cease in what must have seemed to her the financial interests of her richer allies. To make matters worse, these same allies seemed incapable of making the rest of Germany pay reparations on a comparable scale and were preserving the war potential they had undertaken to destroy. From their point of view, the Russians had good reason to complain of the way reparations had been handled.

Over the winter of 1945–6 the dispute had centred on removals of equipment from the Western zones. The Russians denounced the slow pace of dismantling, the almost negligible flow of equipment delivered to them, and the failure to reach agreement on a Reparations Plan within the six months allowed at Potsdam. As early as September 1945, at a meeting with Bevin at the Soviet Embassy in London, Molotov twice brought up the subject of reparations, alleging that Britain was doing all she could to prevent Russia getting reparations and engaging in deliberate delay.[20] When the Foreign Ministers met in December 1945 in Moscow, Molotov returned to the attack. The question of the level of industry, he maintained, was not complicated, so why was it taking so long to reach agreement? The Soviet Union was in a hurry to rehabilitate the country and must get equipment quickly. When told that more was available as reparations than the Russians could transport he commented that the Soviet public would find this reply 'frivolous'.[21]

The central issues came to a head within a month of agreement on the Reparations Plan. At the meeting of the Co-ordinating Committee in Berlin in 8 April 1946, Clay drew attention to the provision in the

[19] See below, pp. 203–4.
[20] Bullock (1983) pp. 132–3.
[21] Roger Bullen and M. E. Pelly, (1985) Document No. 320, p. 800.

Potsdam Agreement for a common export–import plan. Agreement on such a plan was a basic assumption of the Level of Industry Plan. If agreement could not be reached the Plan had no validity, and 'at a suitable time in the not too distant future' the US delegation would call for its revision.[22]

On 27 April 1946 Robertson submitted a paper suggesting that it was time to decide whether each zone was to be run as a separate unit or as part of an economic whole. If the latter, the resources of each zone must be pooled, not treated as its exclusive property. It was not to be expected 'that the British tax payer will defray the cost of all imports to the zone while large quantities of valuable commodities are being transferred without payment to other zones and also while the surpluses of indigenous resources in other zones are not made available to meet the deficit in our zone'. Robertson went on to cite the 'first charge principle' that the proceeds of exports from current production and stocks should be available in the first place for the payment of approved imports and warned that if each zone continued to be run separately from the others, the reparations programme would have to be reconsidered.

Koeltz, the French representative, accepted the proposition that Germany must be treated as a single economic unit but saw no reason why this need imply a central administrative organization. The French had already accepted an Allied Bureau with responsibility for external trade. Dratvin, speaking for the USSR, was in favour of common policies within a single economy but did not accept that the first charge principle had anything to do with reparations. Indeed, to connect the two would be a breach of the Potsdam Agreement. Clay, who was in the chair, was unimpressed by these statements, pointing out that none of the provisions for economic unity had been carried out a year after the ending of hostilities. The Potsdam Agreement must be carried out in its entirety, not just in the parts found convenient. The whole matter of reparations, the export–import balance and central machinery should be referred to governments. In the meantime he would be obliged to halt the work of dismantling, on which 16,000–17,000 men were at work in the American zone.

The Suspension of Dismantling

A week later, on 4 May, the Co-ordinating Committee met again. The main debate was between Robertson and Dratvin. The French

[22] The minutes of the Co-ordinating Committee for March–April 1946 are in PRO FO 371 55424.

reiterated their objections to central administration but otherwise had little to say. The Americans had announced the suspension of dismantling that very day.

Robertson asked whether the Soviet delegation would agree that under the Postdam Agreement no occupying power could remove reparations from their zone from current production and stocks until Germany was self-supporting. As he interpreted their position, the Russians would not undertake to refrain from such removals. If so, this had a direct bearing on the implementation of the Reparations Plan and he would be obliged to seek instructions from his Government whether to follow Clay in suspending dismantling. Dratvin might have replied that it was clearly understood at Potsdam that the Russians could take freely from their own zone. Instead he argued that the Reparations Plan already foresaw an export–import balance in 1949. By that time production would have recovered within the limits set by the Plan and if it was fulfilled, so presumably would be the export–import plan. This was not a very convincing reply since the Reparations Plan already stretched exports to the limit and made no provision for an additional supply in the form of reparations from current production. More telling was the Soviet query on what the Western zones could offer in payment for food from East Germany.

The American suspension of dismantling was followed soon after, without much publicity, by the British and French. They had little option, since the Americans refused to join in the quadripartite valuation of plants for reparations – an essential preliminary. Work proceeded on the 60 factories designated earlier as 'advance reparations' but only about half of these had been allocated among the 18 member nations of the Inter-Allied Reparation Agency at the end of 1946. Work was resumed also at the end of June on the destruction or dismantling of 'war plants', engaged exclusively in the production of munitions of war.[23] But the suspension of dismantling at all other factories was still in force in October 1946 when the IARA Assembly voiced its disappointment in a resolution sent to the Occupying Powers. At the end of 1946, the IARA members had been allocated – but in most cases had not yet received – German equipment to the (pre-war) value of about £5 million. The Russians had done rather better (20,000 tons from the American zone alone by 1 September 1946); but the rate at which industrial equipment trickled out from Western Germany was and remained paltry in comparison with earlier expectations.[24]

[23] *A Year of Potsdam: the German Economy since the Surrender* (OMGUS, Berlin, 1946) p. 46.

The suspension of dismantling was by no means the only cause of the slow rate of deliveries – not even in 1946–7 – but it has been seen as the first step towards a break with the Russians. Others have suggested that Clay's action was directed mainly against the French, on account of their intransigence over the creation of centralized economic agencies.[25] But the issue in the Co-ordinating Committee was not centralized administration; it was economic unity. On this issue much of the running was made by the British, who were undoubtedly more concerned about the Eastern zone than about the French. It would be hard to find in the Foreign Office files any support for the view that the line taken by British representatives in Berlin in April 1946 had much to do with France. Even in official American statements the emphasis is nearly always on economic unity with centralized administration a corollary but a subordinate concern. It was this theme that Secretary of State Byrnes developed at Stuttgart on 6 September 1946, in a speech crystallizing American official policy, returning to the subject several times to show that economic unity was expressly required by the Potsdam Agreement and basic to the Reparations Plan.[26] Clay himself took the view, justifiably, that a common export–import programme, if it was to be effective, required central administration and that the Allied Bureau proposed by the French was not really a central administrative agency at all but merely an extension of the operations of the Allied Control Council.[27] Asked at a press conference on 27 May if he was trying to put pressure on the French, he replied that his primary purpose was not to put pressure on anybody but to face reality and not do damage to the American zone.[28]

In May 1946 British policy was still somewhat ambivalent. In a Cabinet paper circulated on 3 May, the day before Clay's announcement, Bevin posed the question whether it would be best to continue to work towards a unified (but federalized) Germany or, in view of the Russian attitude and the danger of Communist domination of West Germany, work towards a West German state 'more amenable to our influence'.[29] While he did not altogether exclude the possibility

---

[24] Inter-Allied Reparations Agency: *Report of the Secretary-General for the year 1947* (Brussels, 1948) p. 4.

[25] John Gimbel (1968), for example.

[26] Ratchford and Ross (1947) pp. 195, 242–51. The speech made use of a draft by Clay, dated 19 July 1946 (Papers (1947) Vol. I, pp. 236–43).

[27] Ibid., pp. 204, 236.

[28] Ibid., p. 222. As he pointed out in July, the trouble with the French was unwillingness to enter into agreements for German unification; with the USSR it was 'failure to agree on interpretations and methods to carry out previous agreements reached at international conferences' (ibid., p. 244).

of splitting Germany if Russian non-cooperation made this inevitable, the dangers of doing so at once seemed to him greater than those of continuing with existing policies. Ideally, he wanted a federal structure based on regional units with considerable autonomous powers; central administration would be restricted to the co-ordination of the activities of these units.

At that stage, Bevin took a gloomy view of immediate prospects. He expected the Communists to win the forthcoming Berlin election (they suffered a resounding defeat) and was very doubtful whether a nation-wide election under four-power control would yield a victory for the non-Communist parties. There was no likelihood of Germany becoming self-supporting for some time – not even if the Reparations Plan were modified – and there could be no avoiding the major part of the burden of meeting the deficit to be expected. He even toyed with the idea of withdrawal but rejected it because 'disease knows no frontier'. On the other hand, to set about organizing the British zone as an independent unit would mean an irreparable break with the Russians and the end of the facade of four-power control of Germany. This might bring into existence an anti-Soviet block; but the Americans were not ready and the attitude of the French uncertain. It was not far from such a move to the acceptance of a German army into the Western camp. Although a policy of building up the British zone would have many attractions and would offer hope of recovery to the Germans, the dangers still seemed to him to predominate.

Bevin was not able to attend the meeting of Cabinet at which his paper was discussed. His colleagues showed no disposition to challenge his judgement. Morrison rejected the idea that a clash with the USSR was inevitable; Dalton warned against drifting into an anti-Soviet policy; and Bevan thought the prevailing fears of the USSR were exaggerated since Russia's influence would diminish the further west she pushed. The only dissonant note was sounded by Bevin's Parliamentary Under-Secretary (Hector McNeil), who pointed out that the Russians were failing to carry out their agreement to treat Germany as an economic unit and that, in the last resort, this might make it necessary to suspend the application of the Reparations Plan in the British zone.[30]

A week later the Cabinet returned to the subject. When the dismantling issue was raised, Dalton expressed reluctance to agree to a stop in order to put pressure on the Soviet Government (no

[29] 'Policy towards Germany', Memorandum by the Secretary of State for Foreign Affairs, 3 May 1946, CP(46)186, in PRO CAB 129/9.
[30] CM(46)43, 7 May 1946, in PRO CAB 128/7.

mention was made of the French attitude). Others were against withholding reparations for such a purpose, especially when Byrnes, the American Secretary of State, was willing to resume dismantling once the matter was made the subject of a report by the Foreign Ministers' deputies. The conclusion reached allowed Bevin a free hand in default of agreement on the short-term economic proposals then under discussion.[31]

The Cabinet were also informed of five questions posed by Byrnes, of which one related to the Ruhr and Rhineland, one to the western frontiers of Germany and one to the first charge principle.[32] A fourth asked whether during the next 90 days it would be possible to introduce sufficient German administrative machinery to enable Germany to be operated as an economic unit; and the final question ran: 'Will the existing zonal boundaries be continued only for purposes of delineating occupation areas and not as artificial barriers to a reasonably free movement of goods in Germany?'

The Paris Conference

These were indeed pertinent questions, but they · received no satisfactory answers when the Foreign Ministers met in Paris in June/July 1946. By the time of the meeting, the Potsdam Agreement no longer satisfied any of the four Powers represented. The Russians were becoming disenchanted with once-for-all removals, were drawing current deliveries from their own zone and had begun a take-over of 200 of the largest east German industrial enterprises to add to the flow.[33] They now sounded out the Western Powers on current deliveries from their zones as well. The French were still set on severing the Rhineland, the Ruhr and the Saar from Germany and sharing an international control of the Ruhr.[34] The British and the Americans were increasingly concerned at the cost of importing food in order to meet the quite inadequate ration provided, and were frustrated by the difficulties they encountered in reviving the German economy to make it more self-supporting.[35]

[31] CM(46)48, 16 May 1946, in PRO CAB 128/7.
[32] CM(46)48, 16 May 1946, in PRO CAB 128/7. The same questions were raised by Byrnes at the Paris Conference in July (FRUS 1946, Vol. II, pp. 401–2).
[33] *Documents on Germany under Occupation*, Royal Institute of International Affairs (henceforth RIIA), (1955) p. 141. The formation of SAG's, announced on 5 June 1946 was 'in partial settlement of the reparation claims [of] the USSR'.
[34] The French proposals had been submitted to the London meeting of Foreign Ministers in September 1945. As resubmitted in more detail to the Paris meeting on 25 April 1946, they are reprinted in RIIA, *Documents on Germany* (1955) pp. 125–8. For the British attitude to the French proposals, see Rolf Steininger (1982).

Byrnes had hoped to remove Russian suspicions and distrust by offering them a 25-year treaty for the disarmament and demilitarization of Germany. He had the enthusiastic support of Bevin but could not prevail on Molotov, who showed little interest. Byrnes's other initiative was to propose the appointment of special deputies to study economic unity, the future of the Rhineland and the Ruhr, and the other questions which he had circulated in advance. No doubt he hoped in this way to induce the Russians and the French to enter into negotiations and break the stalemate in Berlin.[36]

Again he had no luck. Molotov had no sympathy with French claims. In a speech that was thought at the time to be aimed at offering encouragement to the German Communists (but was equally discouraging to their French comrades) Molotov declared that 'peace and tranquillity', not the destruction of Germany, was Russia's objective and that the Ruhr should not be detached from Germany since without it 'Germany cannot exist as an independent and viable state'. The Ruhr should, however, be under international control as he had demanded at Potsdam. If this were done, if inter-Allied control was established over German industry ('and over the Ruhr industries in particular'), 'we should not hinder Germany from increasing her output of steel, coal and manufactured products for peaceful needs'. While there was no immediate need to raise the level of industry, since current output was far below it, he hinted that this was by no means ruled out. He had no objection to a centralized economic administration; but any future German Government which it served must be a democratic one. 'Above all it must ensure the delivery of reparations to the Allies.'[37]

Coming, as it did, within four months of the Reparations Plan and Sokolovsky's warning that a higher level of steel production would mean war, this was a change of view that could not be dismissed as mere propaganda. It may also have had another purpose. It could have been intended as an offer to accept a revised and higher level of German industry and support the establishment of central administrative agencies as a first step towards the creation of a German Government, provided the Western Allies would undertake to arrange for current reparations to meet Russia's $10 billion claim

---

[35] Throughout 1945–7, the shortages of coal, steel and rail transport interacted with and reinforced one another in the British zone. All were intensified by the shortage of food and low morale (Carden 1979, pp. 541–7).

[36] Baggaley (1980) pp. 585–6.

[37] Speech at the meeting of the Council of Foreign Ministers in Paris on 10 July 1946 (reproduced in RIIA *Documents on Germany under Occupation, 1945–54*) (1955) pp.146–7.

and agree to quadripartite control of the Ruhr. The Russians may have had at the back of their minds the development in the Ruhr of the kind of economic system which they were busy establishing in their own zone.[38]

Neither Byrnes nor Bevin pursued Molotov's suggestions. Bevin had been in favour, earlier in the year, of some form of internationalization of the Ruhr and was also sympathetic to French claims to the Saar. He saw no reason to admit the Russians to a share in the administration of the Ruhr while the British had no say in the administration of Saxony and Thuringia. By April he had come down firmly against internationlization and had decided instead to set up a new province of Rhineland–Westphalia within the British zone. He was driven to the conclusion that, if Germany was not to be treated as an economic whole, the British zone would have to be run on a different footing so as to make sure that no burden fell on the British taxpayer. He made a formal statement to this effect in Paris just before Molotov's speech on 10 July and repeated it next day, explaining that, in the absence of co-operation with other zones 'on a fully reciprocal basis', Britain would be obliged to retain coal and other materials for the rehabilitation of industry in its zone rather than export them, often on credit and at prices well below world levels, to markets in Allied countries.[39]

The Merger of American and British Zones

It was presumably Bevin's intention to bring pressure on Russia. But a threat to halt exports of coal from the Ruhr was far more a threat to economic recovery in France and other European countries where there was a large Communist vote. As such, it cut right across American policy and alarmed Byrnes.[40] He at once responded by proposing a merger between the British and American zones – a proposal which had been under consideration in Berlin for at least a month.[41] The form that Byrnes's proposal took was an offer to merge economically with any other zone, but there was no likelihood that the USSR or France would accept and indeed both countries attacked the proposal and declined the offer.

Bevin did not accept at once: it was not until 29 July, after he had

---

[38] Baggaley (1980) pp. 587–8.
[39] For a fuller account of the evolution of Bevin's thinking on relations with Russia and German unity see Bullock (1983) pp.265–9.
[40] Baggaley (1980) pp. 589–90. See also Gimbel (1976) pp. 106–8.
[41] See, for example, Document 128, in *The Papers of General Lucius D. Clay*, Vol. I.

consulted the Cabinet, that British acceptance was announced and negotiations were put in hand. Bevin was reluctant to engage in any move likely to reduce the chances of ultimate agreement on a unitary Germany, or one that might provoke an open breach with the Russians. As he told Dalton, 'if Potsdam had to be cast aside, he would prefer that Russia should take the initiative in doing so'.[42] On the other hand, it was a basic principle of Potsdam that Germany should be treated as an economic unit and this principle had not been observed. A merger of the two zones was a step towards economic unity – a step which might force the hand of the French Government and bring in their zone too. If the Russians declined to join and went their own way, that was no worse than what was already happening.[43] Bevin urged, however, that they and the French should at least have an offer in writing before any action was taken.

It would be going too far to regard the decision to merge the zones as the critical point at which Europe was split in two. There was no such point. But, as Bevin recognized, it was a turning-point. It tied the USA more firmly to Europe and held out the prospect of an eventual reduction in the drain on Britain's reserve of dollars. Thus it relieved simultaneously the dominant anxieties of the Foreign Office and the Treasury. It also brought some hope of improvement to the Germans and a new emphasis on Germany's place in European recovery. By October Bevin was looking forward to 'conditions which will enable Germany and the world outside Germany to benefit from German industry and resources'.[44]

By the end of the year a fusion of the American and British zones had been negotiated. Then on 12 March 1947 came the Truman Doctrine, followed in May by General Marshall's speech that set in motion the European Recovery Programme. It was to be another year before the final break – when the Russians walked out of the Control Council on 20 March 1948 and made the first moves in the Berlin blockade a few days later. But the rift was widening all the time.

Throughout the debate in 1946 there was a large element of make-believe. However the Potsdam Agreement was interpreted, the deal between Byrnes and Molotov in July 1945 was based on the belief that it would *not* be possible to administer Germany as a single economic whole, with a common programme of exports and imports, a single central bank and normal interchange between

[42] CM(46)56, 6 June 1946.
[43] CM(46)73, 25 July 1946.
[44] H. of C. Debates, 22 October 1946, Vol. 427, Col. 1518.

different parts of the country. Harriman and Pauley, in particular, thought it inevitable that the Russian zone would be separated from the rest of the country.[45] It seemed obvious to some members of the Foreign Office, too, that it would be impossible to get a programme for exports and imports agreed by the Allied Control Council for the whole of Germany, because the Russians would be taking the maximum from their own zone in current deliveries and producing an inevitable disparity between the standard of living in East and West. The result would be an impassable barrier between the zones.[46] The Americans, in an attempt to get over short-term difficulties in the division of reparations removals, had produced unfortunate long-term effects in a division of Germany.[47]

There was therefore nothing very unexpected about the way things had developed over the winter. Bevin had managed to reinsert the first charge principle in Article 19 of Potsdam. Waley had insisted that acceptance of the American proposal on reparations should be subject to the provision in Article 14 that Germany must be treated as a single economic unit with 'import and export programmes for Germany as a whole'. But, as we have seen, they had no expectation that much would come of these provisions. The most Bevin hoped for was 'separate discussions on the exchange of supplies between the different areas of Germany'.

What made the American and British Governments harp on the flouting of the Potsdam Agreement was not concern for economic unity as such – although they realized that loss of economic unity would soon give rise to loss of political unity – but the financial burden imposed by their responsibilities as Occupying Powers. This burden on American and British taxpayers – put by Byrnes and Bevin at $200 million and $320 million a year respectively in 1946 – was attributed by them to the failure to pool German resources. The line taken by Bevin at the Paris meeting of Foreign Ministers in July 1946 was that removals by the USSR from current production and stocks deprived Germany of surplus indigenous resources that should go to pay for necessary imports; and he circulated a paper requiring that 'indigenous resources surplus to approved requirements of one zone must be made available to meet deficits in the approved requirements of other zones'.[48]

[45] Memorandum by S. D. Waley, 2 August 1945, Document No. 600 in Rohan Butler and M. E. Pelly (1984), p. 1257.
[46] Coulson to Cadogan, 31 July 1945, in Butler and Pelly (1984), Document 492, p. 1069.
[47] Ibid.
[48] FRUS, 1946, Vol. II, 11 July 1946, p. 900.

The Debate on Current Deliveries

The Russians, on the other hand, could see no reason to discontinue current deliveries from their zone, particularly when they were in receipt of a negligible trickle from the West. It had been decided at Potsdam at the suggestion of the United States, said Molotov, that 'the Soviet Union should draw reparations mainly from its occupation zone of Germany and partly from the Western zone . . .. Naturally, these reparations must include not only equipment but also commodities out of current production.'[49] Bevin agreed that current deliveries were not excluded but insisted that the text of the Potsdam Agreement made it clear that deliveries should not be taken from any zone until the adverse balance of payments for Germany as a whole had been eliminated.[50]

Thus the debate which began in 1946 with exports, imports and economic unity veered towards the allied issue of current deliveries. None of the Allies had ever set their face in principle against current deliveries. 'Annual deliveries of goods from current production' were one of three forms of reparations included in the Yalta Agreement and the fact that they were not mentioned in the Potsdam Agreement did not rescind the original article. On the contrary, it could be held that, since the purpose of the Potsdam Agreement was explicitly stated to be 'to carry out the Crimea Declaration on Germany', the original agreement still held. The only reference to 'current production' in the Potsdam Agreement was in the requirement that 'the proceeds of exports from current production and stocks shall be available in the first place for payment for (approved) imports'. This was taken by the Western Allies to mean that reparations from current production were permissible only after exports and imports were in balance. Until then they were 'not a matter for immediate consideration'.[51] The Russians, on the other hand, were not conscious of infringing the agreement so long as their own zone was in balance or made no demands on other zones.

Even after Potsdam, the Western Allies did not rule out current deliveries. At the end of January 1946, for example, the Manpower Division of the American Element in the Control Commission was asking whether surplus labour in the Western zones might not be used to produce goods for delivery in reparations and had been told by General Draper that the question was still an open one.[52] But

[49] FRUS, 1946, Vol. II, 10 July 1946, 846.
[50] Ibid., p. 866.
[51] Part X of the Pauley Report to the President.

with the Western zones in heavy deficit, opinion hardened against current deliveries just as the Russians were coming to the conclusion that they were a better bet than removals of capital equipment. Without surrendering their claim to equipment from the West, the USSR had begun to contemplate an upward revision of the level of industry plan in return for current deliveries; by early 1947 they were suggesting the retention of 11 million tons of steel capacity – more than any of the occupying powers had proposed at the end of 1945. The Americans and British, on the other hand, continued to denounce the current deliveries in progress from the Eastern zone and were prepared to give consideration to current deliveries from the Western zones only in substitution for claims to removals of equipment.

The Allies argued that the cost of what was shipped to Russia from the Eastern zone without payment, as reparations, fell ultimately on their taxpayers. The value of those shipments ought to be available in settlement of the bill for food imports into the Western zones. But was this a correct view of the matter? If Russian had had to pay in foreign exchange – presumably in dollars, since the Americans insisted on invoicing German exports in dollars – they could not and would not have paid. There was no real possibility of reducing appreciably the import bill of the Western zones by charging Russia for German exports, whether Germany was treated as a single unit or as four separate zones. If the Russians were told that uniting the zones meant forgoing reparations and paying in cash for all they took, they were unlikely to be in a hurry to welcome union.

However, this was not the way in which the choice was presented. The argument was rather that the removal of reparations in current deliveries reduced the sum total of Germany's resources available to meet her needs. Once she was self-supporting the goods could be spared but, until then, they absorbed resources that might otherwise help Germany to pay her way. Again, one has to ask whether this was really so. Of most deliveries the answer is undoubtedly yes. The deliveries of foodstuffs to Russia might have been made instead to the Western zones. The textiles, engineering products, and other manufactures could have found a market elsewhere.[53] But one has still to ask two questions. First, if delivery had been made to the Western zones how would *they* have made payment? Would such payment not have involved a fresh load on the resources of these zones, exactly equal to the relief offered by the diversion of goods

[52] Murphy to State Department, Telegram 307, 31 January 1946.
[53] For an indication of the kind of goods taken by the Russians in reparations, see Nettl (1951) pp. 211–16.

from the USSR? Or were East German goods to be supplied on credit as a kind of tribute analogous to reparations? The second question follows from the first. Were not the resources of which the Western zones claimed to be denied the counterpart of exactions borne by the inhabitants of the Eastern zone in a lower standard of living and, if so, how did the Western zones intend to prolong these exactions once the Soviet Union had no incentive to compel them?

All this implies that the case against current deliveries – at least from the Eastern zone – lay more in the injustice to the local population (in comparison with their Western neighbours) than in balance of payments considerations. The Russians could see nothing against extending current deliveries to the Western zones when they were successfully levying them in theirs. But the Western powers could with justice resist such efforts if they were convinced that a further depression of living standards should not be allowed. They had no interest, such as they had felt initially in destroying Germany's war potential and removing the spoils in reparations, in a further impoverishment of their zones in the alleged interests of more rapid recovery in the USSR.

There was a further aspect of current deliveries. The extra effort that went to supplying the USSR with goods might do little for the real incomes of the German workers in the Eastern zone. But it did provide them with employment of a kind that might be expected to continue after reparations ceased. A floor to industrial production was provided that was not only of immediate help in keeping capacity and organization in being but also held out hopes for the future. While the Western zones went on arguing over what was to be dismantled (and the Soviet Union did its best to keep them on the hook), the Eastern zone could begin to plan for a steady industrial expansion and recover, in 1946–7 at least, faster than the Western zones.

The fundamental question was, however, political, not economic: who was to control Germany as a single unit? To the Western Allies it looked as if it were Russia's intention to maintain a firm and exclusive grip on her own zone, with instructions from Moscow mediated through Moscow-trained Communists in key positions, and at the same time use the zone as a base from which to infiltrate the Western zones and drum up support for Communist-inspired policies. Russia had already, in a series of *faits accomplis*, installed pliable governments throughout Eastern Europe and built an empire that *she* might regard as a protective belt but which was distinctly alarming to the adjoining countries to the west. If to these conquests she added Germany, neither the UK nor France could provide any real barrier or counterpoise, and one totalitarian state would have replaced another in control of Europe.

The Chiefs of Staff, envisaging just such a situation, had argued in 1944 for dismemberment: a united Germany would never be allowed by the Soviet Union to arm itself, even in self-defence, and might well combine with the Soviet Union against the West, whereas the dismembered parts lying to the west might gravitate to a Western bloc and eventually be allowed to rearm in its support. At that stage, the Foreign Office had reacted in horror at such deliberate sabotage, even in thought, of the continuation into the post-war years of the Anglo-Soviet alliance and the prospect of joint control with the Soviet Union of European affairs. In any event the Soviet was in an excellent position to render the proposed moves by a Western bloc ineffective.[54]

The dilemma posed in 1944 had become a reality in 1946. For two years Bevin wrestled with the problem, fearful of converting a rift with the Soviet Union into a rupture, and precipitating a division of Europe by dividing Germany. Whereas Truman was 'sick of babying the Soviets' by January 1947 and had enunciated the 'Truman doctrine' two months later, Bevin did not give up hope of some accommodation with the USSR until the end of the year, after the London Conference in December 1947.[55] Even then 'he doubted whether Russia was as great a danger as a resurgent Germany might become'. Yet, so long as the Western powers felt obliged to temper their treatment of Germany to Russian demands and to abide by the Potsdam Agreement, they were bound to perpetuate uncertainty in their zones and delay the recovery that would rally popular opinion there to the support of Western policies. It was not until the Marshall Plan in 1947 and the currency reform of 1948 that the Germans in the Western zones could be offered a firm foundation for planning their economic future.

[54] See above, p. 47.
[55] Bullock (1983) p. 269.

8

The Fading Out of Reparations

It is not pleasant for us to face the need to encourage the recovery of past competitors. Nevertheless, the dependence of Europe upon German supplies and upon Germany as a market is one which over-rides the difficulties of fair competition, even bearing in mind that the Western Zones of Germany have been in effect shorn of their home-grown food supplies and must be expected to develop an intensive export drive of their own as a means of life.

Federation of British Industries, September 1947

With the move to merge the American and British zones on 1 January 1947, and in preparation for the ministerial Conference on Germany that was shortly to be held in Moscow, an official committee reviewed the Reparations Plan in the autumn of 1946.[1]

The committee concluded that if modifications were to be made it would be better to propose a comparatively simple formula rather than go through the Plan item by item and face months of hard bargaining and negotiation. For the industries restricted to a fixed level they suggested a flat 50 per cent increase. Permitted steel capacity would thus be increased from 7.5 million tons to 11.2 million tons and the metal and engineering industries would enjoy correspon-dingly greater latitude. The committee were not very optimistic that this would benefit the balance of payments to any great extent, but there would be an improvement in economic activity and employment and in the German standard of living. On the other hand, the loss in reparations would be small because there would still be as much

---

[1] 'Report on Proposed Revision of the *Plan for Reparations and the Level of Post-war Germany Economy*, EIPS/P(46)6, 22 October 1946, in PRO FO 1005/961. The meeting in Moscow did not begin until 10 March 1947.

capital equipment available for allocation as the recipient countries could absorb and put into useful service. For that matter, there would be more than could be shipped to them for use if Frank Pakenham (who had succeeded Hynd as Chancellor of the Duchy of Lancaster) was right in estimating that it would take 200,000 men two years to dismantle all the industrial plants already earmarked.[2]

While there seems to have been agreement on these points, other modifications were contested by departments such as the Admiralty, the Ministry of Supply and the Board of Trade. The Foreign Office, for example, had apparently had second thoughts on the prohibition of ship-building and the ownership of ocean-going vessels. They wanted Germany to have an annual capacity to build 75,000 tons of shipping, allowing her after 20 years to operate an ocean-going merchant fleet of about 1.5 million gross registered tons. The Admiralty and the Ministry of Transport thought this dangerous from the point of view of security and highly detrimental to British shipping. The Ministry of Supply was uneasy at a 50 per cent increase in the permitted level for precision instruments and wanted to couple this with drastic restrictions on clocks and watches and the precision camera industry.

There was also some hesitation over retaining the prohibition on aluminium, magnesium and vanadium (a prohibition that had not formed part of the proposals approved by the Cabinet in September 1945) but it was agreed that the point should not be pressed. A further group of industries on which the committee was in doubt was made up of those where capacity was being retained only until imports could be paid for. They were inclined to favour immediate elimination of synthetic rubber and synthetic oil capacity (apart from Fischer-Tropsch plants used for soap manufacture) and limit synthetic ammonia and ball-bearings capacity to Germany's essential domestic needs.

Preparations for the Moscow Conference

No action was taken on these proposals, presumably because it seemed preferable to wait until after the negotiations in Washington on the fusion of the British and American zones had been completed. But before the Moscow conference Bevin consulted his colleagues on the line he should take. On 2 January 1947 he told the Cabinet that the Soviet Government were pressing their demand for $10 billion in reparations from current production in Germany. Such a

[2] CM(47)2, 6 January 1947, in PRO CAB 128/9

demand could only be met if much of the total came from the Western zones. The US Government might be tempted to go some way towards meeting the demand in return for Russian agreement to treat Germany as an economic unit. Britain, however, could not afford to make concessions involving expenditure beyond what she was already committed to under the fusion agreement. No concessions of any kind should be made that did not bring full agreement on the treatment of Germany; and the Russians would have to supply particulars of what they had removed in reparations or commercial exports. Bevin had already asked for a report from the Control Council on the total value of the goods taken by the Allied powers since the beginning of the occupation.[3]

In pressing for economic unity, Bevin still hoped for a federal system conferring large powers on the provincial governments. He recognized that the Soviet Government would be in favour of a strong central Government, which they would hope to convert to Communism, and that the French would take the opposite view. But, strangely enough, he was uncertain what attitude the USA would adopt.

Bevin was also anxious to see a reduction in the size of the four national armies quartered in Germany at uncomfortably close quarters. This could be achieved with 'really effective co-operation between the four occupying powers' which he was still sufficiently optimistic to think possible. Indeed, Bevin expressed optimism on several different scores: the benefits of economic fusion and the chances of recovering the heavy British expenditure on it; the progress made at the New York Conference of Ministers; and the 'encouraging' prospects for the Moscow meeting.

Six weeks later Bevin submitted a lengthy memorandum to the Cabinet asking for their agreement to the proposals he intended to table at Moscow.[4] These he summarized as follows:

1   That we should resist any claim which may be put forward for current reparation deliveries either from Eastern or Western Germany.
2   That as a principal condition of economic unity we should obtain Russian agreement to bearing a reasonable share in the burden already borne and to be borne by the Occupying Powers in respect of relief imports and external costs of occupation of Germany as a whole.

[3] CM(47)1, 2 January 1947, in PRO CAB 128/9.
[4] 'Main Short-term Problems confronting us in Moscow: summarised conclusions and recommendations', Memorandum by the Secretary of State for Foreign Affairs, CP(47)68, 20 February 1947, in PRO CAB 129/17.

3 The demand for reparations from current production should not be refused outright. It should, however, be made clear that it cannot be considered until Germany has established a favourable foreign exchange balance and has met the expenses incurred by the Occupying Powers.

4 That we should insist on an upward revision of the level of Industry Plan with a minimum steel production level of 10 million tons, the steel-using industries being adjusted to a level appropriate to this steel output.

5 That we should insist on associating the discussion of economic problems with the consideration of the future political structure of Germany.

6 That for the purpose of dealing with the points raised . . . [in 1–4] above, we shall table, at the earliest opportunity in Moscow, a new set of political and economic principles dealing with the treatment of Germany.

Bevin expected the three main topics for discussion to be economic unity, level of industry and reparations. He thought it unlikely that the Russians would accept economic unity and waive their claim to reparations from Eastern and Western zones; but even if they did, there was no guarantee that the cost to the Exchequer would be reduced. The Russian zone was short of raw materials and ill-equipped industrially, so that there would probably be a net inflow of goods into the zone from the West. But would the goods stop there? The Foreign Office thought not. They argued that 'although Russia may pay lip-service to the principles of economic unity and the conception of German central administrative agencies having real control throughout the whole country, the very existence of a Soviet Military Administration in the East would make it difficult for us to ensure that the Russians were living up to their bargain'. There was nothing to prevent them from ignoring any central German authority and shipping the imported goods across Germany's eastern borders into Poland and Russia. This would amount to the continuation of reparations from current production in a disguised form. Why West German exporters should continue to ship goods without payment, or East Germans continue to order them if left to foot the bill, Bevin did not explain.

Instead, he suggested as a 'safeguard' against 'disguised' current deliveries that the United Kingdom 'should only accept unity' if condition 2 above was accepted; that is retrospective acceptance by the USSR of 'a reasonable share' of external occupation costs. Since the USSR claimed 50 per cent of total reparation deliveries from

Germany, this might also be a reasonable share of external occupation costs (including food imports) for her to bear. This was putting the price of economic unity high and making a claim on rather doubtful logic. For good measure, as preconditions for agreement to economic unity, Bevin wanted also to insist on the removal of restrictions on the movement of men and goods between zones and the establishment of genuine freedom of assembly and expression.

If discussion were confined to economic unity, Bevin feared that these conditions would leave him in a minority of one and that if the Conference failed he would be held to blame by world opinion. He would make it his object, therefore, to widen the discussion to the whole field of political and economic principles that he wished to establish. A statement of these principles was circulated to the Cabinet and, in amended form, to the Conference.

The statement was one which the Russians could never possibly have accepted. It put as an aim of the controlling powers the restoration of the German economy to the point at which she could not only balance imports and exports but repay 'as soon as possible' all sums advanced by the occupying powers for imports and external occupation costs. These sums were first to be shared between the occupying powers and then repaid as a first charge on any excess of German exports over essential imports. The controlling powers were to provide the German central administration with an agreed statement of what was owed to them, and this statement was to credit Germany in full with all exports made from current production or stock, whether or not taken as reparations. Until repayment was complete (including repayment of external occupation costs), there were to be no reparation deliveries from current production. Thus Russia would not only have had to stop taking current deliveries as reparations but would also have had to credit Germany with the value of previous takings and furnish to Britain and America a large share (perhaps half) of their disbursements on imports.

More than this. All acquisitions of East German undertakings by the Russians (SAGs) would be null and void, and German property rights usurped by the Russians would be made subject to German law.[5] This would have meant the abandonment of a huge amount of industrial property seized by the Russians and used by them to channel a large slice of industrial output from the Eastern zone to the USSR in reparations.

In addition, the Level of Industry Plan would be radically revised. Steel capacity and the permissible level of steel production would be

[5] See below, p. 205.

raised to 10 million tons. A fresh determination would be made of plant and equipment for removal as reparations and the Control Council would issue a final list not later than 15 August 1947.

Bevin must have been very optimistic if he took seriously the prospect of Russian acceptance of his 'Principles'. He clearly did not mind too much if he was unsuccessful. The Russians, he thought, were too concerned to prevent a split, with the resources of the Ruhr incorporated within a Western bloc, to abandon the principle of quadripartite control. He looked forward to the industrial recovery in the Western zones and the bartering of their steel and other industrial products for foodstuffs and other essential imports from the east. This would cut Britain's dollar expenditure while recovery would strengthen his bargaining position with the Russians. The Eastern zone, on the other hand, was 'likely to change from an asset to a liability as time goes on'. In this Bevin was mistaken; but he was right to count on eventual economic recovery in the Western zones and right also about Russian reluctance (for one year more) to abandon quadripartite control.

When Bevin's paper came before the Cabinet, in the middle of the coal crisis of 1947, it was supported by Cripps and Dalton who attached particular importance to avoiding any increased drain on dollar reserves or other British resources for the benefit of the German economy. Pakenham doubted whether the restrictions on Germany's industrial production could be maintained indefinitely and pointed out that the Land Governments and the trade unions were already in a position, if they chose, to frustrate British policy. Bevin's proposals should be put forward in Moscow as minimum demands. Nye Bevan, however, thought they were impracticable and that the attempt to prevent the creation of a central government in Germany would break down after nourishing the growth of a neo-Fascist movement. If Germany had self-government she would be unlikely to maintain artificial limits on her industrial expansion.[6]

From Bevin's paper it is clear that British policy on reparations was undergoing a number of changes. In the first place, Britain's own commercial interests had come to play a part. In his statement of long-term policy, Bevin used language that would have been repudiated a year earlier: '[Germany] should be left with a sufficient industrial potential to ensure a reasonable standard of living, *but this should be so designed as to interfere as little as possible with our export policy*'[7] (italics added).

Next, Britain's appetite for reparations seems to have increased in

[6] CM(47)25, 27 February 1947, in PRO CAB 128/9.
[7] CP(47)68, 20 February 1947, in PRO CAB 129/17 (italics added).

1946. The Ministry of Supply had its eye on the Hermann Goering Salzgitter Steelworks, the Ministry of Defence on hydrogen peroxide plant, and other ministers (notably Cripps) were pressing for German equipment as an alternative to heavy dollar expenditure.[8] The suspension of dismantling in mid-1946 had led to strong protests from the members of IARA that their reconstruction programmes were being retarded, and in November 1946 General Robertson announced his intention to make RM 100 million of general-purpose machine tools and equipment available for immediate delivery from the British zone.[9]

Bevin now proposed that, after the Moscow discussions, sufficient plants should be declared surplus to meet the urgent needs of the UK and other Western claimants, plus an appropriate allocation to Russia. He was prepared if necessary to do this unilaterally. He also hoped to induce the Americans to agree to a wider definition of 'war plants' so as to include in the scheme covering such plants complete factories in restricted industries.[10]

Thirdly, Bevin had moved a little further towards approving reparations from current production once Germany was in balance on external account. Other countries in addition to Russia were making claims for such reparations but were not pressing them while Germany was supported by the occupying powers. There would be strong protests if they were now told that such claims would never be admitted. Again, it would be a long time before the UK and the USA recovered the money they had advanced, if they ever did. It would be a mistake, therefore, to exclude further reparation payments and what Bevin hoped for was a general statement indicating that such payments would be given consideration once external balance was restored.

It was striking that after the fusion of the British and American zones, Bevin was still in the dark as to some aspects of American policy. For example, when he told his colleagues that he intended to put forward in Moscow a tentative proposal for a European currency and the abolition of tariff barriers in Europe, he expected to enlist support from the Russians but to be opposed by both the Americans

[8] The Salzgitter plant, for which the French shared an equal enthusiasm (below, p. 187 n50), was in the end retained in Germany.
[9] Although parallel action was taken by the French, the equipment actually made available to IARA had a residual value of only RM 42 million (about £3 million).
[10] The British had overdrawn their reparations account through the assignment to them of their share of the German mercantile marine and overseas assets and were impatient to be put in credit by a big increase in the total amount released for allocation by IARA, even if this meant a renewal of deliveries to the USSR under the 25 per cent Potsdam arrangement (ORC(47)IM, 3 February 1947, in PRO CAB 134/597).

and the French.[11] He expected the Americans to 'agree to moderate current deliveries in exchange for Russian agreement on the other Potsdam principles and at the same time increase the level of industry to a greater extent than would be necessitated by these current reparation deliveries alone'.[12]

But a few weeks later in Moscow, General Marshall took a quite different line and would not hear of current deliveries. When Molotov argued that 'acceptance of reparations in the form of current production is an absolute condition of economic unity', Marshall retorted that 'The Potsdam Agreement for economic unity was not conditioned on acceptance of reparations from current production. . . . It looks very much as though the Soviet Union is trying to sell the same horse twice'.[13]

Bevin also believed that 'we go further than the Americans, particularly in the case of steel, as regards the level of industrial capacity which Germany needs to become self-supporting'.

This was based on a remark by General Clay, in New York in December 1946, that 11 million tons of steel would be a security danger – a remark which seems to have prompted Bevin to substitute 10 million tons for the figure of 11 million tons he had used in the House of Commons on 28 October.[15] Bevin thought it unlikely that the Americans would be willing to see steel capacity raised much above 7.5 million tons.[16] On this point, too, Bevin soon discovered that he was misinformed. On his return from Moscow he told the Cabinet that the Americans were now thinking in terms of 14 million tons of steel and a level of industrial production 75 to 80 per cent of the level in 1938 (compared with 55 per cent in the Reparations Plan).[17] Later, in May, he put round a paper on the steel industry, asking to be allowed to go some way to meet the American proposal by accepting a limit of up to 11 million tons.[18]

When this was discussed in Cabinet, Nye Bevan was again the

[11] ORC(47)2M, 24 February 1947, in PRO CAB 134/597.

[12] CP(47)68, Appendix B, para. 16.

[13] Ratchford and Ross (1947) p. 197. Bevin had suggested at an ORC meeting on 3 February 1947 that there were some indications that the Russians were prepared to renounce all or part of their 25 per cent share of Western zone equipment if they could obtain consumer goods (presumably as reparations) from the Western zone.

[14] CP(47)68, Appendix B, para. 19.

[15] Ibid., para. 24.

[16] Ibid., para. 16.

[17] CM(47)43, 2 May 1947, in PRO CAB 128/9.

[18] 'Level of German Industry', Memorandum by Secretary of State for Foreign Affairs, CP(47)163, 19 May 1947, in PRO CAB 129/19. The Americans were pressing for a ceiling of 12.5 million tons, of which 1 million tons was to be for export (Bullock (1983) p. 434).

leading critic. He could see no justification for limiting Germany's steel production on security grounds. The main other argument for sticking to 10 million tons (apart from the need to make plant available in reparations) was the threat of German competition with British exports. This he found even less convincing. When demand for steel was well in excess of supply there could be no case for offering British exporters such protection.[19] As was shortly to appear, others – especially the French – held very different views of security and were passionately opposed to any increase in the level of steel production. Meanwhile, the actual level of output in the Bizone was roughly 3 million tons per annum – far below any of the figures under discussion – while the rated capacity of surviving plant was over 19 million tons.

Revision of the Level of Industry Plan

What was ultimately agreed by the two zone commanders, Clay and Robertson, was that the ceiling to steel production should be 10.7 million (metric) tonnes in the two zones, and 11.5 million tonnes in all Germany if the other two zones elected to join. This was expected to permit of exports of 2 million tonnes to bring Germany's trade nearer to balance. The level for heavy machinery was increased to 80 per cent of the 1936 level and for the chemical industry to 100 per cent. With other relaxations the new agreement was intended to allow industrial production in the bizonal area to regain the level of 1936.

The agreement had its origin in discussions in Moscow between Bevin and Marshall. They concluded that a fresh plan for industry in the bizonal area should be put in hand. Accordingly, a bipartite working party was set up in Berlin charged with the preparation of a plan that would make the Bizone self-supporting as soon as possible and could also serve as a Reparations Plan for the whole of Germany, with an indication of how much capital equipment would be available as reparations. When the working party reported in June some important differences remained between British and American views.

First, there was a difference as to finality. Bevin had wanted to present the new plan at once to the Germans as a firm basis for their efforts by removing the uncertainty surrounding the future of almost every factory. If a new plan was not put into operation very soon it

[19] CM(47)49, 22 May 1947, in PRO CAB 128/9.

would also be impossible to make progress with the dismantling and removal of plant. When Robertson urged this on Clay, however, he encountered strong opposition. To proceed at once to put the plan into operation would be more prejudicial to future negotiations with the French and Russians than the fusion of the British and American zones had been. What Clay proposed was that the plan should be announced as the considered opinion of the bipartite board, intended for use in subsequent negotiations with the other Allies. This dismayed British officials who argued that to submit the plan for quadripartite agreement, when its preparation already flew in the face of such agreement, was to deny it finality and destroy the beneficial consequences it was intended to have.[20]

A second point of disagreement was the permissible level of steel production. The working party proposed that for Germany as a whole, less the Saar, this should be raised to 12.5 million tons per annum with an additional 1 million tons for export, the level fixed for other industries being scaled up correspondingly.[21] This meant more than doubling the permitted level for steel. It would not only be higher than General Clay had in mind – he was willing to accept 11.2 million tons for the bizonal area alone – but well in excess of the 11 million tons for the whole of Germany that was the maximum General Robertson was authorized to consider. If all the working party's proposals were accepted, the total volume of output in Germany would be allowed to regain the 1936 level and would be roughly 40 per cent higher than in the Reparations Plan.[22] Even so, per capita consumption of industrial products in the Bizone would be 25–30 per cent below 1936 levels and no higher than prescribed by the Potsdam Agreement.[23]

There were also disagreements on specific industries. General Clay was not willing to relax the ban on the production of aluminium, magnesium, beryllium and vanadium. On the other hand, General

[20] EIPS(P)(47)4, 'The Future level of German Industry', 1 July 1947, in PRO CAB 134/597.

[21] Jennifer Forsyth to J. M. Fleming, 17 June 1947, in PRO T 230/78. The large upward revision in steel was justified by the need to aim at a value of exports from the Bizone 15–30 per cent higher than in 1936. With a population likely to be swollen in 1952 by 25–30 per cent since 1936, and with much less favourable terms of trade, even this level of exports would pay only for an indispensable minimum of imports, with no tea, coffee, tobacco or other conventional necessities.

[22] EIPS(P((47)4.

[23] This implied a major error in the 1946 Reparations Plan which also claimed to be in accordance with the Potsdam Agreement. Note, however, that the divergence is only in industrial production and consumption, not GNP, relates to the Bizone rather than Germany as a whole, and makes allowance for a big increase in population and less favourable terms of trade.

Robertson was instructed to make no concession on a range of industries from heavy engineering to chemicals and dyestuffs.

In advising ministers, British officials were reluctant, even in June 1947, to challenge the view that security should take precedence over balance of payments considerations. In preliminary instructions to Robertson, the Foreign Office had re-emphasized that 'one of the major objects of HMG's policy in Germany is so to restrict those elements of German industry which are most important to a war economy as to prevent the rapid reconstitution of German war potential at the end of a period of international control.'

There was also some reluctance on the part of supply departments to forgo reparations: they argued that much of the plant that would be retained in Germany under the new proposals would not be operated for perhaps seven to ten years. The Board of Trade continued to harp on clocks, watches and fine optics. It was natural to suspect that, in this and other cases such as dyestuffs, commercial considerations were masquerading under the cloak of economic security.

This British concern for security and for maintaining the flow of reparations seems curious in the light of the struggles of the previous year in Berlin and the crisis through which Britain was passing in the middle of 1947. The Marshall Plan was already under discussion and the need to embark on a recovery plan for Europe as a whole was coming to be accepted. The Russians had themselves been willing to contemplate 11 million tons of steel production.[24] In some of the other industries where the British view was opposed to concessions, the original plan was internally inconsistent and some revision indispensable: for example, the levels fixed for basic chemicals did not square with those for finished chemical products.

The arguments at the official level were repeated at the ministerial. Bevin was anxious at all costs to reach agreement with the Americans, provided the level for steel did not exceed 11.5 million tons. This higher figure would be a last resort and the agreement once reached must be final. The Minister of Supply supported the working party's proposal to relax the ban on aluminium and other non-ferrous metals which the Americans were trying to maintain on commercial, not security, grounds. He and the Minister of Defence were disturbed by the higher figure proposed for the steel industry but

---

[24] At the Paris Peace Conference in July 1946 Molotov said that 'we should not put obstacles in the way of an increase on the output of steel' (FRUS, 1946, Vol. II, p. 871, Minutes of meeting on 10 July 1946). This followed by only four months Sokolovsky's remark in the Co-ordinating Committee that to leave 9 million tons of steel capacity in Germany meant war within a few years.

neither pressed their objections, reserving their fire for the fine mechanics and optics industry and machine tools. The Americans, however, did not regard fine mechanics and optics as having war potential, and all that Bevin could promise was to ask General Marshall to seek military advice on the security aspect. On machine tools, the point at issue was whether to limit production to RM 191 million in the bizonal area, as the Americans proposed, or RM 160 million, which was as high as the Minister of Supply thought advisable. Cripps argued that effective control over the production of machine tools would be very difficult, and the most that Bevin would promise ws to consider the matter.[25] On clocks and watches the Minister of Supply, although anxious to protect the newly established British industry for security reasons, agreed that since 75 per cent of the industry was in the French zone, a concession might be made if necessary.

The Americans took the robust view that security considerations were of negligible importance in any of the industries in dispute – heavy machinery, dyestuffs, watches, precision instruments – and that what risk there was could be justified by the high export value of their products. Officials in Germany were also more conscious than those in London of the political difficulties in continuing to dismantle German factories even on the more limited scale envisaged.

French Objections

Before agreement could be reached in Germany, the French Government entered a vigorous protest against the projected revision of the plan. They saw the proposal to raise the level of German industry as a threat to European security and resented their exclusion from the discussions leading up to the new plan. If the Rhineland and the Ruhr could not be separated from Germany, they should at least be put under international control so that German coal could be used to build up the heavy industry of her neighbours, particularly France, instead of for the re-creation of Germany's industrial preponderance.[26] On 11 July, on the eve of the Conference of 16 European nations to discuss the Marshall proposals, Bidault, the French Foreign Minister, declared that no French Government could consent to a raising of the level of German industry and the abandonment of reparations.[27] A few days later he put the position

[25] Agreement was eventually reached on an output of RM 170 million.
[26] Bullock (1983) p. 431.
[27] Ibid.

graphically to the American Ambassador:

> We have 180 Communists [in the National Assembly] who say: 'The Marshall Plan means Germany first'. If something permits them to say this again . . . I tell you the government will not survive. . . . I am not in a position to overcome the simultaneous opposition of General de Gaulle, the Communist Party, and a not negligible fraction of my own friends.[23]

As Bevin told the Cabinet on 22 July:

> If we and the Americans were . . . to approve and publish the Agreement concluded or virtually concluded in Berlin, not only would the French Government be faced with a very difficult internal situation leading perhaps to their resignation, but the success of the Paris Conference would be gravely threatened and indeed the whole Marshall Plan might well collapse. On the other hand, to postpone the coming into force of the Level of Industry plan obviously has serious disadvantages from the German point of view.[29]

Bevin proposed a postponement of the new plan until the beginning of September, so as to give the French an opportunity of making representations directly to the American and British Governments rather than leave them to make difficulties at the Paris Conference on the Marshall offer. There was to be no repetition of the unfortunate exclusion of the French from the settlement of German questions at Potsdam. On the other hand, they would have to recognize that, until they made up their minds to join the Bizone, responsibility for the area, and for decisions as to its future, must rest exclusively with the two occupying powers.

A tripartite conference between representatives of the three Governments was held in London between 22 and 27 August. It was followed by the publication of the revised plan on 28 August, immediately after the conference. The French 'signed the final communiqué . . . with serious hesitation'.[30] They had been successful in having several general understandings written into the document: for example, the rehabilitation of Germany was to enjoy no priority over that of the democratic countries of Europe. They still expressed reservations in the communiqué about some of the figures in the new

[28] Caffery to Marshall, 18 July 1947, in FRUS, 1947, Vol. II, p. 998.
[29] 'Germany', Memorandum by the Secretary of State for Foreign Affairs, CP(47)209, 22 July 1947, in PRO CAB 129/20.
[30] Minutes of the 4th meeting of the Tripartite Talks, 27 August 1947, in PRO FO 371/65201 (quoted by Mrs Huang Zhongging, 'A Study of the European Recovery Programme', unpublished MS, 1985).

plan.[31] But they gave the plan tacit acceptance, subject to the working out of a satisfactory guarantee of coal exports and an assurance that the limitation on steel production to 10.7 million tons per annum would remain in effect during the period of military occupation.[32]

As usual in French diplomacy in those years, the nub of the matter, apart from security against German military strength, was coal and steel – not enough German coal, too much German steel. The French were apprehensive that Germany's coal requirements would expand with the increase in the permitted level of steel production so that less would be left for export. These fears were taken into account in the formula worked out for the allocation of German coal. French fears of a different kind were mollified by Anglo-American acquiescence in the incorporation of the Saar into the French economy and agreement to the creation of an International Ruhr Authority with French participation.

The release of the new plan was greeted as a plain breach of the Potsdam Agreement by the Russians, while the Americans and British defended it as the inevitable sequel to the failure of the Council over two and a half years to secure the economic unity required by the Agreement. The plan greatly reduced the number of plants available as reparations and involved a reallocation between East and West. The Inter-Allied Reparation Agency (IARA) in Brussels went ahead with a suballocation of specific plants to countries in the West but deliveries remained suspended. As the Soviet representatives came to realize, there were to be no further deliveries of plants from the US zone until German economic unity had been re-established and the resources of the four zones pooled. Plants allocated to the east in the British zone were not being dismantled.[33]

American Pressure

By this time Congress was increasingly disquieted by the incongruity between dismantling plants in Germany and providing dollars to Europe for goods that Germany might be able to supply. Gone were the days of Morgenthau, deindustrialization and a pastoral Germany. Even the violent and widespread attacks on any proposals, like those of the Hoover Report of 1945, interpreted as 'soft' on Germany,

[31] Ibid. See also RIIA, *Documents on International Affairs, 1947–8*, (1952) pp. 625–6.
[32] Clay (1950) p. 321.
[33] Clay (1950) p. 321.

were long forgotten. It was the British who were now attacked for reluctance to suspend the whole dismantling programme.[34] When Clay sought to defend the programme in Washington, a Congressman interrupted his evidence to warn him that a 'peremptory demand to stop dismantling could be put through both Houses of Congress in forty-eight hours'. Yet, as Clay pointed out, Germany's current production was utilizing only about one-third of the capacity it was proposed to leave; steel production, for example, was just over 3.5 million tons per annum – far below the 11 million tons that featured in the Plan. Account had to be taken of the expectations of European countries that they would get at least *some* reparations – and they had had very little. It was also too much to expect that the natural preoccupation of Germany's neighbours with the issue of security would vanish with the Marshall Plan. Clay hinted that he could see something to be said, in the circumstances, for reparations from current production. But this had been consistently ruled out by the US Government as likely to end up as a burden on the American taxpayer.

The revision of the Reparations Plan in August 1947 was not the end of the matter. A succession of American missions visited Germany to make a survey of dismantling and report. One, under Norman Collison, recommended to the US Government that 332 plants listed for delivery as reparations should be retained. Another mission, made up of American industrialists under George Humphrey, reported to Congress through the European Co-operation Administration (ECA) administrator, Paul Hoffman. It too, as we shall see, recommended the retention of a large number of plants in the August list, most of them in the British zone.

The American and British Governments came to accept that the economic unity of Germany must now be a distant objective. In November 1947 Bevin concluded that 'the Soviet Government would, under present conditions, treat any scheme of economic unity solely as a means for forwarding their own interests in the Western zones'; and the Chancellor of the Exchequer (now Cripps) suggested that 'the essential issue now was not one of economic unity but of political unity'.[35]

At the beginning of 1948, after the London Conference of Foreign Ministers, Bevin restated British policy towards Germany. He now wished it to be clearly understood that the guiding principle of the

[34] Clay thought that by the middle of 1948 the French were less restrictive than the British (Clay (1950) p. 323).
[35] ORC(47)8th Meeting, Confidential Annex, 24 November 1947, in PRO CAB 134/597.

Government, in Germany and elsewhere, was that Britain should not be

> a party to creating a situation which can be used to bring about gradually a Communist-controlled Germany on the pattern of the post-war development of events throughout Eastern Europe. . . . We should continue to insist on the firm implementation of our reparations plan and should resist any proposal to suspend deliveries to the Soviet Union and her satellites.[36]

Bevin was still trying to ride two horses. He wanted to promote social democracy in Germany without running any risks of a revival of German militarism. Before long, however, considerations of security began to fade into the background as the rift with Russia deepened. In a matter of months the Communist coup in Prague was succeeded by the Russian walk-out from the Control Council in Berlin and this in turn by the Berlin blockade, following the decision to proceed with currency reform in the Western zones. Thereafter the division of Germany and, with Germany, of Europe was inevitable.

Fresh Modifications of the Level of Industry Plan

In August 1948 Bevin returned to the level of German industry circulating yet another set of proposed modifications. The British Control Commission had produced a new plan as a basis for discussion with the Americans and subsequently the French. The most important change was in the attitude of the Ministry of Defence, who had come at long last to question the value of imposing restrictions (as distinct from outright prohibitions) on the level of German industry. Since such restrictions could not be enforced after the end of the Occupation (hardly a new reflection), the Chiefs of Staff now thought them lacking in any security value. As they put it in more involuted language: 'no continuing restriction on the production of industries needed for war but also essential to the German economy and European recovery need be regarded as essential on security grounds'.[37]

This drew from Marcus Fleming the wry comment: 'what the

[36] 'Policy on Germany', Memorandum by the Secretary of State for Foreign Affairs, CP(48)5, 5 January 1948, in PRO CAB 129/3.

[37] 'Level of German Industry', Memorandum by the Secretary of State for Foreign Affairs, CP(48)203, 13 August 1948, in PRO CAB 129/29. The phrase is repeated in CM(48)56, but with a redundant negative.

Economic Section thinks today, the Ministry of Defence thinks four years hence. I argued strongly on these lines [in 1944]'.[38]

The ostensible reason for proposing yet another 'final' revision to the plan was that a decision as to the duration of the restrictions on German industry had never been included in previous plans. But what gave urgency to this consideration was 'the forthcoming establishment of a Western German Government' after the expected fusion of the French zone with the bizonal area. The fear of permanent restriction should be lifted wherever possible, both because restriction would soon cease to be practicable and because it was 'necessary to offer some assurance of a hopeful economic future to the German people in the Western zones'. The existing reparations programme was meeting with strong and increasing German resistance and any further extension beyond well-defined limits would be difficult to enforce. Finally, Germany had an important role to play in the Marshall Plan that was difficult to reconcile with continuing restrictions.[39]

Clay was already pressing for the abandonment of all restrictions other than that on the steel industry and the ban on industries like aircraft manufacture. The French, on the other hand, looked on most of the restrictions as indefinite limitations on German productive capacity in the interests of European security. They still felt strongly that Germany had more than enough industrial capacity to maintain a reasonable standard of living, and that her war potential gave grounds for anxiety and fear. They could hardly be expected, therefore, to welcome Clay's proposals.

The Americans might, however, be willing to accept a compromise to avoid the political repercussions in France of surrendering to the American view; and it was in this light, as a middle course, that Bevin presented his new plan.

The prohibitions and limitations in the plan were lengthy, circumstantial and complex. The proposed prohibitions were to be maintained in the Peace Treaty when concluded, but the limitations, setting an upper limit to production, would expire.[40] Even at that late stage, a fresh proposal to ban the production of ball- and roller-bearings was included, but Bevin was obviously doubtful whether there was much chance of American agreement.[41] There had also

[38] Manuscript note on minute by Miss J. M. Forsyth to J. M. Fleming *et al.*, 30 July 1948, in PRO T 230/78.
[39] 'Level of German Industry', 13 August 1948, CP(48)203.
[40] This included the limitation of steel production in the Bizone to 10.7 million tons.
[41] Ball-bearings were listed among the prohibited industries in the Reparations Plan of 1946, but production facilities were to be retained until exports and imports were in balance.

been suggestions that various chemicals such as sulphuric acid and chlorine should be banned, but these were excluded and, on the advice of the Chiefs of Staff, Bevin also ruled out the limitations sought by the Ministry of Supply on optics and precision instruments.

The new proposals were attacked in Cabinet as too restrictive and incapable of being maintained effectively for any length of time.[42] Moreover, it was argued, they would prejudice Germany's contribution to European recovery and throw an added burden on the occupying powers. These criticisms were met by pointing to the need for a compromise with French views. Another exchange was on the position of the USSR, which was now proposing that an output of 14–15 million tons of steel should be allowed, with a view to substantial reparations from current production – reparations that would not be possible at the level agreed between the UK and the USA in August 1947. On one view, restrictions were necessary on German industry in case at some time the Soviet Union gained full control. Against this it was argued that a reasonable standard of life was the best antidote to Communist propaganda.

Meanwhile the Americans were exerting pressure in pursuance of section 115(F) of the European Co-operation Act which called on the US Secretary of State 'to obtain the agreement of those countries concerned that such capital equipment as is scheduled for removal as reparations from the three Western zones of Germany should be retained in Germany if such retention will most effectively serve the purposes of the European Recovery Program'.

The Secretary of State was not at first aware that dismantling was still in progress on many unallocated plants in the British zone, and had given Senator Vandenberg to understand that dismantling had ceased at all of the plants which the USA had declined to 'release' for reparations after the review in the spring of 1948. Bevin, for his part, was annoyed by the 'hesitant and procrastinating policy' of his American allies, and had left them in no doubt as to his views.[43] He had agreed six months previously to give consideration to the retention in Germany of a small number of plants, probably 20 to 30, but no list had ever been submitted to him. Instead, a Technical Mission had gone to Germany and had reported without his seeing a copy of its report. Moreover, the list of plants to be dismantled, issued in the autumn of 1947, had omitted plants in prohibited industries, and a year later there were still no final decisions on those

---

[42] CM(48)56, 16 August 1948, in PRO CAB 128/13.
[43] 'Reparations and the European Recovery Programme', Memorandum by the Secretary of State for Foreign Affairs, 14 October 1948, CP(48)234, in PRO CAB 129/30.

plants. So if dismantling stopped, all of them would remain, although they were the most important plants from the security point of view.

Bevin had now to decide what response to make to a formal request from the USA to cease dismantling about 200 plants in the British zone. An American committee, under George Humphrey, had been appointed in August to help in making final decisions about dismantling within 90 days, and would require the fullest information on these plants. Emotion in Congress was running high and the second ERP appropriation was at risk.

Bevin declined to call a halt at plants where dismantling had already begun. If he did so there would be little or no possibility of restarting. The Germans, he said, don't want to pay reparations but have been carrying on with dismantling 'with a fairly good grace'. Any pause would convince them that the critics were justified. To stop for three or four months, as seemed now to be proposed, would be the end of reparations.

In exchanges with General Marshall, Bevin explained that of the 176 plants not yet released from consideration by the US Government, 37 had been completely dismantled, 74 were being dismantled, and although work had not yet started on the remaining 64, it was due to begin shortly. (Work on those 64 plants would be deferred until after 15 December and action on particular plants in the list of 74 would be taken if decisions were reached quickly.) Bevin insisted on having a list of plants released for allocation, including those already dismantled, before the Humphrey Committee proceeded with its investigation. Dismantling would continue in the British zone, pending the completion of the investigation, but it would be of such a character that it would not prevent the eventual retention in Germany of plants (other than those already allocated) that were found to be required in the interests of the European Recovery Programme.

In mid-November it was agreed to authorize the suspension of dismantling on 35 plants in the British zone under review by the Humphrey Committee. A month later Bevin reported that the Humphrey Committee now wanted to retain 167 out of a total of 381 plants under review, while Bevin was willing to agree only to 117.[44] In April 1949 the Prime Minister told the Cabinet that agreement had now been reached on the retention of 159 out of the 167 plants. The other eight, however, represented 30 per cent of the capacity of

---

[44] CM(48)74, 18 November 1948, and CM(48)82, 22 December, 1948, in PRO CAB 128/13.

the 167. All of these were plants that IARA had been led to believe 18 months previously would be released and allocated for reparations.[45]

The End of the Story

By this time the demand for reparations had faded, and complaints that they would be reduced if levels of industry were raised had been abandoned. Some departments continued to attack relaxations on grounds of security but 'no one seriously imagines that the next war will be against Germany'.[46]

With the creation of the Federal Republic of Germany in 1949 the process of withdrawing restrictions and winding up reparations accelerated. Although deliveries did not cease until 1951, no further allocations were made after 1949.

The rest of the story is of a gradual whittling down of the list of plants earmarked for reparations, and of a relaxation of the restrictions on German industry. Opinion in Congress had swung round enthusiastically in favour of the reconstruction of Germany and was impatient with all talk of dismantling in the interests of security. The Americans took the view that plans for the level of industry were means to establish what could be removed as reparations but had no continuing force as ceilings on activity in almost any industry except steel. The French, at the opposite extreme, wanted to retain all the limitations they could for as long as they could in the interests of economic security.

Bevin tried to balance security ('the overriding consideration') against the needs of the Marshall Plan and the importance of Germany to European recovery. He kept reciting the case against reducing dismantling, starting with security: the effect on other countries in IARA that were counting on receiving reparations; the boost to German nationalism if the occupying powers yielded to the campaign against dismantling; the suspicion of the USSR that it was done deliberately to deprive them of reparations. But the recital carried less and less conviction, while the practical difficulties of getting Germans to do the work of demolition multiplied. By the end of 1949 it was the strong probability that the programme would break down for lack of the labour to carry it out that made Bevin finally agree to its virtual abandonment.[47]

---

[45] 'Germany: Reparations and the Prohibited and Limited Industries', Memorandum by the Prime Minister, 5 April 1949, CP(49)76, in PRO CAB 129/34.
[46] Miss J. M. Forsyth to J.M. Fleming, 30 July 1948, in PRO T 230/78.

In August 1947 General Clay had refused to consider the future of the prohibited industries or to agree to the removal from them of surplus plant. Negotiations broke down over the American insistence on the complete removal of the ban on shipbuilding, coupled with French and (to a lesser extent) British insistence on the prohibition or limitation on grounds of security of a large number of comparatively small industries of commercial value to Germany. Agreement between the three countries was finally reached in April 1949. Attlee, in reporting the agreement to the Cabinet, took satisfaction from the inclusion of a ban on synthetic oil and rubber plants which he regarded as 'our most important security objectives'. But by November the ban had gone, and over 400 of those plants were removed from the dismantling list.

Other industries banned in April were the production of magnesium, beryllium, radioactive materials and electronic valves; limits were retained on steel, electric arc and high frequency steel, aluminium, ball-bearings, chlorine, styrene and synthetic ammonia. Ship-building yards with a capacity in excess of 277,000 gross registered tons were to go, and no seagoing vessels were to be built until Germany's coastal fleet had been built up. The duration of these restrictions was the subject of disagreement between the USA (which wanted a three-year limit) and France (which wanted the restrictions to continue indefinitely). It was agreed that they should continue until a Peace Treaty was signed and lapse in 1953, if not renewed after further review.[48]

What was thought to be a definitive agreement lasted roughly seven months until the Petersburg Agreement of November 1949.[49] This more or less ended dismantling (although it lingered for another 18 months) but retained the tripartite agreement on prohibited and restricted industries, including the limit on steel production. The opposition to dismantling and the difficulty of getting labour to undertake it led Bevin to agree to leave the High Commissioners discretion to retain many of the plants affected, including all synthetic oil and rubber plants and all steel works except two.[50] This was on

[47] 'Germany: Meeting of the United Kingdom, United States and French Foreign Ministers, 9th and 10th November 1949', Memorandum by the Secretary of State for Foreign Affairs, CP(49)237, 16 November 1949, in PRO CAB 129/37 Part II; for the Cabinet discussion, see CM(49)67, 17 November 1949.
[48] CP(49)76.
[49] Bullock (1983) pp.738–40. For the text of the Petersberg Agreement, see FRUS, 1949, Vol. III, pp.343–8.
[50] CP(49)237. The two steel works were Krupps, Essen and the Hermann Goering Salzgitter works of which Schumann said that 'his political life would be lost if dismantlement ceased at Salzgitter.'

assurances from the Germans as to security and evidence of good intentions, for example, towards the International Ruhr Authority.

These moves were accompanied by a gradual change of attitude towards Germany. In October 1948 Pakenham (now Minister of Civil Aviation) suggested that the time had come to look on Germany as a valuable ally. Other Ministers, however, thought the rehabilitation of German industry could yet pose a menace to British security.[51] In December Bevin raised the question again: was Germany to be treated as an ally or as a future aggressor? He accepted the need to allow Germany to become self-supporting at a reasonable standard of living. But beyond that what ought to be done? He rejected the idea that Britain should refrain from rebuilding German industry because it might fall into the hands of the USSR: the same danger applied to France and Belgium. He then posed a question to which a different answer had been returned in 1945. Would rearmament not be prevented more effectively by controlling the finishing stages of the engineering industry rather than the basic industries like steel that were essential to peace-time production? At that point he hesitated. What of resurgent German nationalism? What of the French who were certainly not content to see a full-scale restoration of German industry? It was not possible to ignore the possibility of a revival of the German threat to world peace, and Germany must therefore remain militarily weak. It was also wholly unreasonable to let her retain an industrial capacity beyond her peace-time needs, especially when it had been inflated by drawing on the resources of occupied countries in wartime.[52]

The Korean War swept away hesitations of this kind, and from then on the only question was how to overcome French opposition to German rearmament. By September 1950 Bevin was reviewing the Prohibited and Limited Industries Agreement of 1949, and asking for the removal of many limitations that were now 'inappropriate'.[53] He could not endorse the opposition of the USA and France to allowing German diplomatic representation in their capitals. After one more year it was the finance of Germany's defence contribution that was causing perplexity. Occupation costs alone had cost Germany 5–6 per cent of her GNP in 1950–1, and this might rise to 7–9 per cent in 1951–2. To add to this an additional burden of rearmament would not be easy and might produce suggestions that occupation costs should be borne by the occupying powers. If that

[51] CM(48)63, 15 October 1948, in PRO CAB 128/13.
[52] CM(48)82, 22 December 1948, in PRO CAB 128/13.
[53] CM(50)56, 6 September 1950, in PRO CAB 128/18.

happened an additional £180 million would fall on the UK budget and balance of payments.[54]

As for the debts incurred for post-war expenditure on economic aid to Germany by the Allies, the prospect of repayment seemed remote. In September 1950 Bevin recognized that such debts were likely to take second place to the repayment of pre-war debts (to which the USA gave priority) and had in mind a possible 25 per cent repayment. However, in the debt settlement of December 1951 (when Germany had recovered from the balance of payments crisis of the previous winter), British claims were written down only from £201 million to £150 million, with no interest, to be repaid in equal instalments over 20 years, while the USA remitted a full $2,000 million from claims amounting to $3,200 million.[55]

Reparations from the Western Zones

We may end with a brief examination of what was actually dismantled and removed from Western Germany, leaving until the next chapter a discussion of Soviet takings from the Eastern zone.

By no means all that was removed from the Western zones took the form of dismantled equipment that was allocated by IARA. War booty, armaments of all kinds (including what survived of the German navy), gold, stocks of raw materials, patents and trade secrets, German external assets held in the belligerent countries, the services of prisoners of war and a good deal of miscellaneous research equipment, were all taken without allocation by IARA; of these, much the largest items were German external assets and the services of prisoners of war.

The three main recipients of reparations were the USA, the UK and France, of which the first two, for most of the time, professed no great desire to take reparations but received nevertheless more than other Western countries. From IARA alone they received approximately $124 million and $106 million respectively while France received $87 million and the USSR a mere $26 million (all at pre-war prices).[57] The total allocated by IARA to all recipients (again at pre-war prices) came to about $500 million, made up as shown in table 8.1

---

[54] 'German Defence Contribution: Economic and Financial Implications', Memorandum by the Prime Minister, 30 August 1951, CP(51)238, in PRO CAB 129/47.
[55] *The Economist*, 15 December 1951.
[56] PRO T 236/1505, 'Reparations'.
[57] These figures are based on the Reports of IARA (Brussels, 1948–50 and 1961). The Final Report in 1961 gave a total of $520.4 million, but did not show sub-headings within this total.

Table 8.1   Reparations from Western Zones allocated by IARA

	$ million
German external assets (in neutral hands)	269
Industrial capital equipment	143.5
Shipping	44.1
Captured enemy supplies	14.7
Reciprocal deliveries from USSR	1.5
Other	17.5
Total	502.3

The figures in table 8.1 are all in terms of the values reported to IARA, and there is no way of knowing how far these departed from fair market values. It is quite possible that some of the figures are a considerable understatement.[58] This seems to have been true of shipping[59] and it may also have been true of German external assets. A German estimate of total foreign assets owned in Germany at the end of the war puts them at RM 10 billion (about $3 billion), quite apart from patents, trademarks and other intangible assets which, it is claimed, came to as much again.[60] Very little of all this remained to Germany after seizure of assets in the belligerent countries, seizure by neutrals of assets allocated subsequently by IARA, and seizure by the USSR of German assets in Eastern Europe. The Western Allies laid claim to $400 million,[61] IARA distributed $269 million and the USSR seized at least as much. But the total reported falls far short of $3 billion and this may be due in part to undervaluation.

These doubts aside, it is evident that industrial capital equipment, the focus of the controversy over dismantling, was by no means the largest item and amounted to less than $150 million. Half of the total consisted of plants devoted entirely to the production of armaments. Equipment removed from the iron and steel industries was valued at about $30 million. No equipment at all was taken from the synthetic oil and ammonia plants.

[58] According to Sir Desmond Morton (PRO T 236/1505 'Reparations') all valuations were reached by a complicated process which 'competent technical observers' would agree 'writes down the average real monetary value of industrial capital equipment, even on a 1938 basis, by at least two-thirds'.
[59] Ibid.
[60] Stolper (1967) p. 179.
[61] PRO T 236/1505.

The number of plants scheduled for dismantling or destruction was progressively reduced after the first wave of advance factories had been put in hand. The 1,683 plants listed after the Reparations Plan in March 1946 had fallen to about 700 by April 1949 (of which roughly half were war plants), and by the end of 1949 dismantling had virtually ceased.[62] Different sources gave different figures, partly no doubt because the term 'plant' was ambiguous and was used by IARA to cover everything from an operating company to a single piece of equipment.[63] Moreover, what was listed, or notified to IARA, or even allocated by IARA, was not the same as what was ultimately despatched. Not that much had been allocated when it most mattered, in the first two years or so after the war. Up to October 1947, when the Bizone at last submitted a new list of plants allocated under the revised Reparations Plan, the only industrial assets available to IARA consisted of 60 plants designated as advance deliveries, 189 war plants and some general purpose equipment. At that stage, as Molotov complained at the December 1947 Conference of Foreign Ministers in London, deliveries to 20 Allied countries, including the USSR, had reached only $33 million. Bevin in reply claimed that equipment to the value of RM 400 million (say $120 million) had been allocated, but this is not quite the same as delivered. Even including advance deliveries, only RM 274 million (about $80 million) in industrial equipment had been notified to IARA for allocation by the end of 1947.

The removal of industrial equipment had no appreciable effect on West German production. There was little or no pressure on physical capacity in the post-war years, although much of the equipment needed extensive overhaul and the future of much of it was left in doubt for some years. From 1945 onwards Germany's capital stock was appreciably higher than in 1939, in spite of the bombing and war damage. For the years 1945–8, indeed, one German scholar puts the loss from depreciation and inadequate maintenance above the loss due to dismantling.[64]

[62] Clay (p. 324) gives an initial total of 1,546 plants valued at $600 million. General Marshall at the Moscow Conference in March 1947 gave figures showing 174 plants already allocated, 1,322 approved for valuation and 'several hundred others' at various stages of approval, making about 2,000 in all selected for reparations.
[63] Backer (1971) p. 79.
[64] Krengel (1958) pp. 93–6, 105. Clay's estimate (1950, p. 325) of a loss of $275 million includes the value of 719 plants due to be dismantled under the 1947 Plan. Only 400 plants *in all* had been notified to IARA by the end of 1948 and of those notified later nearly all were 'reprieved' under the Petersberg Agreement in November 1949. Harmssen (1951) uses an estimate of $625 million, but even if dismantled plant was undervalued this is certainly too high.

A total of $150 million for removals of capital equipment is far below what was taken from the Soviet zone, as we shall see in the next chapter. The larger total of $500 million allocated by IARA from beginning to end is no greater than the *annual* level of payments under the Dawes and Young Plans. Even Austria paid as much, if confiscated property is included, and what Russia received from the Eastern zone was between 10 and 20 times greater. The inflow of aid from abroad – about $4,000 million – far exceeded the outflow in reparations, in spite of all war-time resolutions to the contrary. It is little wonder that IARA kept complaining that the outflow was too little and too late, and pointing to the RM 8,000 million in gold marks that Germany paid within two years of the ending of the First World War.

But the $500 million distributed by IARA was not the whole story. Apart from German external assets in the hands of belligerents, estimated at $400 million, two additional items in particular imposed a heavy burden. The first was the gain derived by France, Czechoslovakia and other Allies from imports of German coal. At a time when coal was the main bottleneck in industrial production, the loss to Germany and the advantage to the importing countries far exceeded the value of the coal that was shipped; the fuel shortage was perhaps the most powerful factor delaying German recovery. Yet the coal moved for some considerable time without payment and eventually at an export price far below that of alternative supplies. From mid-1946 German coal was invoiced at $8 per ton, while American coal delivered at Le Havre was fetching $22 a ton.[65]

A second item was labour services. No estimate has ever been made of the value to Allied countries of the work done after the war by German prisoners of war retained in captivity. Inevitably it took time for the 7 million soldiers in Allied hands at the end of the war to be disbanded and returned home. Many, if not most, were held outside Germany and there was no great difficulty in finding work for them pending their return, whereas in Germany, food, housing and jobs were all alike scarce. Whether this justified delaying the release of prisoners once transport and other facilities were available is another matter, not disposed of by citing Nazi precedents or ensuring adequate pay and conditions. The economic loss to Germany may have been relatively small, at least for the first year or two, but the advantage to Allied countries was considerable.

In the British case, as we have seen, there were at least 200,000 prisoners of war in the UK in September 1945, of whom over half

[65] Gimbel (1976) pp.156–9; Balabkins (1964) p. 124; Abelshauser (1975) p. 143.

were in employment.[66] A year later there were said to be nearly 400,000 and 500,000 more in other parts of the Commonwealth.[67] By that time the French held nearly 1 million and it was not until April 1948 that they completed their release. The USA had already reached that stage in June 1947.[68] In Western Europe the services of German workers, if we adopt Keynes's assumption of £40 per head per year, must have been at least comparable in value with reparations in kind and quite possibly greater. In the Soviet Union, with far more prisoners – on one estimate, 3,500,000[69] – retained for far longer and on rather different terms, the value of the work done may well have run into billions of dollars.

[66] Above, p. 103.
[67] Balfour (1956) p. 164.
[68] Ibid.
[69] *The Economist*, 21 November 1946, quoted by Balfour (1956). The official Soviet figure at March 1947 was 890,000.

9

Soviet Reparations
from East Germany

There is no magic which distinguishes Soviet success in extracting reparations from Germany from Western failure, unless there is magic in the commonplace that if you really want something very much, you put it ahead of other things. The Russians . . . have sacrificed Allied goodwill, they have sacrificed the German Communist Party, and they have alienated German public opinion.

Peter Nettl, 'German Reparations in the Soviet Empire' (1951)

Soviet Policy on East Germany

In any government there are always competing interpretations of events and competing proposals for action. These differences are often associated with the interests and perceptions of particular departments, fed with different information, bearing different responsibilities, alive to different dangers, subject to different pressures, and above all with their own peculiar ethos and tradition. Within departments too there are disagreements, often peculiarly intense, between the individuals able to influence a policy that from the outside bespeaks a single view of things. Sometimes the disagreements are purely intellectual and there is no constancy in the line-up of supporters from one issue to the next. More commonly, there are ideological affiliations, and groups sharing a common outlook join forces along a wide front, like members of a political party. Common interests may also bind individuals together in a common loyalty to divisional chiefs. Thus in reviewing the history of policy on any major issue such as reparations we have to allow for twists and turns that reflect the influence of particular individuals and groups, an influence that may fluctuate widely for reasons unconnected with the issue in question.

Zhdanov

This is particularly true of the Soviet Union where, in the days of Stalin at least, policy took shape in a struggle between factions for power and dominance.[1] As is now well-known, one faction was led by Zhdanov and Voznesensky and one by Malenkov and Beria. While each espoused particular policies, their attachment to these policies was subordinate to their efforts to strengthen their following and weaken the opposing faction.

As Chairman of the Supreme Soviet's Foreign Affairs Committee and one of the four secretaries of the Central Committee of the Party, Zhdanov had been influential in promoting the Ribbentrop–Molotov Pact in 1939 and the subsequent Winter War with Finland. In June 1939 he had made a strong attack in *Pravda* on British and French plans for a mutual assistance pact with the USSR, and in 1940 continued to take a pro-German line, arguing that Germany could not successfully conduct a war on two fronts.[2] Although demoted after the German invasion, he remained in charge of the Leningrad military district and took credit for the successful defence of Leningrad. His co-ordination of the evacuation of industrial equipment from Leningrad during the siege of the city was later contrasted with the failure of his rival Malenkov to organize effectively the dismantling and removal of German industrial plants. Once the war was over his star rose rapidly and in 1946–7 he resumed the role of crown prince with increasing arrogance. Stalin, who had already got rid of two earlier Leningrad party bosses in Zinoviev and Kirov, appears to have become alarmed and may have had a hand in Zhdanov's sudden death in August 1947.[3] The more prominent members of his faction were removed a year later in the so-called 'Leningrad affair'.

Malenkov

Malenkov, another of the four secretaries of the Central Committee in 1939, was a more influential figure in the war; with Beria, he was for a time virtually running the newly created State Defence Committee. In 1943 the two of them were nominated to the Committee for the Rehabilitation of the Economy of Liberated Areas. The following year Malenkov became Chairman of the Special Committee set up to deal with the dismantling of German

[1] G. D. Ra'anan (1983) pp. 8–10.
[2] Ibid., pp.14–15.
[3] Ibid., pp.149–51.

industry. Thus, so far as East Germany was concerned, it was Malenkov who was in charge of reparations.

Malenkov's policy, soon to come under attack, was to do as much as possible to cripple German recovery. Economic disarmament took precedence over reparations, but so far as the two were compatible every possible advantage should be taken of the dismantling of German industry to obtain plant for reassembly in the USSR. Malenkov and Beria appear to have expected an eventual Soviet withdrawal from Germany and the reabsorption of the Soviet zone into a unified but disarmed Germany. They favoured, therefore, stripping their zone of its industrial infrastructure as quickly as possible, deliberately destroying some that could not be transferred, and pressing on with dismantling without regard to the limited facilities for packing, storing, transporting and reassembling. The result, discussed below, was something of a fiasco, denounced as such by Zhdanov and his allies.[4]

In parallel with the dismantling, but under other auspices, a programme of social and economic restructuring was being carried out. In the early stages this proceeded cautiously with no sweeping or irrevocable measures, in advance of the Potsdam Agreement, to restructure the economy and society of the Soviet zone.[5] But there were those who accepted from the start the goal of Sovietizing the zone and, later, the whole of Germany. Even Stalin, who was more anxious than other Soviet leaders to avoid a confrontation with the West, took it for granted that 'whoever occupies a territory also imposes on it his own social system. Everyone imposes his own system as far as his army has power to do so. It cannot be otherwise.'[6]

The Views of the Zhdanovites

For Zhdanov, Voznesensky and their supporters, the case was even simpler. The war was hardly over when they fell to denouncing Western imperialism, following the familiar totalitarian practice of attributing to less aggressive regimes the sins they were themselves engaged in committing. They took the lead in a militant, anti-Western stance in foreign policy, combining this with efforts to promote a *rapprochement* with Germany, starting with the Soviet zone. By consolidating their control over the zone they could hope to incorporate it gradually in the 'progressive camp' and use it as a

---

[4] Ibid., pp.22, 88.
[5] G. W. Sandford, *The Commanding Heights*, p. 92.
[6] M. Djilas, *Conversations with Stalin* (1962), p. 105.

base from which to win over (or perhaps liberate) the rest of Germany.

The Zhdanovite group regarded capitalism as in its third and final stage of crisis. World markets would narrow as more and more countries withdrew into the 'progressive camp' and the conflicts between capitalist countries would become more acute. As Vosnesensky was to put it in 1948: 'Imperialist expansion of the USA is moving towards a new war as a means of seizing world domination, and as a means of crushing democracy, preventing an economic crisis, and opposing the working class within the country.'[7]

Such views, which are descended from Lenin's *Imperialism*, were clearly shared by the Zhdanovites well before 1948. They were combined with a lurid picture of the economic (and political) prospects facing the Western world: the imminence of an early crisis of world capitalism, chronic unemployment because of the high level of productivity in the USA, and violent political upheavals, including war between the competing capitalist countries. More important, they treated conflict with the West as axiomatic, the demonstrable outcome of an accepted ideology. Zhdanov's stress on ideology, and the particular ideology he embraced, implied an unaccommodating line in negotiations over the future of Germany.

Within the zone, the Soviets made use of the group of Communists under Walter Ulbricht, whom they despatched from Moscow at the end of April 1945. In due course they arranged a shotgun wedding between the KPD (the Communist Party) and the SPD (the Social Democratic Party) to form the SED (Socialist Unity Party), which thereafter assumed office as the Government under Soviet direction. The formation of the SED was inspired by Zhdanov's representative in Germany, Colonel S. I. Tiul'panov, who worked closely with Ulbricht to remake the zone in the image of the USSR.

This implied a willingness to see the zone split off from the rest of Germany and many observers had come to the conclusion by the middle of 1946 that such a split was virtually inevitable.[8] On the other hand, Malenkov and Beria worked on the assumption of an eventual abandonment of the zone, Beria even after the creation of the East German state in 1949.[9] Stalin, himself, appears to have

---

[7] G. D. Ra'anan (1983) p. 69, quoting N. A. Voznesensky, *The Economy of the USSR during World War II* (1948).

[8] In June 1946, for example, Litvinov agreed that Germany would obviously be broken up into two parts. Each side wanted what it could not have, a unified Germany under its control. (See FRUS 1946, Vol. VI, p. 763.) An official of the Foreign Office was quoted to much the same effect (ibid., p. 758).

[9] Ra'anan (1983) p. 89.

198 *Soviet Reparations from East Germany*

looked toward German reunification until at least the middle of
1947, but had concluded by 1948 that 'the West will make Western
Germany their own and we shall turn Eastern Germany into our own
state'.[10]

Soviet Policy on Reparations

As the prospect of substantial reparations from the Western zones
faded, the Russians concentrated on squeezing their own zone hard.
They were determined to reach the total of $10 billion they had
demanded as their share at Yalta within the period of ten years they
had suggested; and there is every reason to think that they either
reached that total or came close to it. However much the Western
Allies might harp on the absurdity of such a target and the
formidable problem that large international transfers presented alike
to those who paid and those who received reparations, the Russians
were free of doubts and inhibitions in their pursuit of the goal they
had set themselves well before the end of the war.

No one knows with any precision how much the Russians took
from Germany. No one knows with certainty what they took from
other enemy countries: Austria, Finland, Hungary, Italy, Romania
and the rest.[11] Nor do we know what proportion was absorbed in
strengthening the Soviet Armed Forces rather than in promoting
economic recovery. Nevertheless it is clear that, in the absence of
loans and grants such as other European countries drew from the
USA, reparations must have made a substantial contribution to the
rehabilitation of the Soviet economy. Their target for German
reparations alone of about $10 billion at pre-war prices, or about
$20 billion at post-war prices, was well in excess of the $12.5 billion
received by Western Europe under the Marshall Plan, and what was
actually taken in reparations was at least comparable with Marshall
Aid. On the other hand, a larger proportion of Russia's takings than
of the total aid provided by North America (including the 1945 loan
of $5 billion to the UK) came after 1947, while it was the first three
post-war years that were most critical.

[10] Djilas (1962) p. 139.
[11] One estimate ('The Economic Situation of East Germany, 1950', Department of
State, OIR5202, 7 August 1950) yields a total of $880 million at current prices for the
value of assets acquired by the USSR in Eastern Europe. Over two-thirds of this was
from Austria. The other countries included are Bulgaria, Finland, Hungary and
Romania.

war booty of the closing months of the war and the early post-war period. Some of this was on private account by members of the army and the 70,000 Soviet officials, all in uniform, who roamed Eastern Germany in the summer of 1945.[12] Even in 1947–8, officers transferred back to the USSR were allowed to send home up to 2.5 tons of personal property while generals could send up to 10 tons.[13] Much larger amounts were commandeered by army units acting on instructions from Moscow. Special 'trophy units' were organized for the purpose of confiscating and sending back a wide variety of industrial and consumer goods. Army divisions were given detailed lists specifying the quantities of each commodity to be collected, and woe betide commanders who failed to comply in full. One list, for example, started with 100,000 tons of food grains, flour, sugar, cheese, etc., went on to 30,000 cattle, 40,000 sheep, 1,000 automobiles, 4,000 trucks, 500 tractors, etc., and finished with a long list of household goods including 5,000 pianos, 1,500 accordions, 12,000 rugs and 3,000 water-closets.[14] Even electric wiring was removed from private houses to meet a shortage in Russia.

These requirements were regularly fulfilled – whatever the necessary damage to property and physical violence to persons. The cumulative effect was a severe setback to economic recovery. The livestock population fell to half or less of its war-time level.[15] Agricultural production also suffered through lack of implements and fertilizers, and the general shortage of transport. What was left for the population was further reduced by consignments of food-stuffs to Russia. One official stated that in two months he personally sent back two trainloads of grain every ten days, that is, twelve trainloads in all.[16] By the autumn of 1946 there were fears of famine in what had been a region with a large export surplus of food.

Another form of reparations was the financial assets taken over by the Russians. These included the assets of the banks, all of which were closed down without compensation to shareholders and depositors. The funds so obtained, and the additional currency put into circulation, helped to meet occupation costs, but were also used

[12] V. Rudolph, 'The Administrative Organisation of Soviet Control, 1945–1948' in Robert Slusser (1953). Uniforms were worn partly in order to provide a legal basis for demanding the return of deserters.

[13] V. Yershov, 'Confiscation and Plunder by the Army of Occupation', in Robert Slusser (1953).

[14] Ibid. Only a third of the livestock survived the journey to their destination in the USSR because of inadequate supervision and lack of food. Shipments continued until the end of 1947, the final shipment consisting of 200,000 animals.

[15] Nettl (1951) p. 257.

[16] Yershov, in Robert Slusser (1953).

to acquire works of art and other valuables from Germans. The chief of the purchasing office in Brandenburg expended over RM 10 million in one month in this way, and the central office in Berlin despatched an entire trainload every week to the Ministry of Foreign Trade in Moscow with a cargo worth RM 50 million at 1938 prices.[17]

Another important source of reparations was the dismantling of industrial plants in the Russian zone. In the months before the Potsdam Agreement this went on at breakneck speed, apparently from fear that the Agreement might set limits to what could be taken in reparations. The result was a great deal of destruction, with relatively little economic benefit to the USSR.

Dismantling took place in waves. In May and June 1945 about 460 works in the Berlin area, many of them in industries of no military importance, were completely dismantled and removed. At first the chief targets were coal mine installations, railway repair shops, locomotive building plants, electrical works and power stations. In the summer and autumn, equipment was taken also from industries such as brick-making, textiles, papermaking and sugar-refining, and the second track was lifted from parts of the railway system in the Soviet zone. The next wave was in the spring and summer of 1946 when removals of track continued and 200 more works were dismantled: thereafter the rate of dismantling decreased and a number of works originally scheduled for dismantling were taken off the list. During the winter of 1946–7, however, there was further dismantling at the Zeiss works at Jena, power stations, printing works and some arms factories that had continued in production to meet Soviet requirements. Further removals took place in the autumn of 1947 and again in the spring of 1948, the first of these including about 700 miles of railway track as well as coalmining machinery and electricity generating equipment, while the second was largely confined to the partial dismantling of three of the SAG works.[18] In all, over 1,200 plants were totally or partially dismantled, a few of them repeatedly, and nearly one-third of the total value of movable industrial capacity was taken.[19] The process of dismantling was punctuated by announcements that dismantling was about to end, the first by Sokolovsky in May 1946, and the second – promising no further dismantling once work in hand on war industries was complete – in January 1947.[20] Nonetheless, it continued all through 1947 and spasmodically in 1948.

[17] V. Rudolph, ibid., p. 36.
[18] *DDR Handbuch* (3rd edition 1985, p. 1121); Nettl (1951) p. 301.
[19] Nettl (1951) p. 301.
[20] Ra'anan (1983) p. 91.

The experience of 1945–6 is well documented and is of interest for the light it throws on Soviet administration.

Conflict of Aims

From the beginning there was friction within the different agencies of the Soviet Government. In the first place there was a conflict of aims. Was the Soviet zone to be plundered *à outrance*, so as to reap the maximum immediate benefit to Soviet recovery, or would it be enough to dismantle German industry to the point at which there was no danger of a rapid revival and a renewal of German military strength? What priority was dismantling to enjoy in relation to the need to enlist German support for a programme of Sovietization that would turn East Germany into an outpost of the Soviet Union? Might it not be better to leave more plant in the zone, subject always to considerations of security, and milk it by drawing on the output so permitted in the form of current deliveries of reparations?

There seems no doubt that the Russians put military security first; and since, with dismantling, this could be made to yield a dividend in deliveries of plant and equipment from the dismantled factories, the secondary aim of reparations could be served simultaneously. But security might be better assured if the Soviet zone were to remain under Soviet control or was bound hand and foot to the Soviet economy, or was reconstituted as a 'People's Republic', that is, sufficiently in the image of a Communist regime to make it a natural friend and ally. These purposes were not promoted by dismantling which, if carried too far, made it more difficult to retain control, or link the two economies, or win support for a puppet government. Unless the means to a thriving economy were left in the Soviet zone it was unlikely to prove a dependable ally.

The impact on the rest of Germany had also to be considered. Germany held a central place in Soviet thinking. Fears of yet another invasion after a swift German recovery, recollections of how nearly Germany had gone Communist between the wars, hints that the USA might soon pull out, combined to incite the USSR to contemplate an extension over the whole of Germany of the kind of grip it already had on the Eastern zone. But such an extension would fail if the industry of the Eastern zone were left in ruins and its people in sullen destitution. Dismantling would not make the zone an inviting example of the future under a Communist regime.

Equally, dismantling might do little to speed up recovery in the USSR in comparison with the contribution that could be made through the mobilization of German manpower and plant in order to make the goods that Russia needed. For reasons given below, the loss of productive capacity to Germany when plant was dismantled far exceeded the value of the additional capacity established in the USSR. Even when the plant was successfully transferred, it took a great deal of time and extra expense to reassemble it and get it to work. Once in working order it still failed to produce the goods required soon enough, because of the lack of skilled workers and managers with the necessary experience.

Conflict Between Factions

The conflict of aims was compounded by a conflict of personalities struggling to assert themselves in the Soviet baronial power-structure.[21] A policy of dismantling German industrial plants, designed to weaken the German economy and strengthen the USSR through deliveries of capital equipment in reparations, was backed by Malenkov in particular. In 1944 he established the 'Special Committee under the Council of People's Commissars', which controlled the progress of economic disarmament in occupied territory, overriding both the military commanders on the spot (the GSOVG) and the authorities responsible for the military government of Germany (the SVAG). The Special Committee was represented in Berlin in the summer of 1945 by Saburov, Malenkov's protégé, who in 1949 became head of the State Planning Commission;[22] other representatives of the Special Committee were posted in each of the five Soviet provinces into which the Eastern zone was divided.

Malenkov encountered opposition from Zhdanov on political grounds, and from Mikoyan on economic grounds. Zhdanov was anxious to play on German nationalism and win support for a policy of Sovietizing East Germany. Mikoyan, as Minister of Foreign Trade, was more alive to he practical limitations of reliance on dismantled plant in rebuilding Soviet industry and to the advantages of using German capacity to produce what the USSR needed for the fulfilment of its plans. Among members of the Zhdanov faction was Voznesensky, then chairman of the State Planning Commission. Beria, the head of the secret police, although siding with Malenkov,

---

[21] On this see Gavriel D. Ra'anan (1983); and the testimony of Soviet refugees, in Robert Slusser (1953). Ra'anan seems to me to lay too much emphasis on the clan structure of the Soviet hierarchy, with attitudes to particular policies governed by alignments behind competing chieftains, and too little on inter-departmental in-fighting, with political figures acting as spokesmen for departmental interests.

[22] Saburov attended the Potsdam Conference as Deputy Chairman of SVAG. He was recalled to Moscow on other duties after the Conference.

and anxious to obtain German equipment for the NKVD's economic enterprises, was also, as the minister in charge of atomic research, opposed to the dismantling of German heavy industry required in exploiting the uranium deposits in Saxony.[23] Doubts about dismantling were also voiced by General Meklis of GSOVG, who was in charge of Soviet agitation and propaganda in Eastern Europe and found himself handicapped by a paper shortage. This led him in May 1945 to enter a protest against the dismantling of German paper factories and printing plants.

There is some reason to think that initially the Politbureau expected the Western Allies to insist on conditions of peace that would make it impossible to engage successfully in a policy of Sovietizing Germany, or even the Soviet zone of Germany.[24] Given Soviet fears of a rapid economic recovery of Germany, this reinforced the case for taking immediate action to dismantle or destroy plants within the Soviet zone and so under Soviet control. Later, in the months before the Potsdam Conference, the need for speed may have come from expectations that the Allies would call a halt to wholesale dismantling in favour of a systematic agreement on reparations. The more could be removed as war booty in advance of such an agreement the better.[25]

Whatever the reason, in the first half of 1945, dismantling went ahead with all possible speed and little apparent opposition. The aim appeared to be to dispose of the maximum number of enterprises in the shortest possible time, without much regard to the uses to which the equipment could be put. There was little or no general direction of the dismantling drive. Twelve hundred enterprises were dismantled in a fortnight, but even this pace was not considered sufficient and trophy units were given orders to switch from looting to dismantling. Only a fraction of what was dismantled could be moved and much of it lay out in the rain and weather. If it got to the marshalling yards at Brest-Litovsk there were no covered warehouses and goods had to be stacked on bare ground, subject to pilfering and exposure, unprotected even by a barbed wire fence, until the end of 1945.[26]

Loading was very disorderly. There were no inventories or bills of lading, and often no address or indication of destination, so that Soviet ministries spent years trying to trace missing items of

---

[23] Ra'anan (1983) p. 22n.

[24] V. Rudolph, 'The Administrative Organisation of Soviet Control, 1945–1948' in Robert Slusser (1953).

[25] V. Alexandrov, 'The Dismantling of German Industry' ibid.

[26] Ibid. Twenty-five trainloads from the Bluchermacher chemical plant were still on the ground several yeas later, rusting away.

equipment. There was no indication of the connection between one piece of equipment and another, and machinery from different factories became mixed up. When the equipment came to be assembled, blueprints and layouts were often missing because the dismantling crews had made a bonfire of all the paper in factory offices.[27]

It is little wonder, in these circumstances, that the Zhdanov faction gained ground and that dismantling became more discriminating. Before the end of 1945 a few dismantling orders had been countermanded because the plant was needed for use in Germany. The Military Government was in conflict with the Special Committee almost from the beginning, since its plans for the use of German factories and its efforts to make a systematic survey of available capacity were constantly being upset by fresh dismantling. In Moscow, Mikoyan, as the man responsible for carrying out the Reparations Plan (for production to meet Soviet requirements) had particular reason to seek more orderly arrangements. A tentative economic plan, submitted to Moscow for approval, was introduced in the final quarter of 1945, and as this evolved it naturally enveloped the arrangements of the Soviet authorities for milking the East German economy through current reparations deliveries. It was these deliveries that were threatened by the continued removal or destruction of capital equipment. Mikoyan and Malenkov were on a collision course.

The opposition to Malenkov's policy developed gradually and did not come to a head until well into 1946.[28] Mikoyan began by getting the activities of the Special Committee in Germany brought under the control of the SVAG. This made for more orderly arrangements but did not stop departments in Moscow from finding a way round and contriving to have German factories allocated to them for dismantling even when this interfered with SVAG's plans in Berlin. At the beginning of December 1945, Mikoyan succeeded in bringing all members of the staff of SVAG under the Ministry of Foreign Trade for pay and rations, where before their loyalty was to their parent department in Moscow from which they were seconded to SVAG.

The following month he made a more decisive move to secure priority for current deliveries over capital removals. The move arose

---

[27] Ibid.
[28] Ra'anan (1983) p. 91. In a speech in Berlin on 21 May 1946, Sokolovsky had already announced that dismantling virtually ceased on 1 May. A few war plants might still have to go but, that apart, removals were over ('USSR: Policy in Germany', PRO FO 943/308).

in connection with plans to bring 30 excavators from Germany in order to boost the production of cement. The output of cement in the USSR in 1945 was no more than about 4 million tons; a drive to expand production had been inaugurated by Kaganovich with the slogan 'Cement means the Five Year Plan'. It was planned to raise the output to 10.5 million tons by 1950 and to make use of German plant. But the only excavators that could be found in the Russian zone were at the V1 and V2 plants at Nordhausen and these were commandeered by the MVD for uranium mining. Mikoyan proposed to include in the Reparations Plan for 1945–7 24 cement factories with a total annual capacity of 6.5 million tons, and pointed to the advantages of leaving intact in Germany the necessary engineering equipment for this purpose. He suggested, however, that if Malenkov insisted on a safeguard, the enterprises producing the cement plant should be taken into Soviet ownership. This argument prevailed and was the origin of the idea of Soviet-owned corporations (SAGs) in Germany.[29]

Mikoyan did not, however, get his way in everything. A scheme for leaving SVAG in Berlin to co-ordinate the Reparations Plan was opposed successfully by Malenkov and Beria, with some support from Kaganovich and Bulganin who feared that the new arrangements would deny them access to reparations. The Plan (for which Mikoyan retained general responsibility) turned out to be a series of bids from the different ministries in Moscow without much regard to available capacity (which was an unknown quantity and shrinking). For this and other reasons, by the autumn of 1946 the Plan was falling scandalously short of fulfilment, and not a single set of equipment for cement manufacture had been completed.[30]

Meanwhile, in mid-1946 Zhdanov and Voznesensky set on foot an inquiry, under Mikoyan, into the dismantling process. Although this did not report until May 1947, Malenkov suffered immediate demotion and his policy lost ground. Mikoyan was able to call for the re-establishment of some of the industrial capacity of the zone, the cessation of removals except for iron and steel constructional material and equipment, the exclusion of 200 of the largest enterprises and their conversion to Soviet-owned corporations, and the winding up of the Special Committee after the despatch of the plants already dismantled. This programme was adopted and with

[29] Much of the argument developed over the Krupp–Gruson plant in Magdeburg after the withdrawal of Allied forces from the town.
[30] The electrical engineering industry in the Soviet zone had been so completely destroyed that it was unable to supply the electrical equipment needed by the cement plants.

the submission of the report in May 1947 the Special Committee ceased to exist. Many of its functions had already been transferred to the SVAG in the autumn of 1946, when the major change of policy occurred.[31]

On this interpretation of events, the changes in Soviet policy in 1946 had nothing to do with any Allied activities after the Potsdam Agreement and were a response to purely domestic pressures, not to those activities or to what was said and done in quadripartite negotiations.

Conflict between Departments

Finally there was a conflict between departments. Most of the Soviet officials who swarmed over the Eastern zone in 1945 had been seconded to the Soviet Military Government (SVAG) but they still looked to their parent department for pay and a career. Thus when they lent a hand to the dismantling process it was usually with an eye to some need of their parent department in its efforts to meet the programme laid down for it by the Soviet planning authority, Gosplan. If they spotted some likely piece of equipment they could usually make use of a colleague from the same ministry to get them the necessary authorization for its removal. In this way, 'aviation factories were allocated to the Ministry for the Meat and Dairy Industry merely because they contained metal-working lathes needed in the repair shops of the enterprises subordinated to that ministry'.[32] The Minister for Heavy Machine Construction, Kazakov, on a visit to Berlin, could arrange for Koval, a senior member of his ministry acting as Deputy Chief of SVAG, to take time off and show him round in the spring of 1946, so that he could pick and choose the equipment he wanted and then, on his return to Moscow, draw up specifications for reparations orders, confident that they would be met.

Departments fought one another to have equipment allocated to them, each seeking all it could get from Germany. The battle was not confined to officials since they inevitably brought in ministers in support and the issue might only be resolved by the Council of Ministers or even the Politburo.

The confusions of policy, the ministerial battles, and the departmental in-fighting were perhaps less important than the practical difficulties in the way of moving plant and equipment from Germany to Russia and getting it back into working order. These difficulties

[31] This account rests largely on V. Rudolph, in Robert Slusser (1953).
[32] Ibid., p. 21.

arose partly from haste and inexperience, and partly from an acute shortage of storage and transport facilities. It is easy, as one reads the horror stories of waste, destruction and intrigue, to overlook what *did* get to Russia and *was* of use. There is some evidence that where the military were directly involved, as with aero-engine factories, or the equipment was for the hush-hush First Administration (uranium mining and the atom bomb), much greater care was taken, from packing to transport and delivery. It may have been the low priority items that tended to rust in the open or be mislaid, or be incapable of reassembly. All one can say is that the Russians clearly overdid dismantling and would have been much wiser – certainly in retrospect and perhaps even if they were right to fear too rapid a German recovery – to have destroyed much less and started earlier to plan for current deliveries from the remaining plant.

Estimates of Russian Takings

How much did the Russians take from East Germany? We may begin by looking at Russian statements.

There could be no concealing the large demands made by the Russians on the German economy; periodic announcements about them were made both by the Russians themselves and by leading Germans in the zone. Ulbricht, for example, announced that in 1948 reparation demands would amount to 17 per cent of planned net industrial production and occupation costs to a further 8 per cent. It appeared to be implied that if there were a shortfall in the Plan it would not fall on reparation demands; and since production did not in fact show the expected growth, the actual proportions must have been correspondingly larger.[33]

In May 1950 the Russians announced that they would consider the amount paid to the end of 1950 as $3,658 million out of the Yalta total of $10 billion which they now proposed to reduce to $6,829 million by cutting the outstanding amount in half.[34] The balance of $3,171 million was to be paid in 15 annual instalments of $211 million. Three years later, in August 1953, when they agreed to end reparations in the following year, the figures published implied that three annual instalments had been paid since 1950 and no more, bringing the total to $4,292 million. This total excludes occupation costs, for which official figures have been published in respect of the years after

[33] 'Economic Position in the Soviet Zone' PRO FO 944/670.
[34] Department of State, 'The East German Economy at the end of the First Five Year Plan', OIR 7131, 15 June 1956, p. 16. All these figures are at pre-war prices.

1948.[35] In 1949–53 these averaged about DM 2 billion, and the figure for 1948 is known to have been similar. Assuming a slightly lower average in 1945–7, we can put the total for 1945–53 at about $3.2 billion in pre-war dollars. Thus the Soviet Union acknowledged a total call on German goods and services (without payment) in those years of $7.5 billion in pre-war dollars (and about double that figure, i.e. $15 billion, in current dollars).

There are good grounds for regarding this total as too low. Several estimates by German writers yield much higher figures; Bevin quoted an estimate of $7 billion at the meeting of the Council of Foreign Ministers at Lancaster House on 15 December 1947; and American intelligence reports put the takings, other than occupation costs, at nearly double the acknowledged amount.

The estimate quoted by Bevin came from a brief by A. W. Bechter.[36] This gave a total of $7.2 billion, presumably at current prices, to the middle of 1947, made up of $4 billion in industrial capital equipment, $1.2 billion in railway track and equipment and public utilities plant, and $2 billion in current deliveries. Between the end of June and the end of October the total might have risen to about $7.75 billion through the removal of brown coal and briquetting plant to the value of $300,000, and a further $250,000 in current deliveries. The total excluded anything taken from territory now occupied by Poland, labour services and financial and other assets such as cash, gold, foreign exchange, works of art, etc.[37] Bechter pointed out that the Soviets had taken plant from industries which it had been agreed at Potsdam should not be restricted. What they took from current production was charged to reparations account at prices related to 1938 levels, while higher prices might have to be paid by the German authorities in meeting production costs.

Bechter's estimates are not very circumstantial or sophisticated and may be too high.[38] He estimated that 70 per cent of current production (presumably GNP) went to the USSR and doubted

---

[35] The official figures include large payments for 'goods deliveries to the occupation authorities', a substantial part of which consisted of machinery, basic chemicals, etc. and may be reparations in disguise. The fact that the proportion of goods deliveries to the occupation authorities to total goods deliveries rose from 21 per cent in 1947–9 to 33 per cent in 1953, strengthens this suspicion. (OIR 7131, p. 16n.)

[36] 'Economic Conditions in the Soviet Zone', December 1947, in PRO FO 371/64312.

[37] On Soviet removals of gold and other assets from the Reichsbank, see Sayer and Botting, *Nazi Gold* (1984). The Soviet Army removed from the Reichsbank negotiable bonds payable in gold or dollars to the value (in 1945) of $400 million. In 1950 the German Federal Government enacted legislation validating pre-war bonds but only if the bearer could prove ownership on 1 January 1945.

[38] He says that US estimates were 'at one time much lower' ('The Two Year Economic Plan for the Soviet Zone', in PRO FO 644/670).

whether more than 5 per cent of the output of producer goods and 10 per cent of the output of consumer goods were absorbed into the German economy.

American Estimates

A fuller picture of German takings in the early post-war years is given in an American intelligence report dated 15 November 1948.[39] A summary is given in table 9.1:

Table 9.1 Reparations from the Soviet Zone, 1945–48

	Value in 1938 RM million
Capital removals and acquisitions	
Industrial equipment	
from the Soviet zone and Berlin	3,300 – 4,300
from the Western zones	140
Transportation equipment	
rail	170
shipping	94
Real assets of Soviet Corporations	1,600 – 2,000
Other industrial property and real estate	200
Total	5,500 – 6,900
Current production	
Industrial and mining output	
reparation orders	3,600
other deliveries to the USSR	3,200
Uranium ore mining	140
	6,940
Less raw materials supplied by USSR	400
Agricultural output	700
Transportation services	300
Total	7,540
External assets	500
Grand total	13,540 – 14,940

[39] OIR Report No. 4792, *Soviet Takings from Germany 1945–48* (Department of State, Division of Research for Europe).

Taking a rate of 30 cents to the Reichsmark, and omitting external assets and equipment from the Western zones, these figures yield a total of $3.9–4.3 billion at 1938 prices to the end of 1948. The estimates were intended to represent 'values delivered to the borders of the Soviet zone or to Soviet consumers within the zone', rather than the loss to the German economy which might be appreciably higher.

Three of the items call for special comments: (1) the assets of German corporations acquired by the USSR; (2) the estimate of removals of industrial equipment; and (3) uranium mining.

The assets of 213 industrial plants in the Eastern zone were taken over by the Soviet authorities in mid-1946, and subsequently organized as Soviet-owned Corporations (SAGs). They were not removed from East Germany and were later given back (although not to their original owners). The last 33 plants, accounting for about 20 per cent of East German industrial production, were returned without compensation in 1953, but payments to an unknown extent were made on earlier transfers to the East German Government. Whatever the figure credited to reparations account in 1948 (which table 9.1 puts at RM 1,600–2,000 million), a different figure would be appropriate in 1953, and not necessarily a lower one.[40]

The figure for industrial equipment removed may well be an underestimate. It starts from an estimate for 1939 of the industrial capital of the Altreich (i.e. Germany within the 1937 frontiers), adds 10 per cent for new equipment installed during the war, deducts 20 per cent – surely far too much – for war damage, and divides the total by three to get the share of the Eastern zone. This is then reduced by a quarter to get the fair market value, allowing for undermaintenance and dismantling. Finally, US estimates that 30–40 per cent of industrial capacity was removed are applied, yielding the RM 3,300–4,300 million shown in table 9.1.

The RM 140 million shown for uranium mining is almost certainly an underestimate. By 1950, according to a later American report, expenditure for this purpose was up to RM 700 million a year. In 1953 it was estimated that 250,000 workers, 3 per cent of the working

[40] OIR 7137 (1956) pp. 9–10. In February 1947 74 plants were returned to the German authorities and in 1950, 23 more. The remaining 116 plants employing about 325,000 workers were organized in 30 holding companies (SAGs), which had diminished to 12 by early 1952. They accounted for nearly one-third of total industrial production and about half their output went for reparations. More plants were returned in 1952 and only 33 larger plants remained under Soviet control by 1953. It is likely that payments by the East German authorities amounted to at least RM 500 million at pre-war prices; they may well have been a good deal more.

population of East Germany, were engaged in uranium mining and supporting operations, financed by the German authorities for the sole benefit of the USSR.[41]

Table 9.1 brings out the wide variety of things taken in reparations. The RM 170 million of railway equipment, for example, includes rolling stock, signalling equipment and one-third of the entire railway track (including all second track). All this was removed when East (and West) Germany was chronically short of transport. The figure for shipping represents the Soviet share of Germany's merchant marine; that for agriculture is about 10 per cent of the value of agricultural output; and the RM 500 million for transportation services assumes that freight costs added 4–5 per cent to the value of goods shipped to the USSR.

There is a great deal that is not included. Military equipment, the value of territory annexed, personal property confiscated, the property of expellees, intangible assets, stocks, and services of all kinds other than transport are all omitted. Nothing is shown for money appropriated: banks and other financial institutions were mulcted of RM 3 billion and additional currency was issued to the value of RM 8–12 billion in the form of military marks.[42] Similarly, nothing is shown for levies on the East German budget or the profits of Soviet trading organizations or back pay made over to Soviet troops in 1945; budget appropriations in 1945–8 may have totalled nearly RM 17 billion.[43] It would be wrong, however, to count both the value of what was transferred and the money with which the various transactions were financed.

A later American intelligence report in 1956 includes estimates covering the period 1945–53, which are shown in table 9.2.

If we leave out occupation costs, this yields a total for 1945–53 of RM 20.5 billion or $6.15 billion at the pre-war prices in which the Soviet figures were calculated. This is nearly $2 billion higher than the total of $4.3 billion officially acknowledged for the same period. One reason for the discrepancy is that the American estimate assumes that Soviet takings continued at much the same rate after 1950, while the Soviet figure assumes a sharp drop. Instead of the official $634 million the American total adds nearly $2 billion for the

[41] US Department of State, 'The Economic Situation in East Germany', IR No. 6415, 28 October 1953. The DDR Handbuch (1985) gives a figure of 225,000 for 1951. Bechter in 1947 put the total at 50,000, not all at one time (PRO FO 371/64312). Nettl (1951, p. 195) gives an estimate of 40,000 for 1946.
[42] OIR No. 5202, 'The Economic Situation in East Germany 1950', 7 August 1950.
[43] For the period 1945–52 German sources put total annual payments from public budgets to the Soviets at RM/DM 4.5 billion or a total of DM 37 billion (OIR No. 7131, p. 13).

Table 9.2 Soviet takings from East Germany, 1945 – 53

	1945–48	1949	1950	1951	1952	1953	1954–53	1945–53 in $ billion of 1936 purchasing power[a]	1945–53 in $ billion at current values[a]
Industrial & transportation equipment	4.0	–	–	–	–	–	4.0	1.2	2.4
Current deliveries of reparations & other unrequited goods	(5.5)	1.6	1.5	1.4	1.3	1.1	12.5	3.75	7.5
Uranium mining	(0.4)	(0.4)	0.7	0.9	0.9	0.9	4.0	1.2	2.4
Services for Soviet troops and authorities	(5.3)	(1.3)	1.1	1.1	1.1	1.1	11.0	3.3	6.6
Direct takings	(15.2)	3.3	3.3	3.4	3.3	3.1	31.5	9.45	18.9
GNP at market prices			19.2	21.8	23.5	24.9			
Soviet takings as percentage of GNP at market prices			17.2	15.6	14.0	12.4			

[a] Converting at the rate of 30 cents per RM (rather than the official rate of 40 cents) and taking current prices to be double pre-war prices in dollars.
Source: Department of State, 'The East German Economy at the end of the First Five Year Plan', OIR 7131, 15 June 1956, table 8.

three years 1951–3. This by itself accounts for $1.32 million out of a divergence of $1.85 million. In other words, a comparison made for the years 1945–50 would show a far smaller discrepancy than one including the years 1950–3.

The Soviet figures also assume that no reparations deliveries were made after 1953, whereas US estimates indicate a further delivery of

RM 500 million in 1954–5, together with an annual expenditure in those years, met by the East German authorities, of RM 900 million on uranium mining and an equal amount on occupation costs.[44] On top of this, American intelligence reports show an additional levy from 1951 onwards in the form of less favourable terms of trade than similar transactions at world prices would have involved. In other words, the Soviet authorities are alleged to have rigged the prices at which German exports were exchanged for imports from the USSR so as to exploit the East German economy. The amounts involved are substantial. The US figures show a rise from RM 500 million in 1951 and 1952 to RM 1 billion in 1953 and RM 1.5 billion in 1954 and 1955. The implication is that as reparations deliveries faded out, the USSR relied increasingly on purchases at artificially favourable prices.

These estimates yield an aggregate for 1954–5, excluding occupation costs and the terms of trade effect, of RM 2.3 billion or $0.7 billion (at 1936 prices), bringing the total for 1945–55 up to $6.85 billion (again, in pre-war dollars). If the terms of trade deterioration is included, the US estimate for the 11 years 1945–55 reaches $8.35 billion, while the addition of occupation costs brings the total to $11.5 billion, of which $6.7 billion falls in the six years after 1949 and $4.8 billion in the five years 1945–9. This may appear to imply an increasing burden over the decade on the East German economy. But since GNP was increasing rapidly from the very low level to which it sank in 1945–6, a constant absolute level of Soviet takings of goods and services (there was little change between 1949 and 1953) was consistent with a perceptible fall in the proportion they bore to GNP. Excluding the terms of trade effect, the US estimates imply a drop in the total burden on the East German economy from over 17 per cent in 1950 (and substantially higher figures in earlier years) to 12.4 per cent in 1953 and to a little over 7 per cent of GNP at market prices in 1955.[45]

German Estimates

Many other estimates of Russian takings have been made, especially by German writers.[46] The DDR Handbuch, for example, gives a total for the period up to 1953 of DM 66.4 billion, presumably at

---

[44] These figures and all others in this paragraph are at 1936 prices.

[45] The US estimates are taken from OIR 7131 (1956), table 8.

[46] Among non-German writers see Gottlieb (1960), Nettl (1951) and Nutter (1962). Gottlieb (p. 138) estimates the pre-war value of all industrial equipment removed from the Soviet zone at RM 3.75 billion. This excludes office equipment, railway track and wagons and public utility (e.g. power station) equipment. Nettl (pp. 237–8) gives a total to the middle of 1948 (at 1936 prices) of RM 11.5 billion, of which RM 4.1 billion

current prices.[47] If we deduct DM 16 billion included as occupation costs (the American report gives a figure of DM 17.5 billion) and convert to dollars at current prices, using the official exchange rate of DM 4.2 = $1, we get a total of $12 billion. Since dollar prices in the middle of the period were roughly double dollar prices before the war, this suggests a total in pre-war dollars of about $6 billion, that is, much the same as the $6.5 billion given above for the period to 1953. However, the official rate probably undervalued the Deutschmark, so conversion at the official rate is likely to yield too low a total in pre-war dollars. Once allowance is made for 1954 and 1955 and 15 per cent is added to bring the total into line with Maisky's calculations at Yalta, we get a minimum of $7.7 billion, excluding occupation costs and 'exploitation in trade', and more probably a figure of between $8 billion and $9 billion. The German total is reached by a different route and includes the items set out in table 9.3.

Some doubt attaches to the DDR Handbuch estimate because of the risk of double-counting when data on financial appropriations are combined with data on 'real' transactions. It is not altogether clear what the Soviet authorities did with the bank assets they confiscated and the military marks that they put into circulation. Their holdings of cash were not written down in value when the currency reform took place in 1948 and private holdings were reduced in value by 90 per cent. But how far these funds were applied to the finance of occupation and other costs, and how far they added to the flow of reparations in ways not recorded in table 9.2 is impossible to establish.

There is also some uncertainty about the last three items in the German estimate for which no specific provision is made in the American figures. Payments towards the repurchase of SAGs before the handing back of the remaining plants in 1953 *may* have been as high as DM 2.55 billion; the American report is content to suggest a

represents dismantled capital goods, RM 4.4 billion current production and stocks, RM 1 billion food and RM 2 billion shipments from the SAGs. He also indicates that in addition the Soviet authorities held a reserve of RM 7 billion as the excess of receipts and subsidies from German public bodies over all outgoings. Nutter (p. 352) gives a figure in 1938 dollars of $6.2 billion for total reparations from East Germany.

Of early German estimates the best known are those of Harmssen (1951).

[47] DDR Handbuch, 3rd edn, 1985, pp. 1121–4. These estimates are based on the work of Franz Rupp, published in *Bonner Berichte aus Mittel- und Ostdeutschland*, 1951, and 1953. The conversion of current DM into pre-war dollars is inevitably rather arbitrary and there is a further difficulty in converting East German marks into West German marks. According to Dr Johannes Kuppe (letter of 24 November 1985), the Russians generally used a conversion rate of 2.5 to $1 but others have used rates as low as 6:1.

Table 9.3 German estimate of Soviet takings

	DM billion
Works of art and other booty	2
Dismantled equipment	5
Products bought with looted cash or occupation notes (including uranium mining DM 7.5 billion)	15
Current deliveries charged to reparation account	34.7
Transport and other costs involved	2.85
Subsidies to SAG enterprises	3.3
Working capital for SAGs and capital removals from them	1.0
Cost of repurchase of SAGs	2.55
Total	66.40

Source: DDR Handbuch, 3rd edition, 1985.

minimum of DM 870 million. Half the output of the SAGs went at subsidized prices to the USSR, but whether the allowance of DM 3.3 billion in the German figure went wholly for this purpose, or is partly duplicated under other headings, is not altogether clear. On the other hand, the American report makes no attempt to evaluate separately 'unofficial takings' financed out of SAG profits (DM 1.2 billion in 1951 alone); and it admits that there is a substantial gap between aggregate funds available to the Soviet authorities over the period and the various outgoings for which it is able to account.

Russian Success in Extracting Reparations

What was taken from East Germany dwarfs what was taken from Western Germany. Reparations from current production in the Western zones were negligible and the value of capital plant (at pre-war prices) delivered to the end of 1949 was under RM 500 million, compared with about RM 4 billion taken from the Eastern zone. Against this has to be set the cost to the UK and USA of paying for German imports of food. In some post-war years Britain alone was spending more than RM 500 million *annually* for this purpose.[48]

[48] In the 18 months from 1 January 1947 to 30 June 1948, the UK spent £113 million on relief imports, involving a net drain of $260 million from Britain's almost negligible reserves (PRO T236/1018).

Thus Russia succeeded in extracting reparations on a scale which Western observers regarded as virtually impossible. That the population of East Germany suffered severely from these exactions need not be doubted. The population of the Soviet Union suffered too over the same years, as a result of the destruction the Germans had wrought. In spite of the dismantlings and removals and the heavy burdens they continued to bear when all that ceased, the East Germans recovered remarkably fast, even if they lagged well behind their West German neighbours. That they did so in spite of their handicaps is not without its implications for theories of economic growth and development. Given peace, stability and a widening market, an industrious, knowledgeable and strongly-motivated people can overcome many obstacles that prove overwhelming under other conditions and in other countries.

There were special features of this experience with reparations that made it very much a special case. One of these was the 'enclosed' nature of the transfer. Neither Russia nor East Germany carried on a large trade with other countries. Even in 1960 Russia's trade was no greater than Switzerland's. East Germany, which had conducted about two-thirds of its trade with West Germany before the war, and only 15 per cent or so with Russia and Poland, began to trade almost exclusively with the USSR while the volume of its trade with West German fell to negligible proportions and even in 1951–2 had reached only 5–10 per cent of its pre-war volume.[49] The market which East Germany supplied was not one in which it faced foreign competition, and it was a market that grew automatically with the supply. Thus there were none of the transfer difficulties and disruptions of international markets that are likely to accompany the efforts of one industrial country to make large-scale payments of reparations to another.

A second relevant feature was that the paying country was prostrate and in the firm grip of the receiving country. Neither the consumer nor the taxpayer could withstand the demands made upon them, nor could they evade them by bringing the country to a stand-still through strikes, campaigns against higher taxes, or demands that produced hyperinflation. The Soviet authorities could insist on levies that added up to 17 per cent or more of East German GNP without meeting with effective resistance until the riots of 1953 obliged them to moderate their claims. Without the powers that the USSR could exert and the anomie of the defeated Germans, it would not have been possible to channel so much of East Germany's trade to unfamiliar destinations in the USSR. The deliveries of reparations

[49] ECE, *Quarterly Bulletin for Europe*, Third quarter 1949, p. 26.

on which the Russian planners counted were also built into the plans of the East Germans after scrutiny and approval by Gosplan. There was no question of competition or price adjustments. The transfer was an international transfer only in a Pickwickian sense.

Impact on East Germany

The Soviets persevered with a target of $10 billion for reparations from Germany to be delivered over a period of ten years. They received little from Western Germany but held for many years to their target, hoping to make up from their own zone what they were denied from the rest of Germany.

When the Soviets were obliged by the aforementioned riots of 1953 to modify their plans in East Germany, they would appear to have received goods to the value of over $5 billion – and this apart from miscellaneous forms of loot and labour services (perhaps another $1 billion or so). The loss to East Germany, given the conditions under which dismantling was conducted, would be somewhat greater. Much the largest element in the total was the flow of goods from current production which initially took about half the net value added by industry in the Soviet zone, about one-third in 1948, and a diminishing proportion thereafter as industrial output expanded. Capital removals were largely confined to the first two years and did not much exceed $1 billion. By 1953 the costs of uranium mining borne by the East Germans had reached a similar total and were still continuing.

The burden on East Germany, including occupation costs and the forfeiting of trade gains resulting from the prices fixed in trade with the USSR, can be roughly estimated at $23 billion over the years 1945–55, or about $18.5 billion (at current prices) to the end of 1953. As a proportion of GNP, Soviet takings still came to over 17 per cent in 1950–1, but had fallen to under 13 per cent by 1955 or, if trading forfeits are excluded, to about 7 per cent.

The burden fell partly on investment which remained relatively low as a proportion of GNP (13–15 per cent in the years 1951–5), but mainly on consumption. Not only did this fall to an extremely low level in the immediate post-war years, when there was near famine in 1946, and a level of consumption per head in 1947 two-thirds below the depressed level of 1936, but in the years after 1950 the proportion of GNP devoted to personal consumption remained obstinately around 50 per cent, compared with over 60 per cent before the war. The East German consumer was the main contributor to reparations through forgoing an exceptionally large slice of what he produced.

Nevertheless, large reparation payments did not prevent industrial recovery and in some ways contributed to it. By 1953 East Germany's industrial production was well above the 1936 level (US estimates suggest by 13 per cent, official figures by very much more), while consumption per head may have been as much as 20 per cent below. East Germany may have lagged behind West Germany but its rate of expansion was impressive. In the six years 1947–53, GNP, even on Western calculations, grew by 70 per cent.

10

Concluding Reflections

Whether life in Germany is tolerable from 1949 onwards will depend
far more on the prosperity of the world than on the precise extent of
removals of capital equipment now.

S. D Waley to E. Playfair, 26 November 1945

If we stand back from the detail of the Reparations Plan and the
rhetoric of inter-Allied disagreements, the picture that emerges is
indeed paradoxical. Western Germany, now probably the richest
country in *Western* Europe, paid about $150 million in reparations in
the form of capital equipment, $350 million in other forms distributed
through IARA, and at least $400 million more in external assets – a
total of about $1 billion. Eastern Germany, now the richest country
in *Eastern* Europe, paid at least $7 billion at pre-war prices and
$14 billion at current prices in capital equipment and current
production (including the value of work in the uranium mines). The
lion's share of reparations from Western Germany was taken by the
UK and the USA, neither of which had shown any overwhelming
desire for reparations; all reparations from Eastern Germany went
to the USSR. Western Germany received about $4 billion in aid,
Eastern Germany little or nothing. The UK, which had financed the
war with the aid of sales of foreign assets and by running up
international debts to the tune of $20 billion, was obliged when the
war was over to subsidize Germany. The USSR, which had probably
suffered a rather smaller net capital impairment (in the form of war
damage within the USSR, not on external account), recovered in
reparations from Germany alone at least half of what it had lost;
indeed on some calculations it may have come close in post-war

years to absorbing capital from abroad, in aid and reparations, equal
to the damage it suffered in war.

We can draw one very obvious conclusion. So far as its purpose
was to make reparations available to Russia and other countries,
dismantling German industry was an utter failure, while the
possibilities of reparations from current production were much
larger than anyone (including the Russians) thought by the end of
the war.

The Possibilities of Agreement between the Four Powers

The figures also prompt a question: was there no way in which an
accommodation could have been reached between the four major
powers that were at loggerheads over reparations?

They started, after all, from much the same premises. Germany's
war potential must be smashed; and if this meant that a vast amount
of industrial equipment was redundant, it could be removed in
reparations without detriment to an eventual recovery of the
German economy. Even the British, in Moscow and at Potsdam,
were never in doubt that there was plenty to spare – although not, it
is true, as much as $10 billion. If there were initial fears that
industrial capital equipment might have suffered heavy loss from
bombing and other war damage, these fears had been set at rest well
before the Potsdam Conference; and after Potsdam there was no
longer an incentive to withhold supplies so as to drive a better
bargain with Russia. The four powers not only could, but did, reach
agreement on a Reparations Plan by March 1946.

By 1947 both sides had learned the difficulties, disadvantages and
disappointments attendant on efforts to take delivery of reparations
in the form of capital equipment. Both were prepared to accept the
need to revise upwards the level of German industry permitted
under the Reparations Plan. Each had at one time or another
contemplated a flow of reparations from current production in the
Western zones. Could they not have foreseen earlier that such a flow
would raise fewer problems and be more in keeping with longer-
term needs? Might they not have reached agreement that, from the
start, reparations should come almost exclusively from current
production? Was it out of the question to satisfy the Russians by
making deliveries of finished goods from Western Germany on an
increasing scale, comparable with the deliveries Russia obtained
from the Eastern zone from 1946 onwards? If the Eastern zone could
do it, why not the rather more industrial part of the country in the
West?

To all these questions only a dusty answer can be given. By 1947 reparations were far from the only source of disagreement between Russia and the Western powers, and accommodation to Russian demands had come to be viewed as appeasement. The question what form reparations should take could not be reconsidered dispassionately in that atmosphere. There had never been, even in wartime, a great deal of trust on either side; active collaboration at the working level such as existed between the Western Allies had been extremely limited; the ideas, values and long-term aims of East and West were far apart. Each wanted to remake Germany in its own image, and each assigned Germany a different role in European reconstruction. The UK and the USA became increasingly alive to the central importance of German economic recovery in European reconstruction and the solution of the dollar problem. For Russia, on the other hand, what economic recovery was permitted must lag behind her own and accrue to her benefit first and foremost; the last thing she wanted was a German recovery over which she had no control. As Russian suspicions and insecurity came to the surface, Soviet policy overreacted, awakening a similar alarm in the West: Russia's attitude to her Western Allies once the war was over seemed more and more akin to her attitude to Germany in 1940. Under these conditions, the quadripartite rule was poisoned by distrust and fear that the military strength of Germany would pass into the hands of 'the other side'. Where competition for German support began to take the place of collaboration in keeping Germany down, the Western powers had little incentive to placate the Russians by imposing fresh burdens on their zones, weakening the German economy and antagonizing the population.

Other difficulties prevented an earlier agreement on reparations from current deliveries. One cannot assume away the learning process. Both sides were hopeful at the start that substantial capital reparations could be removed within the first two years. They took little account of the heavy burden in skilled manpower, scarce packing materials and still scarcer transport facilities that the dismantling programme involved, of the difficulties of successful re-erection, or of the diversion of effort from more immediate tasks. Until the Russians had suffered severe disappointment through the poor yield from their own efforts and the long delays in the West, they showed little interest in deliveries from current production in the Western zones. The Western powers were equally set initially on a programme of dismantling, and regarded current deliveries as something to come later, if at all, after balance between exports and imports had been restored.

Dismantling in 1945 had become a fixation: it, too, cannot be assumed away. The destruction of Germany's armaments factories and the restriction of her 'war potential industries' were articles of faith that sprang from fears of a renewal of German military power and persisted long after the end of the war. A proposal to take current deliveries in reparations if made in 1945–6 would have been on top of existing demands, not in substitution for them.

While the taking of current deliveries cut across dismantling of capital equipment, some combination of the two was not impossible, as experience in East Germany showed. There was a substantial surplus of capital equipment in 1945, and even if far more had been removed, its loss would have had little or no immediate effect on industrial production. The difficulty in meeting Russian demands did not lie in any setback to industrial expansion from the low point in 1945 that larger reparations would have produced. It lay partly in the practical difficulties of dismantling and shipping, and partly in Western reluctance to offer *both* capital equipment *and* current output to Russia when she was already drawing heavily on her zone and refusing to incorporate it in a single country-wide economy. This reluctance was reinforced by growing German resistance to dismantling and Western awakening to the danger of alienating German opinion when Russia was making a bid to win it over.

One has also to take some account of the magnitudes involved. There was no real prospect of reparations in capital equipment from the Western zones reaching a total within two or even three years of the $2–3 billion that Molotov wanted from the Ruhr, much less the $6–7 billion from the Western zones implied in his original demand for capital deliveries of $10 billion from Germany. Dismantling and shipment on that scale within two years was much too ambitious. Yet out of $6 billion the USSR would have received only $1,500 million; and only $600 million would have been without payment. The rest would have required payment either from the USSR or from East Germany; and if from the latter it amounted to an equivalent sacrifice of deliveries to the USSR and so came to much the same thing. Was it really worth all the fuss for at the very most $600 million of equipment? Moreover, is it not implicit in such a calculation that the demand for reparations from current production was a new and additional demand?

On the other hand, if the deliveries from current production that the Soviet really wanted took the form of steel and heavy machinery, would it have been any easier to organize a flow of those goods to the USSR worth $600 million in the first two to three years? There was no steel to spare because there was no coal with which to make more. It would probably have been necessary to deprive other countries of some of the coal they were assigned and boost the German steel production, partly at the expense of the French. Yet nobody ever accused the French of being the main obstacle to current deliveries. Steel apart, the task of supplying $600 million in manufactures from the Western zones by, say, the end of 1948 would have been an entirely reasonable requirement – far less than the Eastern zone supplied over those years. Even if one multiplies by four to allow for takings by countries other than the USSR, current deliveries of $2.4 billion over three years would have been nearer to the bounds of possibility than $2.4 billion in capital equipment.

This still leaves unexplained the contrast between the successful extraction of reparations from the Eastern zone and the continuing large deficit of the Western zones. How was it, one may ask, that West German recovery needed $4 billion in aid (just as British recovery needed $5 billion, without counting Marshall aid) while East German recovery enabled a much larger sum to be *paid* in reparations?

The answer is in part that the East German standard of living fell even lower than the West German. No one can pretend that the figures are at all reliable, but the impression they give is that, in spite of the enormous refugee population which may have added nearly 20 per cent to the numbers in the Western zones, consumption levels there were better maintained than in the Eastern zone. In 1947, for example, personal consumption per head in the Eastern zone is said to have been only 34 per cent of the level in 1936, while in the Bizone it was 49 per cent.[1] In later years the difference was just as perceptible – at least 25 per cent in 1950. At the same time, production in the West was slower to recover. In the Soviet zone industrial production in 1946 is estimated to have been 49 per cent of the level in 1936 (and 67 per cent in the final quarter) whereas it was no more than 31 per cent in the British zone.[2] The Soviet authorities gave priority to the production of industrial raw materials such as

[1] For East Germany, I have used the estimate in 'The East German Economy at the end of the Five Year Plan' (OIR 7131, 15 June 1956). For the Bizone I have used the *Statistical Handbook of Bizonal Recovery Programs* issued by the Military Government in January 1949.

[2] Nettl (1951) pp. 162, 165. Industrial production in the Soviet zone dropped steeply at the beginning of 1947 and at the end of 1949 was little higher than three years earlier. In the Western zones, on the other hand, the set-back in 1947 was much less marked and the subsequent expansion over the next two years much stronger (ibid., p. 241). Official figures for the Eastern zone showed production in 1947 at 60 per cent of the 1936 level while British estimates put the proportion at only 40 per cent. ('The Two Year Plan for the Soviet Zone', 7 September 1948, in PRO FO 644/670).

coal, timber, metals, potash and chemicals, and although some was taken in reparations, the benefit was also felt by manufacturing activities in the zone. These were, in the main, light industries making consumer goods or light engineering such as precision instruments and optics. The heavy industries of the Ruhr, on the other hand, were held back by a shortage of materials, especially coal, and by uncertainties over dismantling. In this respect the West in a sense *did* make deliveries from current production and starved German industry for the benefit of foreign consumers (especially France). The two-year delay in currency reform – for reasons quite unconnected with reparations – was a further factor in the slow recovery of West German industry. From 1948 onwards, however, industrial production shot ahead of production in the Eastern zone and by the end of 1950 was back to the pre-war level while in East Germany it was still at least 20 per cent below.

These facts go some way to show the contrasting effects on the two economies of removing reparations from the one and feeding aid into the other. They do not demonstrate that deliveries of reparations from current production by the Western zones would have been at the expense of the balance of payments of the area and hence financed by the occupying powers. That would undoubtedly have occurred had output been completely inelastic to reparations orders (unless consumption had been lowered still further by the occupying powers). Output was probably a good deal more inelastic in the West than in the East but by, say, 1947 it is hard to believe that all the limitations on output were on the side of supply and that there would have been no response in output to the placing of reparations orders. It might well have required, however, a substantial investment in imported materials which would have been hard to procure and which Britain at least would have been unable to finance.

Other Possibilities of Accommodation

A second possibility of accommodation would have been to let Russia have a loan or a grant in consideration of dropping her demand for reparations from the West. If a grant of the $2–$3 billion mentioned by Molotov at Potsdam would have settled the reparations issue it might have been less expensive than the bickering that followed (including the Berlin airlift, the war in Korea and the costly rearmament in 1950–3).

But it is by no means clear that the Russians would have agreed to withdraw their demand in exchange for a grant. When Molotov asked for a loan of $6 billion in January 1945, with low interest and easy terms of repayment, he presented the request almost as a favour to the USA, to help them out of trouble in the expected depression after the war.[3] What he wanted from the Ruhr was not just the dismantled equipment. It was also the dismantling; and a grant would not have brought that with it.

A third possibility would have been a combined effort of reconstruction embracing the whole of Europe and requiring contributions from ex-enemy countries in lieu of reparations. Marcus Fleming's idea of seeking reconciliation by helping countries in need, whatever their war record, and then requiring payment as soon as these countries could contribute, with reparations taking the form of disproportionate contributions, was highly imaginative. But, in practice, the USA was virtually the only country in surplus in 1945–7, and the scheme would have had to be financed almost exclusively by her – when she already bore a large part of the burden of UNRAA and was providing the world with more finance even than under the Marshall Plan. It was too much to hope that the USA would announce something like the Marshall Plan in 1945–6 *on top of* UNRAA, the British Loan and other major contributions to world recovery.

Apart from this, Russia's needs were enormous and urgent, entitling her to some priority and making any share-out a delicate matter. When she was in the mood to pillage Germany she would hardly have wanted to take part in a scheme for Germany's rehabilitation. The fact that the USA was likely to be the sole source of funds would have redoubled her suspicions since in the language of which the USSR was so fond, it would have been an open invitation to join the camp of the imperialists. Russia found it impossible, not surprisingly, to join the Marshall Plan; she would have had equal difficulties a year, or even two years, earlier in joining a similar plan for European recovery.

An accommodation between the powers had to be a political as much as an economic matter. The struggle between them was not really over reparations but over Germany. If they had seen eye to

---

[3] For fuller details of the proposed loan see Herring (1973) and Peterson (1973); also FRUS, 1945, Vol. V, pp. 937–1030; Mastny (1979) p. 215; Nettl (1951) p. 40; and Feis (1970) p. 247.

Stalin was asking visiting Congressmen in September 1945 why the US Government had not replied to the Soviet proposal. He had apparently not been informed of the progress of the negotiations and seemed unaware that the USSR had been told at an early stage that a loan was not constitutionally possible, since it required Congressional approval, and that an approach should be made instead to the Export–Import Bank (PRO FO 371/47860).

eye over the regime they wanted to encourage in Germany they might have come to an understanding also on reparations. But they were far from seeing eye to eye and their disagreements on reparations drove them further apart.

So long as there was a common enemy, the Alliance had held – a little precariously because of suspicions of overtures for a separate peace. It collapsed when the enemy was defeated and without a government. Germany had been not only the most powerful military nation in the world, but also the economic heart of continental Europe, pumping out the investment goods that drove the economy forward. If Germany went Communist, Europe was likely to follow; if she held out against Communist rule, Europe might do so too. The Western powers who had fought a long war against one totalitarian power could hardly relish the prospect of submitting to another, however warmly they had felt towards her as a military ally. If a line had to be drawn it would inevitably run through the middle of Germany and the partition that nobody really wanted would come to be the only settlement acceptable to everybody.

At first both sides united in demanding economic security. This was soon followed by the suspicion that the security needed was not against a revival of German military strength, or not against that alone, but against the use of Germany as a tool by a former ally. The Russians believed that only a socialist regime assured them of peace while the restoration of a capitalist economy spelt eventual aggression and war. The Western Allies, on the other hand, concluded that they had allowed Russia much too free a hand in seeking security behind a long crescent of satellite states, and that the time had come to be blunt and firm in announcing the limits they would tolerate in future. The series of *faits accomplis* presented to the Allies had to be accepted. But they aroused antagonism, distrust and a disinclination to yield more ground.

It is hard to see how things could have taken a radically different course. The Western Allies had not, until far too late, asked themselves how they could find enough common ground to run Germany together. They knew, or should have known, the kind of regime the Russians were establishing in their zone. Yet at Potsdam, Byrnes gave them freedom to go on stripping it of reparations. As Waley commented at the time, it looked as if the Americans 'had now given up hope of collaborating with the Russians in the administration of Germany as a single economic unit'.[4]

No doubt the Americans were doing little more than recognizing a

[4] Waley at staff conference with Prime Minister and Foreign Secretary, 31 July 1945, in Document No. 486, Butler and Pelly (1984) p. 1053.

fait accompli, and hoping that it would be possible later to co-ordinate activity in the different zones on a basis still to be worked out. But there were some, like Willard Thorp, who recognized that the zonal freedom Byrnes conceded would make it

> extremely difficult in practice to ensure uniform economic treatment in all zones of occupation.... In consequence, it would be difficult, if not impossible, to reach agreement on the inter-zonal adjustment of surpluses and deficits and on an import programme for Germany as a whole, including the respective shares of the occupying powers in the financing of such imports. It is quite likely that the result would be to orient the economy of Eastern Germany towards the Soviet Union and Eastern Europe and that of Western Germany towards Western Europe.[5]

The fact is that each of the four occupying powers wanted a hand in the control of Germany but was unwilling to let the others interfere with the control it exercised over its own zone. The Americans were anxious to prevent the Russians from having a hand in the Western zones – the major preoccupation of Byrnes at Potsdam.[6] The British were opposed to letting other countries participate in control of the Ruhr.[7] The French guarded jealously their freedom of action in their own zone. It was not only the Russians who wished to safeguard control over their zone.

Once the Russians and the French were on German soil they were not likely to quit until they were assured of a Germany either incapable of waging war or committed to policies of which they could approve and subject to controls that could be enforced. It was hard enough for the USA and the UK to induce France to accept the establishment of a German Government in the Western zones. How much more difficult it would have been to find a German Government acceptable to the Russians too. Yet, in the case of France, the difficulties had nothing to do with reparations and there was no ideological barrier such as divided Russia from her Allies. Even with the Russians, indignation and anger over reparations were not the prime obstacle to agreement. That lay in an ingrained distrust of the intentions of the West – a distrust inflamed by what

[5] Memorandum by Willard Thorp, Department of State, 28 July 1945, quoted by Kuklick (1972) p. 162.
[6] So Harriman recalled, long afterwards (Kuklick (1972) p. 156).
[7] In February 1947 Bevin maintained that 'the powers of a central German government should not be such as to interfere with British plans for the development and control of the Ruhr', 'The Ruhr', Memorandum by Secretary of State for Foreign Affairs, ORC (47)13, 21 February 1947, in PRO CAB 134/598.

they saw as trickery over reparations and, far more, by the evident intention of the Western powers to put Germany back on her feet.

The Marshall Plan

From that point of view the Marshall Plan was the last straw. Germany was to be rebuilt, and dismantling to fade away so as to allow her to contribute to the recovery of Western Europe under American leadership. As the Americans saw it, it was impossible to continue with quadripartite rule that gave each of four countries an effective veto over necessary measures, such as currency reform, and made it impossible for Germany – and in consequence for Europe – to become self-supporting again. A start had to be made in restoring the Germany economy to the position it had once occupied, not only in order to put an end to the burden on American taxpayers, but also for the sake of European reconstruction. If that meant a break with Russia and the division of Germany, it was a price that would have to be paid. Western Germany must be saved from Communism, and Europe too, through a comprehensive programme of sustained economic expansion.

That was not how it appeared to the Russians, or to those in the rest of Europe who still feared renewed German aggression. Germany was still potentially a formidable military threat, and had shown under Hitler how short a space of time was required to build an almost irresistible military machine. To see a restoration of the German economy under American auspices, with the vast addition to its capital stock since 1936 still largely intact, was bound to arouse strong feelings throughout the Soviet empire. There was also, no doubt, a 'jealous rage' against the wealth of America that enabled her to pour resources into Western Europe just when the outlook for a slide towards Communism in France, Italy, and perhaps even Germany, was beginning to look so promising.[8]

There was only one Germany but two ideologies, two systems of government. The clash betwen them was almost bound to end in a division into two Germanies. That division could have been avoided only if the necessary understandings had been reached while the war was still in progress, and of that there was little chance. In the absence of ideological differences, with a genuine democracy in Russia, differences over Germany would not have excited the same hostility. The 'safe' Governments that Russia installed in neighbouring countries would also have been more democratic and more acceptable

[8] Feis (1970) p. 249.

who were planning in the USSR for the peace had backed the use of existing resources for the benefit of Germany's victims in preference to removing industrial equipment in reparations. It needed no great insight to appreciate that the value of equipment removed could be equalled or surpassed *every year* by what that equipment would produce if left in place and brought into operation. But such considerations weighed little when the stock of equipment was far in excess of what could be operated, and when the removal of a great deal of it was thought indispensable to future security.

It took only one, or at the most two years, for the two discarded ideas – current reparations and reconstructing Europe – to return to favour. The USSR soon rediscovered the first, while the second – a little later – seized the imagination of the USA. The UK – more particularly at the official level – had always kept an open mind about current reparations, but on two conditions. One was that German exports should first be sufficient to meet the cost of necessary imports; it was because there seemed no immediate likelihood that this condition would be met that Britain was opposed to current deliveries in 1946–8. The second was that German industrial recovery, and with it the revival of German exports of manufactures, should not take precedence over British recovery and the re-establishment of a level of British exports adequate to meet the cost of imports.

The UK had also a keener sense than either of her principal Allies of the importance of reabsorbing Germany into the European economy. It was not just revulsion at the spectacle of a starving Germany that brought Britain into conflict with Russia over reparations: the British Government had always insisted on a 'decent minimum' for Germany. It was also conscious that Germany must be able to earn her living and that in the past she had done so in ways central to the growth and development of Europe. By the winter of 1946–7 the acuteness of the dollar problem was coming to be associated with the absence of an alternative source of supply in Germany. European recovery seemed on the verge of being halted and reversed for lack of dollars and some at least of the shortage was due to the existence of an economic vacuum in what had been the heart of the European economy.

The turning-point in the whole affair was the acceptance by the USA that without her assistance European recovery would collapse. Collapse was likely to mean the spread of Communism over Western Europe, starting perhaps with Germany. On the other hand, if recovery was to be enduring, Germany had an essential part to play. But a deliberate attempt to rebuild Germany and make her the pivot of European reconstruction, meant an end to co-operation with the Russians – and an end also to reparations, if Germany was henceforth to be an ally.

The struggle over reparations was thus largely incidental to struggles of a different kind. There had never, even in wartime, been a great deal of trust on either side; active collaboration at the working level such as existed between the Western Allies had been extremely limited; the ideas, values and long-term aims of East and West were far apart. Each wanted to remake Germany in its own image, and each assigned Germany a different role in European reconstruction. The UK and the USA were increasingly alive to the central importance of German economic recovery in European reconstruction. Russia, on the other hand, required Germany's economic recovery to lag behind her own and accrue to her benefit first and foremost; the last thing Russia wanted was a German recovery over which she had no control.

These differences intensified Russian suspicions and insecurity, making them difficult allies and leading them to pursue courses of action that made the West equally suspicious and uneasy. The two regimes in Germany, east and west, could not fail to be regarded as alternatives, and hence in competition with one another. Neither was willing to give way to the other or move out while the other remained; and the Russians had no intention of moving out until their demands had been met and the Soviet zone was tied firmly to the Soviet economy. They were prepared to speak softly to the Americans for the short time that they were likely to remain; but their co-operation was as wary as their collaboration with Germany had been in 1939–41.

No country emerges from the story with much credit. But on the whole the stance of British policy is perhaps the least discreditable. Churchill's lapse at Quebec apart, the Morgenthau Plan received no support from British ministers in the Coalition Government. Their first and only intervention on reparations was to back Churchill at Yalta in refusing support for Molotov's demand for $20 billion when Stettinius throught it 'reasonable'. In the negotiations leading up to the Reparations Plan, Labour ministers defended a much higher level of steel production than any of the other countries and had the satisfaction in December 1947 of securing quadripartite agreement – by that time almost unheard of – to the level of steel production they had approved in September 1945 (11.5 million tons). In March 1946 their agreement to the Reparations Plan was qualified by three important reservations when the other delegations put forward none. Later, it is true, they showed less enthusiasm for upward revisions in the level of industry than America and perhaps, at one stage, Russia. But this largely reflected their concern for French susceptibilities.

What British policy would have been, had no other power been involved, no one can be sure. The chances are that it would have been along the lines of the first British plan of November 1945, perhaps with a rather higher figure for steel since the Cabinet had agreed to 11.5 million tons. This would have involved acceptance of a level of industry similar to that underlying the revised plan of August 1947, that is, the 1936 level of production, and up to 40 per cent higher than the Quadripartite Plan of March 1946. If that had been the starting point it is a fair assumption that it, too, would have been relaxed progressively, if only because of the burden on the British Exchequer. In the absence of fears of Russian manoeuvres, relaxation might not in the end have gone so far or so fast; and there might well have been no such integration of Germany into the European community as eventually took place. For that, American aid and American pressure on the one side, and the compulsions on France to opt for reconciliation under the Schuman Plan on the other, were the operative factors rather than British policy as such. Nevertheless, Britain had contributed to this outcome by making it a prime object of policy to persuade the Americans to stay in Europe and by her constant efforts from 1944 onwards to promote the economic and political recovery of France. No country with Britain's enormous debts and major adjustments in attitude still to be made could have hoped to accomplish much more in the first three crucial years after the war. If British policy was rarely decisive it was at least rarely regrettable.

The Lessons of the Reparations Story

There are plenty of lessons in the reparations story for the student of politics. But what of the student of economics?

Nearly all the lessons offered by the Western zones are in striking contrast to those one might derive from the Eastern zones. One at least, however, they share. Both zones provide ample testimony to the difficulty at the end of a war of making available, dismantling and re-erecting capital equipment, and transporting it intact from one country to another. Given ample time, skilled labour, packing materials and information, these things can easily be done. But the necessary conditions are unlikely to be fulfilled after a long war when the programme has to be completed in a hurry, within a time-limit, when the labour and material required are scarce, communications are restricted and the information needed to bring plant back into operation is lacking.

When we turn from capital to current deliveries, we find the Western zones making little or no such deliveries, except in the form of coal supplied – most of it to France – at much too low a price. The Western Allies did, however, incur heavy occupation costs which were debited to the budgets of the zonal authorities or, later, the Federal Government. On the other hand, they had to plough in large sums in payment for imports, first of foodstuffs and later of raw materials as well. The net effect, over the years when it mattered most, between 1945 and 1949, was a substantial net payment to Germany. In the British case, payments for imports into Western Germany involved a heavy outlay in dollars when the UK was desperate to find dollars for its own necessary imports. Russia, on the other hand, was taking goods from her zone that in 1946 absorbed half the value added by industry and mining, and even in 1948, when output had expanded substantially, one third of value added.[9] In 1949, for which a more reliable estimate is available, Soviet takings were over 10 per cent of GNP or, including occupation costs, over 17 per cent.[10]

The Russians had no difficulty in absorbing reparations. If in doing so they set back East Germany's recovery from the war, the recovery eventually took the East German standard of living well above the Russian. If they forced extreme hardship on the population it may well have been no greater than the hardship borne by many parts of the Soviet Union simultaneously. They were right to say that they could deal with the transfer problem by taking goods in kind. But they took cash as well and it hardly mattered whether what they took was in one form or the other, since they had no intention of spending the money elsewhere and would have been unlikely to find takers if they had tried. What did matter was that they had effective control over budgetary appropriations since *somebody* had to pay for the goods they took from current production. The really significant contrast between the failure of the Allies after the First World War and the success of the Russians after the Second World War is in their power to force the German authorities to raise 17 per cent (or more) of GNP for transmission to the Russians as command over German resources.

On the other hand, it is true that the transfer dislocated trading patterns. East Germany traditionally conducted over half her trade with the rest of Germany and very little with the USSR. By 1949 less

[9] 'The Economic Situation in East Germany', OIR 5202, 1950, National Archives.
[10] 'The East German Economy at the End of the First Five Year Plan', OIR 7131, 1956, National Archives.

than 5 per cent was with the rest of Germany and 40–50 per cent with the USSR. Had West Germany been under a similar obligation to make current payments to the West there is every reason to expect that distortions of a somewhat similar kind would have resulted. Germany would have had to find export markets much earlier and would have had to make inroads into unfamiliar markets in which other Western countries were already comfortably ensconced. It was these forced sorties of a competitor, before British exporters were able to supply the goods and establish themselves in the market, that the British feared. Marcus Fleming had some reason to doubt whether the competition would be less damaging to British trade if the reparations transfers were in kind rather than in cash.

What did emerge as the post-war years rolled on, was that the reparations problem was very different in a prosperous and expanding world from what it might have been had the pre-war world depression returned. So long as world markets kept expanding, the process of recovery seemed that much easier. There was less tension within and between industrial economies, and a better prospect of a steady improvement in output and income. But by the time Germany re-entered world markets on a pre-war scale, reparations from the Western zones were virtually at an end.

Bibliography

Books

Abelshauser, Werner, *Wirtschaft in Westdeutschland, 1945–1946: Rekonstruktion und Wachstumbedingungen in der Americanische und Britische Zone*, Deutsche Verlags–Anstalt, Stuttgart, 1975.

Alexandrov, Vladimir, 'Soviet dismantling of equipment in post-war Germany', in Slusser, Robert, 1953.

Backer, John H., *Priming the German Economy: American Occupational Policies 1945–1948*, Duke University Press, Durham, North Carolina, 1971.

Backer, John H., *The Decision to Divide Germany*, Duke University Press, Durham, North Carolina, 1978.

Baggaley, Philip, 'Reparations, Security and the Industrial Disarmament of Germany: Origins of the Potsdam Decisions', PhD Dissertation, Yale University, 1980.

Balabkins, Nicholas, *Germany under Direct Controls: Economic Aspects of Industrial Disarmament, 1945–1946*, Rutgers University Press, New Brunswick, 1964.

Balfour, Michael and Mair, John, *Four Power Control in Germany and Austria 1945–1946*, Oxford University Press for Royal Institute of International Affairs, London, 1956.

Barker, Elizabeth, *The British between the Superpowers 1945–50*, Macmillan, London, 1983.

Birkenhead, Lord, *Walter Monckton*, Weidenfeld and Nicolson, London, 1969.

Brailsford, H. N., *Making Germany Pay?* National Peace Council, London, 1944.

Bullen, Roger and Pelly, M. E., see 'Official documents, etc.' below.

Bullock, Alan (Lord), *Ernest Bevin, Foreign Secretary, 1945–1951*, Heinemann, London, 1983.

Burridge, T. D., *British Labour and Hitler's War*, André Deutsch, London, 1976.

Butler, Rohan and Pelly, M. E., see 'Official documents, etc.' below.

Byrnes, James F., *Speaking Frankly*, Heinemann, London and Toronto, 1947.

Carlyle, M. (ed.), see 'Official documents etc.' below.

Churchill, Winston, *The Second World War: Vol. VI: Triumph and Tragedy*, Cassell, London, 1954.

Clay, Lucius D., *Decision in Germany*, Doubleday, New York, 1950.

Clemens, Diane Shaver, *Yalta*, Oxford University Press, Oxford, 1970.

Cole, G. D. H., *Reparations and the Future of German Industry*, Gollancz, London, 1945.

Djilas, Milovan, *Conversations with Stalin*, Rupert Hart-Davis, London, 1962.

Eden, Anthony (Earl of Avon), *The Eden Memoirs, Vol. II: The Reckoning*, Cassell, London, 1965.

Feis, Herbert, *Churchill, Roosevelt, Stalin: The War They Waged and the Peace They Sought*, Princeton University Press, Princeton, 1957.

Feis, Herbert, *Between War and Peace*, Princeton University Press and Oxford University Press, Princeton and Oxford, 1960.

Feis, Herbert, *From Trust to Terror: The Onset of the Cold War 1945–1950*, W. W. Norton & Co., New York, 1970.

Foschepoth, Josef (ed.), *Kalter Krieg and Deutsche Frage: Deutschland in Widerstreit der Mächte 1945–1952*, Vanderhoeck und Ruprecht, Göttingen and Zurich, 1985.

Gimbel, John, *The American Occupation of Germany*, Stanford University Press, Stanford, California, 1968.

Gimbel, John, *The Origins of the Marshall Plan*, Stanford University Press, Stanford, California, 1976.

Ginsburg, David, *The Future of German Reparations*, National Planning Association pamphlet no. 57/58, Washington, 1947.

Gladwyn, Lord, *The Memoirs of Lord Gladwyn*, Weidenfeld and Nicolson, London, 1972.

Gottlieb, Manuel, *The German Peace Settlement and the Berlin Crisis*, Paine-Whitman, New York, 1960.

Harmssen, G. W., *Reparationen, Sozialprodukt, Lebenstandard: Versuch einer Wirtschaftsbilanz*, F. Trüjen Verlag, Bremen, 1947.

Harmssen, G. W., *Am Abend der Demontage*, F. Trüjen Verlag, Bremen, 1951.

Harrod, R. F., *The Life of John Maynard Keynes*, Macmillan, London, 1951.

Herring, George, *Aid to Russia 1941–1946: Strategy, Diplomacy, the Origins of the Cold War*, Columbia University Press, New York, 1973.

Hessian, C. H., *John Maynard Keynes*, Collier MacMillan, London, 1984.

Hoffmann, Walther G., *Das Wachstum der deutschen Wirtschaft seit der Mitte des 19 Jahrhunderts*, Berlin and New York, Springer Verlag, 1965.

Hughes, R. D., *Soviet Foreign Policy and Germany 1945 to 1948*, PhD thesis, Claremont Graduate School, 1964.

Keynes, John Maynard (Lord), *The Economic Consequences of the Peace*, Macmillan, London, 1919.

Keynes, John Maynard (Lord), *Collected Writings*, Vol. XXII, *Activities 1939–45: Internal War Finance*, 1978.

Keynes, John Maynard (Lord), *Collected Writings*, Vol. XXV, *Activities*

1940–44: Shaping the Post-War World: the Clearing Union, 1980.
Keynes, John Maynard (Lord), *Collected Writings*, Vol. XXVI, *Activities 1940–6: Shaping the Post-war World: Bretton Woods and Reparations*, 1980.
Klein, Burton H., *Germany's Economic Preparations for War*, Harvard Economic Studies, Vol. 109, Cambridge, Mass., 1959.
Klimov, Gregory, *The Terror Machine, the Inside Story of the Soviet Administration in Germany*, Faber and Faber, London, 1953.
Kolko, Gabriel, *The Politics of War: Allied Diplomacy and the World Crisis of 1943–45*, Weidenfeld and Nicolson, London, 1969.
Krengel, R., *Anlagevermögen, Produktion und Beschäftigung der Industrie im Gebiet der Bundesrepublik von 1924 bis 1956*, Berlin, 1958.
Kuklick, Bruce, *American Policy and the Division of Germany: the Clash with Russia over Reparations*, Cornell University Press, Ithaca, New York and London, 1972.
Lewis, Julian, *British Military Planners and Post-war Strategy*, Oxford DPhil Thesis, 1981.
Maisky, Ivan, *Memoirs of a Soviet Ambassador, The War 1939–43*, Hutchinson, London, 1967.
Mastny, Vojtech, *Russia's Road to the Cold War*, Columbia University Press, New York, 1979.
McCauley, Martin, *The German Democratic Republic since 1945*, Macmillan in association with School for Eastern European Studies, University of London, 1983.
McNeill, W. H., *America, Britain and Russia: their Co-operation and Conflict, 1941–1946*, Oxford University Press for Royal Insititute of International Affairs, 1953.
Medvedev, Roy, *All Stalin's Men*, Basil Blackwell, Oxford, 1983.
Mee, Charles L., Jr, *Meeting at Potsdam, N. Evans & Co., New York, 1975*.
Mendershausen, Horst, *Two Post-war Recoveries of the German Economy*, Amsterdam, 1955.
Nettl, J. P., *The Eastern Zone and Soviet Policy in Germany 1945–50*, Oxford University Press, London, 1951.
Nubel, Otto, *Amerikanische Reparationspolitik gegenüber Deutschland, 1941–1945*, Bundesministerium für Innerdeutsche Beziehungen, A. Metzner, Frankfurt-am-Main, 1980.
Nutter, G. W., *Growth of Industrial Production in the Soviet Union*, Princeton University Press, Princeton, 1962.
O'Farrell, H. H., *The Franco-German War Indemnity and its Economic Results*, Harrison and Sons, London, 1913.
Ovendale, R. (ed.), *The Foreign Policy of the British Labour Governments, 1945–1951*, Leicester University Press, 1984.
Overy, R. J., *Goering; the Iron Man*, Routledge and Kegan Paul, London, 1984.
Pakenham, Francis (Lord), *Born to Believe*, Jonathan Cape, London, 1953.
Pauley, Edwin W., *Report on German Reparations to the President of the United States, February to September 1945*, Washington, 1945.
Penrose, E. F., *Economic Planning for the Peace*, Princeton University

Press, Princeton New Jersey, 1953.

Piettre, André, *L'Economie allemande contemporaine, Allemagne Occidentale, 1945–1952*, Editions M.Th. Génie – Librairie de Médicis, Paris, 1952.

Ra'anan, Gavriel D., *International Policy Formation in the USSR: Factional 'Debates' during the Zhdanovschina*, Archon Books, The Shoestring Press, Hamden, Connecticut, 1983.

Ratchford, B. U. and Ross, W. D., *Berlin Reparations Assignment*, University of North Carolina Press, Chapel Hill, 1947.

Ross, Graham (ed.), see 'Official documents etc.' below.

Ruhm von Oppen, B. (ed.), see 'Official documents etc.' below.

Rupp, Franz, *Die Reparationsleistungen in der Sowjetischen Besatzungzone*, Bonner Berichte aus Mittel- und Ostdeutschland (BB), 1951. See also 'Official documents etc.' below.

Sandford, Gregory W., *From Hitler to Ulbricht: the Communist Reconstruction of East Germany 1945–46*, Princeton University Press, 1983.

Sayer, Ian and Botting, Douglas, *Nazi Gold*, Granada, London, 1984.

Scharf, Claus and Schröder, Hans-Jürgen (eds), *Politische und Ökonomische Stabilisierung Westdeutschlands 1945–1949*, Franz Steiner Verlag, Wiesbaden, 1977.

Scharf, Claus and Schröder, Hans-Jürgen (eds), *Die Deutschland Politik Grossbritanniens und die Britische Zone 1945–1949*, Franz Steiner Verlag, Wiesbaden, 1979.

Schmidt, Hans A. (ed.), *US Occupation Policy in Germany after World War II*, The Regents Press of Kansas, Lawrence, 1978.

Schwarz, Hans-Peter, *Vom Reich zur Bundesrepublik: Deutschland im Widerstreit der aussenpolitischen Konzeptionen in den Jahren der Besatzungsherrschaft, 1945–1949*, Neuwied, Luchterland, 1966.

Sharp, Tony, *The Wartime Alliance and the Zonal Division of Germany*, Oxford University Press, 1975.

Slusser, Robert, *Soviet Economic Policy in Post-War Germany*, Research Programme on the USSR, New York, 1953.

Smith, Jean Edward, *The Papers of General Lucius D. Clay* (2 vols), Indiana University Press, Bloomington and London, 1974.

Snell, J. F., *The War-time Origins of the East–West Dilemma over Germany*, Hauser, New Orleans, 1959.

Stettinius, E. R., *Russia and the Russians: the Yalta Conference*, ed. Walter Johnson, Jonathan Cape, London, 1950.

Stolper, Gustav, Häuser, K., and Borchardt, K., *The German Economy 1870 to the Present*, Weidenfeld and Nicolson, London, 1967.

Strang, Lord, *Home and Abroad*, André Deutsch, London, 1956.

Sutton, Antony C., *Western Technology and Soviet Economic Development 1945–1965*, Vol. 3, Hoover Institute Press, Stanford, 1973.

Taussig, F. W., *International Trade*, Macmillan, New York, 1927.

Trachtenberg, Marc, *Reparation in World Politics: France and European Economic Diplomacy, 1916–1923*, Columbia University Press, New York, 1980.

Treue, Wilhelm and Schrader, Käthe, *Die Demontagepolitik der Westmächte nach dem Zweiten Weltkrieg*, Göttinger, 1967.
Watt, Donald C., *Britain Looks to Germany: British Opinion towards Germany since 1945*, D. Wolff, London, 1965.
Webb, Robert Geoffrey, *Britain and the Future of Germany: British planning for German dismemberment and reparations 1942–45*, PhD thesis, State University at Buffalo, 1979.
Wheeler-Bennett, Sir John, *The Wreck of Reparations*, Allen and Unwin, London, 1933.
Wheeler-Bennett, Sir John and A. J. Nicholls, *The Semblance of Peace: the Political Settlement after the Second World War*, Macmillan, London, 1972.
Wilson, Roland, *Capital Imports and the Terms of Trade*, University of Melbourne, Melbourne, 1931.
Woodward, Sir Llewellyn, *British Foreign Policy in the Second World War*, HMSO, London, 1962.
Woodward, Sir Llewellyn, *British Foreign Policy in the Second World War*, Vol. 5, HMSO, London, 1976.

Articles

Boyle, Peter G., 'The British Foreign Office View of Soviet–American Relations, 1945–46, *Diplomatic History*, 1979, pp. 307–320.
Burridge, Trevor, 'Great Britain and the dismemberment of Germany at the end of the Second World War', *International History Review, III*, 4, Oct. 1984, pp. 565–79.
Carden, Robert W., 'Before Bizonia: Britain's economic dilemma in Germany, 1945–46', *Journal of Contemporary History*, Vol. 14, No. 3, July 1979, pp. 535–55.
Foschepoth, Josef, 'Britische Deutschlandpolitik zwischen Yalta und Potsdam', *Vierteljahrshefte für Zeitgeschichte*, Vol. 30, 1982, pp. 675–714.
Gottlieb, Manuel, 'The German economic potential', *Social Research*, Vol. 17, 1950, p. 77.
Keynes J. M., 'The German transfer problem', *Economic Journal*, 1929, p. 1.
Keynes, J. M., 'The reparation problem: a discussion. II A rejoinder', *Economic Journal*, 1929, p. 179.
Keynes, J. M., 'Views on the transfer problem. III A reply', *Economic Journal*, 1929, p. 404.
Krieger, Wolfgang, 'Was General Clay a revisionist?', *Journal of Contemporary History*, Vol. 18, April 1983.
Moseley, Philip, 'Dismemberment of Germany: the Allied negotiations from Yalta to Potsdam', *Foreign Affairs*, April 1950.
Munting, Roger, 'Lend-lease and the Soviet war effort', *Journal of Contemporary History*, Vol. 19, 1984, pp. 495–510.
Nettl, Peter, 'German reparations in the Soviet empire', *Foreign Affairs*, 1951, pp. 300–7.
Ohlin, Bertil, 'The reparation problem: a discussion. I Transfer Difficulties, Real and Imagined, *Economic Journal*, 1929, p. 172.
Ohlin, Bertil, 'Mr Keynes' Views on the transfer problem. II A rejoinder', *Economic Journal*, 1929, p. 400.

Paterson, Thomas, 'The abortive loan to Russia 1943–46', *Journal of American History*, Vol. 56, 1969, pp.70–92.

Pollard, Robert A., 'Economic security and the origins of the cold war: Bretton Woods, the Marshall Plan and American rearmament, 1944–1950', *Diplomatic History*, Vol. 9, No. 3, Summer 1985.

Rueff, Jacques, 'Mr Keynes' views on the transfer problem. I A criticism', *Economic Journal*, 1929, p. 388.

Steininger, Rolf, 'Die Britische Deutschlandpolitik in den Jahren 1945/46', *Politik und Zeitgeschichte*, Supplement to *Das Parlament*, 9 Jan. 1982.

Wagner, R. Harrison, 'The decision to divide Germany and the origins of the cold war', *International Studies Quarterly*, 24, June 1980, pp. 162–73.

Warner, Geoffrey, 'The division of Germany 1946–1948', *International Affairs*, Vol. 51, 1975, pp.60–71.

Official Documents, etc.

Bonner Berichte aus Mittel- und Ostdeutschland (BB): Die Reparationen der Sowjetzone in den Jahren 1945 bis 1953 (continuation of the work of Franz Rupp), 1953; *Die Sowjetische Hand in der deutscher Wirtschaft, Organisation und Geschäftsgebaren der Sowjetischen Unternehmen*, 1953.

DDR Handbuch (3rd edn), Cologne, 1985.

Documents on British Policy Overseas, Vol. I, Rohan Butler and M. E. Pelly (eds), HMSO, 1984; Vol. II, Roger Bullen and M. E. Pelly (eds), HMSO, 1985.

Documents on Germany under Occupation 1945–54, 1955, B. Ruhm von Oppen (ed.), Royal Institute of International Affairs, 1956.

Documents International Affairs, 1947–1948 and *1949–1950*, Margaret Carlyle (ed.), Royal Institute of International Affairs, 1952.

Economic Survey of Europe since the War, Economic Commission for Europe, Geneva, 1953.

The Foreign Office and the Kremlin: British Documents on Anglo-Soviet Relations, 1941–45, Graham Ross (ed.), Cambridge University Press, 1984.

Inter-Allied Reparations Agency, Annual Reports of the Secretary-General, Brussels.

Foreign Relations of the United States (FRUS), US Department of State, Government Printing Office, Washington, DC.

The Plan for Reparations and the Level of Post-War German Economy, Allied Control Authority, Berlin, April 1946.

'The Reparations Plan and the Future Level of Industry in Germany', unpublished official report by A. K. Cairncross, April 1946.

Statistical Handbook of Bizonal Recovery, Special Report of the United States and United Kingdom Military Governors, January 1949.

Statistisches Jahrbuch für die Bundesrepublik (annual).

Three Years of Reparations, OMGUS, Berlin, November 1948.

A Year of Potsdam: the German Economy since the Surrender, OMGUS, Berlin, 1946.

Index